LIBRARY OF NEW TESTAM

595

Formerly the Journal for the Study of the New Testament Supplement Series

Editor
Chris Keith

A BAPTISM OF JUDGMENT IN THE FIRE
OF THE HOLY SPIRIT

John's Eschatological Proclamation in Matthew 3

Daniel Wayne McManigal

t&tclark

LONDON · NEW YORK · OXFORD · NEW DELHI · SYDNEY

T&T CLARK
Bloomsbury Publishing Plc
50 Bedford Square, London, WC1B 3DP, UK
1385 Broadway, New York, NY 10018, USA

BLOOMSBURY, T&T CLARK and the T&T Clark logo are trademarks of
Bloomsbury Publishing Plc

First published in Great Britain 2019
This paperback edition published in 2021

Copyright © Daniel W. McManigal, 2019

Daniel W. McManigal has asserted his right under the Copyright, Designs and Patents Act,
1988, to be identified as Author of this work.

For legal purposes the Acknowledgments on p. x constitute an extension
of this copyright page.

A catalogue record for this book is available from the British Library.

A catalog record for this book is available from the Library of Congress.

Library of Congress Cataloging-in-Publication Data

ISBN: HB: 978-0-5676-8396-0
PB: 978-0-5676-9992-3
ePDF: 978-0-5676-8397-7
eBook: 978-0-5676-8400-4

Series: Library of New Testament Studies, 2345678X, volume 595

Typeset by Deanta Global Publishing Services, Chennai, India

To find out more about our authors and books visit www.bloomsbury.com
and sign up for our newsletters.

CONTENTS

ACKNOWLEDGMENTS

I would like to express my sincere thanks to Dr. Ian K Smith, for his constant encouragement, penetrating questions, helpful comments, and generosity of time in reading over and interacting with the present work. Revs. David Thommen and Jeremy Baker, Mrs. Rina Kroes, Drs. John Davies, Lee Irons, Alistair Wilson, David Turner, and Peter Bolt kindly read over early manuscript drafts and provided thoughtful challenges, corrections, input, and suggestions. Any remaining errors belong solely to the author.

Kate Scott (librarian, Christ College Sydney) and Alice Hamstra were a great help in securing monographs and articles for the present work. My profound gratitude is offered to Rev. Clayton Willis whose biblical dialog, unceasing encouragement, friendship, and editing skills were constant aids in seeing this project through to the end. I would also like to thank the session and congregation of Hope Presbyterian Church, Bellevue, Washington, for their kindness and support. Thank you for permitting your pastor to pursue this piece of writing to its completion.

A special thanks to Chris Keith for accepting the present work for the LNTS series. Dominic Matos, Arub Ahmed, Sarah Blake and Sweda R are also to be thanked for their help and attention to the many details of the publication process.

Finally, I wish to give thanks to the Lord for my family. Carmen Duran and Willa McManigal provided help with the children and other duties so that I could immerse myself in this project. Wayne McManigal made numerous corrections to every draft chapter. To my wife Jill, and my children Caleb and Ellie, thank you for being a part of this long and demanding process (Prov 18:22; 3 John 4). I am grateful for your love, patience, and prayers through it all.

GENERAL ABBREVIATIONS

BCE	Before Common Era
CE	Common Era
cf.	*confer*, compare
ch./chs.	chapter/chapters
comm(s).	commentary, commentaries
ed./eds.	editor/editors
e.g.	*exempli gratia*, for example
esp.	especially
ET	English Translation
et al.	*et alii*, and others
etc.	*et cetera*, and so on
frag.	fragment
HB	Hebrew Bible
i.e.	*id est*, that is
MT	Masoretic Text
n.	footnote
n.d.	no date
NT	New Testament
OT	Old Testament
repr.	reprint
trans.	Translator, translated by
v./vv.	verse/verses
vol(s).	volume(s)

Abbreviations of Versions of the Bible

ASV	Authorized Standard Version
ESV	English Standard Version
KJV	King James Version
LXX	Septuagint
NASB	New American Standard Bible
NET	New English Translation
NIV	New International Version
RSV	Revised Standard Version
Vulg.	Vulgate

Abbreviations of the Names of Biblical Book

Gen Genesis

Song or (Cant) Song of Songs
(Song of Solomon, or Canticles)

Luke Luke

Exod Exodus

Isa Isaiah

John John

Lev Leviticus

Jer Jeremiah

Acts Acts

Num Numbers

Lam Lamentations

Rom Romans

Deut Deuteronomy

Ezek Ezekiel

1–2 Cor: 1–2
Corinthians

Josh Joshua

Dan Daniel

Gal Galatians

Judg Judges

Hos Hosea

Eph Ephesians

Ruth Ruth

Joel Joel

Phil Philippians

1–2 Sam 1–2 Samuel

Amos Amos

Col Colossians

1–2 Kgdms 1–2
Kingdoms LXX

Obad Obadiah

1–2 Thess: 1–2
Thessalonians

1–2 Kgs 1–2 Kings

Jonah Jonah

1–2 Tim 1–2 Timothy

1–3 Kgdms 3–4
Kingdoms LXX

Mic Micah

Titus Titus

1–2 Chr 1–2 Chronicles

Nah Nahum

Phlm Philemon

Ezra Ezra

Hab Habakkuk

Heb Hebrews

Neh Nehemiah

Zeph Zephaniah

Jas James

Esth Esther

Hag Haggai

1–2 Pet 1–2 Peter

Job Job

Zech Zechariah

1–2–3 John 1–2–3 John

Ps/Pss Psalms

Mal Malachi

Jude Jude

Prov Proverbs

Matt Matthew

Rev Revelation

Eccl (or Qoh) Ecclesiastes
(or Qoheleth)

Mark Mark

Deuterocanonical Works and Septuagint

Jdt — Judith
1–4 Macc — 1–4 Maccabees
1 Esd — 1 Esdras
Sir — Sirach/Ecclesiasticus
Wis — Wisdom of Solomon
Bar — Baruch
Tob — Tobit

Dead Sea Scrolls

1Q28b — *Rule of the Blessings*
1 QS — Serek hayyaḥad (*Rule of the Community, Manual of Discipline*)
1 QH — Hôdāyôt (*Thanksgiving Hymns*) from Cave 1
1QM — *1Q War Scroll*
1QpHab. — *1QPesher to Habakkuk*

1QSb	*1Q Rule of benedictions*
4Q16	*Isaiah Pesher[b]*
4Q161	*(4QpIsa[a]) 4QIsaiah Pesher[a]*
4Q162	*(4QpIsa[b]) 4Q Isaiah Pesher[b]*
4Q252	*4QCommentary on Genesis A*
4Q285	*4Q War Scroll[g]?*
4QFlor	*4Q Florilegium [4Q Midr Eschat[a?]]*
11Q1Q	*Sefer ha-Milḥāmāh 11Q14*
CD-A	*Damascus Document[a]*

Abbreviations of the Names of Pseudepigrapha

1 En.	*1 Enoch* (Ethiopic Apocalypse)
3 En.	*3 Enoch* (Hebrew Apocalypse)
4 Ezra	*4 Ezra*
T. Ab.	*Testament of Abraham*
T. Asher	*Testament of Asher*
T. Levi	*Testament of Levi*
T. Jud.	*Testament of Judah*
T. Isaac	*Testament of Isaac*
Tg. Ps.-J.	*Targum Pseudo-Jonathan*
Jub.	*Jubilees*
2 Bar.	*2 Baruch* (Syriac Apocalypse)
4 Bar.	*4 Baruch*
2 Esd	*2 Esdras*
Sib. Or.	*Sibylline Oracles*
Pss. Sol.	Psalms of Solomon
Aris. Ex	Aristeas the Exegete

Babylonian Talmud and Mishnah, Tosefta

b. Hag.	*Hagigah*
b. Sanh.	*Sanhedrin*
b. Yebam.	*Yebamot*
m. Sanh.	*Sanhedrin*
t. Sukk.	*Sukkah*

Josephus

Ant.	*Jewish Antiquities*
J.W.	*Jewish War*
B.J.	*Bellum Judaicum*

Abbreviations of Periodicals, Reference Works and Serials

AB	Anchor Bible Commentary
ACNT	Augsburg Commentary on the New Testament
AOTC	Apollos Old Testament Commentary
AYBC	Anchor Yale Bible Commentary
BBR	Bulletin for Biblical Research
BDAG	A Greek-English Lexicon of the New Testament and Other Early Christian Literature (Third Edition)
BECNT	Baker Exegetical Commentary on the New Testament
BETL	Bibliotheca Ephemeridum Theologicarum Lovaniensium
BJRL	Bulletin of the John Rylands University of Manchester
BSac	Bibliotheca sacra
BZ	Biblische Zeitschrift
BZAW	Beihefte zur ZAW
BZNW	Beihefte zur Zeitschrift für die neutestamentliche Wissenschaft
CBQ	Catholic Biblical Quarterly
ConBNT	Coniectanea Biblica New Testament Series
CTJ	Calvin Theological Journal
DNTB	Dictionary of New Testament Background
DOTP	Dictionary of Old Testament Prophets
DSD	Dead Sea Discoveries
EBC	Expositor's Bible Commentary
EQ	Evangelical Quarterly
ET	Expository Times
FRLANT	Forschungen zur Religion und Literatur des Alten und Neuen Testaments
HBT	Horizons in Biblical Theology
HSM	Harvard Semitic Monographs
HTKNT	Herders theologischer Kommentar zum Neuen Testament
HTR	Harvard Theological Review
ICC	International Critical Commentary
INT Interpretation:	A Journal of Bible and Theology
IVP	InterVarsity Press
JBL	Journal of Biblical Literature
JJS	Journal of Jewish Studies
JPTSup	Journal of Pentecostal Theology Supplement Series
JSNT	Journal for the Study of the New Testament
JSNTSup	Journal for the Study of the New Testament—Supplement Series
JTS	Journal of Theological Studies
LNTS	Library of New Testament Studies
NA^{27}	*Novum Testamentum Graece*
NAC	New American Commentary
NBC	New Bible Commentary
NCBC	New Collegeville Bible Commentary
NDBT	New Dictionary of Biblical Theology

NIBC	New International Bible Commentary
NICNT	New International Commentary on the New Testament
NICOT	New International Commentary on the Old Testament
NIDB	New Interpreters Dictionary of the Bible
NIDNTTE	New International Dictionary of New Testament Theology and Exegesis
NIGTC	New International Commentary on the New Testament
NIVAC	New International Version Application Commentary
NovT	Novum Testamentum
NPNF	Nicene and Post-Nicene Church Fathers
NSBT	New Studies in Biblical Theology
NTAbh	Neutestamentliche Abhandlungen
NTS	New Testament Studies
P&R	Presbyterian and Reformed
PTUS	Patristische Texte Und Studien
RSB	Religious Studies Bulletin
SBL	Society of Biblical Literature
SBLSP	Society of Biblical Literature Seminar Papers
SNT	Studien zum Neuen Testament
SNTSMS	Society for New Testament Studies Monograph Series
SPCK	Society for Promoting Christian Knowledge
SPS	Sacra Pagina Series
TBT	The Bible Translator
TDNT	Theological Dictionary of the New Testament
TJ	Trinity Journal
TPINTC	TPI New Testament Commentaries
TWOT	Theological Workbook of the Old Testament.
TynBul	Tyndale Bulletin
UBSHS	United Bible Society Handbook Series
VT	Vetus Testamentum
WBC	Word Biblical Commentary
WMANT	Wissenschaftliche Monographien zum Alten und Neuen Testament
WTJ	Westminster Theological Journal
WUNT	Wissenschaftliche Untersuchungen zum Neuen Testament
ZAW	Zeitschrift für die alttestamentliche Wissenschaft
ZECNT	Zondervan Exegetical Commentary on the New Testament
ZTK	Zeitschrift für Theologie und Kirche

Chapter 1

INTRODUCTION

The Backlighting of Matthew 3:11

When readers of Matthew's Gospel step into his narrative world, they encounter a dutiful scribe who has undertaken to tell Jesus's story through the lens of Israel's past. Through the use of OT citations, allusions, and typology Jesus is presented as the promised offspring of Abraham, David's royal son and prophet. In Jesus, Israel comes face to face with the fulfillment of the nation's prophetic past. Matthew repeatedly reminds his readers that Jesus has come, "In order that it might be fulfilled," but will that mean blessing or curse for Israel? The hope of blessing (1:1) and the possibility of curse (1:11) hinge upon how Israel will respond to Jesus, and Matthew will not allow his readers to linger long over Israel's decision and its outcome. Jesus will be rejected according to the scriptures, but this also fulfills a plan that was announced in the OT and will be the decisive event whereby the nations will be gathered to the people of God (Matt 8:11; 28:19–20).

In ch. 2, Matthew sets up the expectation of a future crisis. Under the specter of death God once more calls his son out of Egypt (Hos 11:1; Matt 2:15). The subsequent slaughter of the innocents (2:16–18) and the quotation from Jeremiah preview the coming judgment upon Israel. And yet the dark foreboding is balanced by an implicit message of hope that runs through the events of ch. 2. As the true king of the Jews (2:2), Jesus has come to experience the exodus on behalf of his people. Chapter 2 also hints that Jesus will escape death and lead his people out of Israel.

In ch. 3 some thirty years of narrative silence are passed over as Jesus goes from infancy to adulthood. In the wilderness, the silence is broken. When John the Baptist arrives he announces that Israel must submit to the assessment of heaven (Matt 3:2). Those who refuse and hold to their status as the biological children of Abraham (3:9) will undergo the judgment. John condemns the leaders of Israel by announcing that the one who is coming after him is coming to destroy them. They will experience the Spirit's fire and there will be no escape. The messianic judgment will chop down the unfruitful trees and cast out the chaff into the unquenchable fire. Both of these symbolic pictures are placed on either side of the baptism in the Holy Spirit and fire and help to elaborate its meaning. *This study will argue that the baptism of the Holy Spirit and fire is the eschatological judgment that will come upon the unrepentant nation in Jesus's generation, upon Jesus himself as he hangs upon the cross for the sins of his people, and upon the wicked on the last day, when the judge returns in glory.*

The Reason for This Book

Our aim is to advance a fresh Matthean reading of John's words, "He will baptize you in the Holy Spirit and fire" (Matt 3:11). We will argue that the future baptism, as conceived by Matthew, is not the gift of Pentecost. It is not two baptisms: one for the good and the other for the evil. It is not a baptism of fire through which all must pass. The Gospel of Matthew presents the baptism of the Holy Spirit and fire as the judgment of God upon the nation of Israel, and the regathering of a people around Jesus. In the second place we will argue that the meaning of John's water baptism mirrors the future messianic baptism of judgment upon Israel. Because the two baptisms have been brought together in Matt 3:11, they are best understood in light of one another and in light of Matthew's larger narrative concerns with regard to Israel's national failure and future. The outcome of this nuanced narrative reading is that the baptism with water and the baptism in the Holy Spirit and fire are mutually explanatory and distinctively one-sided in meaning.

The Plan of This Book

The present work explores and explains the meaning of the logion of Matt 3:11, ἐν πνεύματι ἁγίῳ καὶ πυρί, in its Matthean form. Grammatical details effecting the interpretation are also explored, followed by a survey of the main interpretations proposed by scholars. We then go on to offer an explanation of the baptism in the Spirit and fire as eschatological judgment upon Israel, taking note of the structural and contextual aspects that confirm such a reading.

We next turn to several OT passages to explore the underpinnings of John's eschatological announcement. Isa 11, Mal 3–4, and Dan 7 provide announcements of the arrival of the day of the Lord and of a coming figure(s), the root of Jesse and Son of Man. The characteristics both of the day of the Lord and the ruler to come are the soil from which Matthew's eschatological material grows.

The narrative context of Matt 3:1–12 will establish the reason for the arrival of John the Baptist and the reason for his eschatological message and sign. John's message and baptism are closely related even though not easily understood. As we will argue, John's preaching and baptism are auditory and visual pronouncements of judgment. Consideration must therefore be given to John baptizing Jesus. What are the implications of John's prophetic sign for Jesus's messianic work? Is the judgment carried out during Jesus's ministry (Matt 11–12)? Should the cross be considered a baptism in the Holy Spirit and fire? To this we fill out the last of our textual treatment of the messianic baptism of Spirit and fire with the Olivet Discourse (Matt 24–25).

Because John's preaching and baptism are future-oriented and are best understood as a prophet with an apocalyptic message, we conclude by defining the descriptive terms used throughout the pages that follow.

Messianic

When it comes to the word(s) messiah/messianic the multiplicity of definitions is hardly surprising. For Collins, "What matters is the expectation of a Davidic king, of an ideal priest, of an eschatological prophet. Besides, there was no Jewish orthodoxy in the matter of messianic expectation, and so we should expect some variation."[1] John the Baptist does not describe the one to come as the messiah, but such a requirement is not necessary.[2] Matthew's narrative presents Jesus as (1) John's "one to come," and (2) Israel's messiah. The activities of the one to come (3:11) and his identity as "Χριστός" (1:1) tell us that Matthew has conceived of John's expected figure as Jesus the messiah. John's self-professed unworthiness to carry the sandal straps of the "Coming One" (3:11) and his question as to whether or not Jesus was ὁ ἐρχόμενος (11:3) indicate that John was looking for some sort of powerful figure to set things right. Matthew presents Jesus in the role of an agent of deliverance and judgment. In sum, Jesus is the Christ, the fulfillment of the OT eschatological proclamation of the prophets and the agent of salvation and judgment.

Eschatology

Traditional definitions of eschatology narrowly define it as, "The end of this world's time—that is to say, when it refers to a consummation of the historical process in events which lie beyond the scope of the world's history."[3] Our usage of eschatology is broader in scope than the "last things." With regard to the prophets in particular, there is not always a distinction "to be drawn between Jahweh's action within history and his action at the end of it, and there is consequently no need to confine the term 'eschatological' to the latter."[4] Future, temporal events in history that involve the activity of God in salvation and judgment and are described with end-time language (darkness, shaking of the heavens, heavenly armies, the overthrow of God's enemies) will be designated as "eschatological." This use of the term is not

---

1. John J. Collins, *The Scepter and the Star: Messianism in Light of the Dead Sea Scrolls* (Grand Rapids/Cambridge: Eerdmans, 2010), 18.

2. Andrew Chester, *Messiah and Exaltation*, WUNT 207 (Tübingen: Mohr Siebeck, 2007), 193–201, esp. 193–96.

3. Geerhard von Rad, *Old Testament Theology*, 2 vols., trans. D. M. G. Stalker (New York: Harper & Row, 1965), 2.114.

4. Von Rad, *Old Testament Theology*, 115.

intended to imply the end of history in every given situation, though it could convey such depending upon the event.[5]

Apocalyptic

Matthew's Gospel in general and John's preaching in particular contain traits of apocalypticism.[6] Hagner states that "from beginning to end, and throughout, the Gospel makes such frequent use of apocalyptic motifs and the apocalyptic viewpoint that it deserves to be called the apocalyptic Gospel. Nearly every major section of the Gospel bears the stamp of apocalyptic in one way or another."[7] David Sim articulates eight characteristics of apocalyptic eschatology: a dualistic world view, a deterministic understanding of history, the belief in a series of eschatological woes preceding the end, the arrival of a savior figure, the judgment, descriptions of the fate of the wicked, the fate of the righteous, and an expectation of the end as imminent.[8] The literary genre of the Gospel of Matthew is not that of an apocalypse proper (e.g., Daniel, 1 Enoch, 4 Ezra, Apocalypse of Abraham, or the book of Revelation), but it does contain the themes enumerated by Sim. John proclaimed that the end was near, that there were only two types of people: the wheat and the chaff, fruitful and unfruitful trees; he proclaimed the imminent arrival of the kingdom of heaven and announced the coming separation which would be either to the eternal fire or to the barn of the one wielding the winnowing fork (3:12). Such descriptive activities in Matthew's Gospel will be designated "apocalyptic."

Conclusion

Matthew 3:11 is an important part of John the Baptist's apocalyptic eschatological proclamation. Matthew's narrative framework identifies Jesus as the messianic agent who will bring to pass the eschatological utterances and action of John. The combination of broader judgment themes found in Matthew and the prophets along with a close reading of Matt 3:11 in its narrative context will break new ground on the baptism in the Holy Spirit and fire and the baptism of John as the symbolic pointer to the reality he proclaimed.

---

5. Cf. E. P. Sanders, *The Historical Figure of Jesus* (London: The Penguin Press, 1993), 93.

6. Leopold Sabourin, "Apocalyptic Traits in Matthew's Gospel," *RSB* 3.1 (1983): 19–36; Donald Hagner, "Apocalyptic Motifs in the Gospel of Matthew: Continuity and Discontinuity," *HBT* 7.2 (1985): 53–82; Daniel M. Gurtner, "Interpreting Apocalyptic Symbolism in the Gospel of Matthew," *BBR* 22.4 (2012): 525–45.

7. Hagner, "Apocalyptic Motifs," 60.

8. David C. Sim, *Apocalyptic Eschatology in the Gospel of Matthew*, SNTSMS 88 (Cambridge: Cambridge University Press, 1996), 31–52.

Chapter 2

THE GRAMMAR OF THE LOGION

Introduction

In this chapter we will present arguments for interpreting βαπτίσει ἐν πνεύματι ἁγίῳ καὶ πυρί as a single, future outpouring of the Holy Spirit in judgment. The textual indicators for a single baptism are the following: the solitary preposition governing the two datives, the close connection of water and spirit, and the parallelism of βαπτίζω to the same group (ὑμᾶς). Grammatically, πνεύματι ἁγίῳ and πυρί are united into a single baptism both by the ὑμᾶς and by the singular ἐν.[1] Additional evidence for a single event in Spirit/fire will include analogous grammatical constructions in the NT and alternative constructions available to Matthew for distinguishing subjects/object.

Interpreters have sometimes thought John's prophecy to be of two baptisms, largely upon the basis that the baptism of the Holy Spirit would be understood positively, sometimes in terms of Pentecost or OT prophecy, and fire as the symbol of final judgment.[2] Even though the majority position favors a single

---

1. Craig L. Blomberg, *Matthew: An Exegetical and Theological Exposition of Holy Scripture*, NAC 22 (Nashville: Broadman Press, 1992), 80. James D. G. Dunn, *Baptism in the Holy Spirit: A Re-examination of the New Testament Teaching on the Gift of the Spirit in Relation to Pentecostalism Today* (Philadelphia: Westminster Press, 1970), 11. D. A. Carson, *Matthew*, EBC 1 (Grand Rapids: Zondervan, 1995), 105. William J. Dumbrell, *The Search for Order: Biblical Eschatology in Focus* (Grand Rapids: Baker, 1994), 162; James D. G. Dunn, "Spirit-and-Fire Baptism," *NovT* 14 (1972): 84. Donald A. Hagner, *Matthew 1-13*, WBC 33A (Nashville: Thomas Nelson, 2000), 52. M. J. Harris, *NIDNTTE*, 3.1178.

2. "Er 'tauft mit Feuer' will sagen: er taucht alles Gottwidrige in das Gerichtsfeuer hinein. Zugleich 'tauft er mit Geist,' d.h. er gießt den Geist Gottes wie Wasser über die Menschen aus." Leonhard Goppelt, *Theologie des Neuen Testaments* (Göttingen: Vandenhoeck & Ruprecht, 1980), 90. "The Spirit is for the righteous, the fire for the wicked." J. Steinmann, *Saint John the Baptist and the Desert Tradition* (New York: Harper & Brothers/ Longmans, n.d.), 69. Robert L. Webb, *John the Baptizer and Prophet: A Socio-Historical Study*, JSNTSup 62 (Sheffield: Sheffield Academic Press, 1991), 289–95. Holy Spirit and fire are two separate phases in the messianic mission.

future baptism (be it positive or negative in outlook), there have been sufficient challenges to warrant further examination of the prepositional phrase in question before offering an interpretation of the Holy Spirit and fire which depends, in part, upon the validity of a single, future baptism in Spirit and fire.[3]

The Significance of the Preposition's Repetition?

According to A. T. Robertson, "When several nouns are used with the same preposition the preposition is repeated more frequently than in the earlier Greek."[4] With specific reference to Matt 3:11 Harris observed that

> generally speaking, a preposition tends to be repeated before a series of nouns joined by καί more frequently in biblical Greek (under Semitic influence) than in non-Biblical Greek. Sometimes, therefore, the non-use of a second or third preposition in NT Greek may be theologically significant, indicating that the writer regarded the terms that he placed in one regimen as belonging naturally together or as a unit in concept or reality . . . in Matthew 3:11 the phrase en pneumati hagiō kai pyri points not to two baptisms . . . but to a single baptism in spirit-fire.[5]

Webb has argued that ἐν is implied (ellipsis) in the second baptismal-clause (πυρί) and that ὑμᾶς indicates two groups of people and by implication two baptisms.[6] It is a linguistic mistake to refer to John's announcement as a future "baptism" (a singular event) rather than a future "baptizing."[7]

Juxtaposing the statements of Harris and Webb raises an important question, "How much weight can be laid upon the lack of repetition of the preposition?" If it is not necessary or theologically significant, are there any other contextual factors that would favor a second baptism rather than a hendiadys?

---

3. "More and more, however, the two are being seen as a hendiadys." Grant Osborne, *Matthew*, ZECNT (Grand Rapids: Zondervan, 2010), 116.

4. A. T. Robertson, *A Grammar of the Greek New Testament* (Nashville: Broadman, 1934), 566. Likewise Turner, "A strong tendency to repeat the preposition in a series is consistently maintained on part of the different writers of the New Testament": Nigel Turner, "An Alleged Semitism," *ET* 66 (1995): 253.

5. Harris, *NIDNTTE*, 1178. But see Moule's warning about building exegetical conclusions upon prepositions; C. F. D. Moule, *An Idiom Book of the New Testament* (Cambridge: Cambridge University Press, 1982), 48–49.

6. Webb, *John the Baptizer and Prophet*, 289–95.

7. Ibid., 290–91.

OT Semitisms

The influence of Semitisms might be one of the main reasons for the reduplication of the preposition.[8] Matthew Black made the observation that one of the characteristic features of Semitic usage is the repetition of a preposition before every noun of a series which it governs.[9] In his study of the B-text of Ezekiel, Turner shows that repetitions with the preposition occur seventy-eight times out of a possible ninety-three. In the NT, the percentage drops dramatically.[10] Turner's findings raise the possibility that the lack of recurrence of the preposition might not be so significant.

NT Inquiry In order to gain greater clarity, a NT search was made for ἐν + dative + καί + dative (without variables). Synoptic parallels were included in the final count. The solitary preposition occurs forty-three times in the NT. This number becomes all the more significant when it is compared to the ἐν + dative + καί + ἐν + dative pattern (without variables), yielding twenty-six results in the NT. This specifically narrow NT inquiry confirms and brings a caution to bear: unlike the LXX, the NT's *exclusion* of the preposition ἐν is statistically more likely than its *inclusion*. To appeal to the absence of the preposition in Matt 3:11 proves very little.

Because the omission of the preposition is nearly twice as likely as its inclusion, our focus will be upon similar grammatical constructions. A search was made for all the ἐν + dative + καί + dative constructions in the NT, with parameters set for one- to three-word variables.[11] Of the 115 occurrences, 59 were excluded

---

8. Benjamin G. Wright III, "A Note on Statistical Analysis of Septuagintal Syntax," *JBL* 104.1 (1985): 111–14. David A. Black, "New Testament Semitisms," *TBT* 39 (1988): 215–23. For an overview of Semitisms in the NT see James H. Moulton and Wilbert F. Howard, *A Grammar of the Greek New Testament* (Edinburgh: T&T Clark, 1929), 413–86.

9. Matthew Black, *An Aramaic Approach to the Gospels and Acts* (Oxford: Oxford University Press, 1979), 114–15.

10. Repetition occurs 58 percent of the time in Romans and 1 Corinthians, 37 percent in Ephesians, 17 percent pastorals, Revelation 63 percent, John 53 percent, Mark 38 percent and Matthew 31 percent. Nigel Turner, *A Grammar of New Testament Greek* (Edinburgh: T&T Clark, 1976), 4:93; cf. 3:275.

11. Matt 2:16; 3:11; 4:16; 6:2, 5; 11:21; 13:57; 14:6; 23:20, 21; 24:19; 26:69; Mark 5:3, 5; 13:17; Luke 1:6, 17, 75, 79; 2:44, 52; 3:16; 4:36; 7:25; 7:32; 8:15; 10:13; 16:10; 18:30; 21:23, 25, 34; 24:19, 44; John 4:23, 24; 5:14, 26; 18:20; Acts 1:8; 2:46; 7:22, 36; 16:2; 17:17; Rom 15:9; 1 Cor 1:5, 10; 2:3; 10:2; 14:21; 2 Cor 1:12; 2:15; 8:7; 11:27; 12:10, 12; Eph 1:1, 8; 3:21; 4:24; 5:9, 19; 6:4, 10, 18; Phil 1:1, 7, 9, 13; 4:6, 12; Col 1:2, 9; 2:7, 11, 13, 16, 18, 23; 1 Thess 1:1, 5, 7, 8; 4:4; 2 Thess 1:1, 4; 2:9, 13, 17; 3:8; 1 Tim. 2:2, 7, 9, 15; 5:17; 2 Tim 1:13; 4:2; Titus 3:3; Phlm 16; Heb 12:23; 1 Pet 3:19; 2 Pet 3:11, 18; 1 John 2:8, 24; 3:18, 24; 5:6; 2 John 3; Jude 1; Rev 1:9; 6:8; 14:10; 18:16.

for grammatical reasons.[12] The remaining fifty-four support an interpretation of βαπτίσει ἐν πνεύματι ἁγίῳ καὶ πυρί as a hendiadys. In what follows, we offer seven representative NT samples with brief comments, after which we will draw several conclusions.

NT Parallel Arrangements   Matthew 11:21 οὐαί σοι, Χοραζίν, οὐαί σοι, Βηθσαϊδά· ὅτι εἰ ἐν Τύρῳ καὶ Σιδῶνι ἐγένοντο αἱ δυνάμεις αἱ γενόμεναι ἐν ὑμῖν, πάλαι ἂν ἐν σάκκῳ καὶ σποδῷ μετενόησαν. This is a hypothetical statement that highlights the culpability of Chorazin and Bethsaida. "Sackcloth and ashes" are coordinating symbols of a singular concept, repentance (Esth 4:1, 3; Isa 58:5; Dan 9:3). A sequence of events is rendered unlikely: first they repented with sackcloth, later with ashes. A comparison is also not easily maintained: some will wear sackcloth, others ash.

Luke 4:36 καὶ ἐγένετο θάμβος ἐπὶ πάντας καὶ συνελάλουν πρὸς ἀλλήλους λέγοντες· τίς ὁ λόγος οὗτος ὅτι ἐν ἐξουσίᾳ καὶ δυνάμει ἐπιτάσσει τοῖς ἀκαθάρτοις πνεύμασιν καὶ ἐξέρχονται. Jesus commands (ἐπιτάσσει) the unclean spirits (accusative case and plural) with authority and power (dative and singular). There is no possibility of separating ἐν ἐξουσίᾳ καὶ δυνάμει as these datives are descriptive of the singular exorcism (v. 35).

Luke 1:17 καὶ αὐτὸς προελεύσεται ἐνώπιον αὐτοῦ ἐν πνεύματι καὶ δυνάμει Ἠλίου. The datives explain the way in which John the Baptist will go before Jesus. To have the spirit of Elijah is no different than to have the power (2 Kgs 2:13–15).

Luke 1:74–75 ἀφόβως ἐκ χειρὸς ἐχθρῶν ῥυσθέντας λατρεύειν αὐτῷ ἐν ὁσιότητι καὶ δικαιοσύνῃ ἐνώπιον αὐτοῦ πάσαις ταῖς ἡμέραις ἡμῶν. It is unlikely that in the future some will serve in holiness and others in righteousness.

John 4:23 ἀλλ᾽ ἔρχεται ὥρα καὶ νῦν ἐστιν, ὅτε οἱ ἀληθινοὶ προσκυνηταὶ προσκυνήσουσιν τῷ πατρὶ ἐν πνεύματι καὶ ἀληθείᾳ· καὶ γὰρ ὁ πατὴρ τοιούτους ζητεῖ τοὺς προσκυνοῦντας αὐτόν. To worship the Father in spirit is to engage in true worship, which suggests that πνεύματι and ἀληθείᾳ are not descriptive of two different types of worship but of one.

Luke 1:79 ἐπιφᾶναι τοῖς ἐν σκότει καὶ σκιᾷ θανάτου καθημένοις, τοῦ κατευθῦναι τοὺς πόδας ἡμῶν εἰς ὁδὸν εἰρήνης. The locative datives ("darkness" and "shadow") describe the singular eschatological situation. The aorist infinitive has as its object the substantival participle of κάθημαι. Luke has bracketed the dative nouns by placing them between the article and its corresponding participle. The darkness is the shadow of death.

---

12. Reduplication of ἐν: Matt 2:16; 6:2, 5; 11:21; 13:57; 23:20, 21; 24:19; Mark 5:5; Luke 16:10; 18:30; John 5:26; 18:20; Acts 1:8; 7:36; 26:29; 1 Cor 1:10; 2:3; 10:2; 14:21; 2 Cor 2:15; 11:27; Eph 3:21; 6:10; Phil 4:12; Col 2:16; 1 Thess 1:5, 7, 8; Phlm 16; 1 John 2:8, 24; 3:24; 5:6; Rev 6:8. Lists (names, places, things): Acts 16:2; 17:17; 2 Cor 8:7; 11:27; 12:10, 12; Eph 5:9, 19; Phil 1:11 9; Col 1:2; 1 Thess 1:1; 2 Thess 1:1; 3:8; 1 Tim 2:9,15; Rev 18:16. Independent/dependent clauses, compound sentences, disanalagous syntax: Matt 14:6; 26:69; Mark 5:3; John 5:14; Heb 12:23; Jude 1.

This same principle is operative in John 3:5 which contains a similar grammatical construction using a different preposition: ἀπεκρίθη Ἰησοῦς· ἀμὴν ἀμὴν λέγω σοι, ἐὰν μή τις γεννηθῇ ἐξ ὕδατος καὶ πνεύματος, οὐ δύναται εἰσελθεῖν εἰς τὴν βασιλείαν τοῦ θεοῦ. The future aspect of the aorist followed by ἐκ + genitives do not point to two different things separated in time (such as the water of embryonic fluid first and the birth of the spirit second). These genitives describe the nature of the second birth. The parallelism of γεννηθῇ ἐξ ὕδατος καὶ πνεύματος (3:5) and ἐκ τοῦ πνεύματος (3:6) poses a challenge to a twofold birth interpretation.[13] As in the case of the baptism in the Holy Spirit and fire, so also for the new birth in water and the Spirit, both constructions describe a conceptual unity, not diversity.

The above examples have illustrated two principles. First, two datives governed by ἐν do not convey a notion of sequence, or separation of time. The timing of the verb for the second dative is contemporaneous with the first. Second, and more importantly, an antithetical or contrastive relationship of the datives was *not* discovered in all fifty-four samples.[14] The evidence shows that two datives modified by ἐν tend to give either a unified negative impression ("in sackcloth and ashes") or a positive one ("in spirit and truth").[15] How the antithetical gracious baptism of the Spirit and baptism of judgment by fire can be maintained on grammatical grounds remains unclear. These texts demonstrate that an additional dative noun, joined by the coordinating conjunction καί, gives texture to the overall picture; it is a composition of similar but not identical images.[16] On the narrative level, Matthew conceived of one future baptism in the Holy Spirit and fire. If Matthew was describing two different baptisms a disjunctive particle could have made a clear distinction between the two.

13. Linda L. Belleville, "'Born of Water and Spirit': John 3:5," *TJ* 1 (1980): 135. Water symbolizes the Spirit elsewhere (John 7:37–39; 4:10–14). The combination of water with Spirit was not unique (Isa 32:15; 44:3–4; Ezek 36:25–27; 39:29; Joel 3:1–5; Zech 12:10; 1 QS 3. 6–9; 4.21).

14. Philippians 1:7 could be an illustration of contrasting datives: καὶ ἐν τῇ ἀπολογίᾳ καὶ βεβαιώσει τοῦ εὐαγγελίου (defense and establishment of the gospel), or, both serve a unified purpose in Paul's program for the advance of the gospel. In defending the truth Paul was establishing the gospel.

15. See also Sib. Or. 3:287; 14:84; T. Levi 16:5; T. Ab. 13:14; Aris. Ex 37; 4 Bar. 6:23; Pss. Sol. 2:23; 3:8; 4:7.

16. The repetition of the preposition is outside the purview of the argument, but the principle might also apply even when the preposition is repeated, as in the case of 1 Thess 1:5, ἐν λόγῳ μόνον ἀλλὰ καὶ ἐν δυνάμει καὶ ἐν πνεύματι ἁγίῳ. Paul's assertion is that when he preached there was a demonstration of the Holy Spirit and power *attending* their preaching.

Alternative Grammatical Options   Based upon the regular usage of the disjunctive conjunction (examples given below), Matthew had at least two ways to describe two different baptisms. He could have written αὐτὸς ὑμᾶς βαπτίσει ἐν πνεύματι ἁγίῳ ἢ [ἐν] καὶ πυρί (he will baptize you in Holy Spirit or [in] fire), or, αὐτὸς ὑμᾶς βαπτίσει ἢ ἐν πνεύματι ἁγίῳ ἢ [ἐν] πυρί (he will baptize you either in/with Holy Spirit or [in] fire).[17] As the texts taken from Matthew show, when Matthew wished to make such distinctions, he could do so by using ἤ.

Matthew 17:25 οἱ βασιλεῖς τῆς γῆς ἀπὸ τίνων λαμβάνουσιν τέλη ἢ κῆνσον; ἀπὸ τῶν υἱῶν αὐτῶν ἢ ἀπὸ τῶν ἀλλοτρίων; "From whom do kings of the earth take toll or tribute? From their sons or from others?"

Matthew 21:25 τὸ βάπτισμα τὸ Ἰωάννου πόθεν ἦν; ἐξ οὐρανοῦ ἢ ἐξ ἀνθρώπων; "The baptism of John, whence was it? From heaven or from people?"

Matthew 27:17 . . . τίνα θέλετε ἀπολύσω ὑμῖν, [Ἰησοῦν τὸν] Βαραββᾶν ἢ Ἰησοῦν τὸν λεγόμενον χριστόν; "Whom do you want me to release for you, Barabbas or Jesus who is called Christ?"

Matthew 12:33 Ἢ ποιήσατε τὸ δένδρον καλὸν καὶ τὸν καρπὸν αὐτοῦ καλόν, ἢ ποιήσατε τὸ δένδρον σαπρὸν καὶ τὸν καρπὸν αὐτοῦ σαπρόν· ἐκ γὰρ τοῦ καρποῦ τὸ δένδρον γινώσκεται. "Either make the tree good, and its fruit good; or make the tree bad, and its fruit bad; for the tree is known by its fruit."[18]

With regard to Matt 3:11, the above examples demonstrate that the messianic actions of salvation and judgment could have been contrasted with an either/ or grammatical configuration: "Either he will baptize you in the Holy Spirit or in fire." The repentant could expect the former, the unrepentant the latter. How one responds determines which metaphorical reality applies. Like previous expectations, judgment and restoration were twin eschatological realities (Isa 34; 66:24; Joel 3:9–16; Zeph 3:8, 12–13; Mal 3:18; Jdt 16:17; Pss. Sol. 15:3–13; 17:23–46; 1 En. 1; 1 QS 2.16; 4Q280). John shared this eschatological outlook as v. 12 indicates (i.e., the destinies of wheat and chaff). But if Matthew wished to make such a contrast between the righteous and the wicked by two different baptisms one can only wonder why he did not use ἤ to do so. And so, without any textual variants to suggest otherwise, and without a clear grammatical delineation to set up the contrast, the grammar of 3:11 favors a single baptism.

Conclusion

The grammar and NT parallel constructions support a single, future baptism. The single preposition ἐν, followed by two datives joined by καί, usually expresses

---

17. Bruner and Taylor believe that this is what Matthew has in mind but they do not substantiate it grammatically. Frederick D. Bruner, *The Christbook: A Historical/Theological Commentary, Matthew 1-12* (Waco: Word, 1987), 80–81. Joan E. Taylor, *The Immerser: John the Baptist within Second Temple Judaism* (Grand Rapids: Eerdmans, 1997), 140.

18. Cf. Acts 4:7; Rom 4:10; 1 Cor 4:21 and Col 2:16.

either the positive or negative aspect of the controlling verb. No antithetical relationships between the objects are found in similar NT grammatical constructions. The relationship of the datives to the verb is that of providing a cohesive, multifaceted picture of the action (or state of being). While grammarians are right in recognizing the recurrence of the preposition in the LXX, this phenomenon should not be invoked for the purposes of highlighting the importance of its absence in the NT. Finally, we have attempted to show that when a distinction was sought, ἤ ἐν could be used. The announcement of John the Baptist will be rightly understood as a unified picture of distress and judgment portrayed by the singular baptism ἐν πνεύματι ἁγίῳ καὶ πυρί.

Chapter 3

THE MEANING OF THE LOGION

Introduction

In the previous chapter it was argued that the grammar of Matt 3:11 favors one future baptism ἐν πνεύματι ἁγίῳ καὶ πυρί. We now turn to an outline of the three main interpretations of the difficult logion. After surveying and evaluating these oft-discussed explanations, we will go on to offer a fourth that will provide greater clarity to Matthew's placement and theological purpose of the logion and thereby stimulate future exegetical reflection.

Category #1: An Announcement of Purification

The purification interpretation appears to have its roots in the third century with Origen. In his comments concerning the future baptism by Jesus, Origen states, "For his baptism is not that of the body only; He fills the penitent with the Holy Ghost, and his diviner fire does away with everything material and consumes everything that is earthly, not only from him who admits it to his life, but even of him who hears of it from those who have it."[1] The fire which accompanies the

---

1. *Origen's Commentary on John* 6.17 (*ANF* 10:366). Paraphrasing the words of the Baptizer, Origen writes, "For I am come to make ready for the Lord a people prepared for Him, and by my baptism of repentance to prepare the ground for Him who is to come after me, and *who will thus benefit you much more effectively and powerfully than my strength could*" (emphasis mine) *Origen's Commentary on John* 6.17 (*ANF* 10:366). Luz, understands "fire" to mean "purgatory" and cites Origen's homilies on Jer 2:3 and Ezek 1:13. Ulrich Luz, *Matthew 1-7*, Hermeneia, ed. Helmut Koester, trans. James E. Crouch (Minneapolis: Fortress, 1985), 171. Meyer and Dunn think that Origen took "fire" to mean "everlasting punishment." Neither author gives citations from Origen's works. Heinrich A. W. Meyer, *Critical and Exegetical Hand-Book to the Gospel of Matthew*, vol. 1 (Edinburgh: T&T Clark, 1844; repr., Peabody: Hendrickson, 1983), 81; Dunn, "Spirit-and-Fire Baptism," 81. Bock, on the other hand, cites Homilies on Luke 24 for Origen's understanding of "fire" as "judgment"; Darrel L. Bock, *Luke 1:1-9:50*, ECNT 1 (Grand Rapids: Baker, 1994), 322.

Spirit refines and cleanses the individual, purging the person of impurities. Augustine, Theodore of Heraclea, and Chrysostom followed this interpretation as did Calvin.[2]

This interpretation experienced a reasonable measure of success into the twentieth century.[3] Though scholarly opinion has suspected a Christianizing of John,[4] the Dead Sea Scrolls have largely reversed this explanation.[5] The question of the timing of the purification-baptism is either delegated into the indefinite future (from the perspective of John the Baptist) or it is understood to be an announcement of Pentecost.[6]

Category #2: πνεύματι ἁγίῳ as Grace, πυρί, as Judgment

According to others, πνεύματι ἁγίῳ is best understood as a gift for the righteous, while πυρί is a symbol of destruction. This is sometimes understood as one baptism, while others find two.[7] Regardless of whether one holds to a single or

---

2. Augustine, *Sermons on New Testament Lessons* 21.19 (*NPNF* 6:324); for Heraclea cf. Manlio Simonetti, ed., *Matthew 1-13*, ACCS 1a (Downers Grove: Inter Varsity Press, 2001), 47–48; Chrysostom, *Homilies on the Gospel of Saint Matthew* 11.6 (*NPNF* 10:71); John Calvin, *Harmony of the Gospels Matthew, Mark and Luke*, vol. 1, trans. William Pringle (Grand Rapids: Eerdmans, 1972), 127–28.

3. Cf. Luz's comments on the history of influence: Luz, *Matthew*, 1.171.

4. L. W. Barnard, "Matt. 3.11/Luke 3.16," *JTS* 8.1 (1957): 107; Rudolph Bultmann, *The History of the Synoptic Tradition* (Oxford: Basil Blackwell, 1963), 246; Vincent Taylor, *The Gospel According to St. Mark* (London/New York: Macmillan/St. Martin's Press, 1955), 157; William F. Flemington, *The New Testament Doctrine of Baptism* (London: SPCK, 1948), 18–20.

5. Cf. 1 QS 3.7–9; 4.21; 1 QH 16. 11–12. See J. A. T. Robinson, *12 New Testament Studies* (London: SCM, 1962), 19.

6. Robert Jamieson and A. R. Fausset, *A Commentary: Critical, Experimental and Practical on the Old and New Testament*, vol. 5 (Grand Rapids: Eerdmans, 1948), 12; D. A. Carson, *Matthew*, EBC 1 (Grand Rapids: Zondervan, 1995), 105; R. T. France, *Matthew*, TNTC (Grand Rapids: Eerdmans, 1989), 93; David Hill, *The Gospel of Matthew*, NCBC (Grand Rapids: Eerdmans, 1984), 94–95; Robert H. Mounce, *Matthew*, NIBC (Peabody: Hendrickson, 1991), 19–20. Blomberg, *Matthew*, 79; Leon Morris, *The Gospel According to Matthew* (Grand Rapids: Eerdmans, 1992), 62; Luke T. Johnson, *The Acts of the Apostles*, SPS 5 (Collegeville: The Liturgical Press, 1992), 25–26; John B. Polhill, *Acts*, NAC 26 (Nashville: Broadman, 1992), 83.

7. For the single baptism view see Raymond E. Brown, *New Testament Essays* (London/ Dublin: Geoffrey Chapman, 1965), 135–36; George Eldon Ladd, *A Theology of the New Testament*, rev. ed. (Grand Rapids: Eerdmans, 1993), 33; For two baptisms see Webb, *John the Baptizer and Prophet*, 289–95; John Nolland, "'In Such a Manner It Is Fitting for Us to Fulfill All Righteousness': Reflections on the Place of Baptism in the Gospel of Matthew," in

double baptism, the end result is functionally the same: the benefit of the Spirit is given to the righteous and the fire is reserved for the wicked.[8]

Category #3: Both Positive and Negative within Each Term

The third interpretation mediates between grace and judgment. According to Dunn:

> What John held out before his hearers was a baptism which was neither solely destructive nor solely gracious, but which contained both elements in itself. Its effect would then presumably depend on the condition of its recipients: the repentant would experience a purgative, refining, but ultimately merciful judgment; the impenitent, the stiff-necked and hard of heart, would be broken and destroyed.[9]

On this interpretation there is no polarity between Holy Spirit and fire. Both convey the dual ideas of judgment and purification (1 Cor 3:10–15; Isa 4:4; 44:3; T. Isaac 5.21–5; 4 Ezra 13.8–11).[10]

With the first interpretation, category 3 affirms the role of the Spirit with regard to purification. Yet it is correct to see more in John's preaching than a promise for the repentant. It is here that category 3 is similar to category 2, but instead of two groups (repentant and unrepentant) as the recipients of two different symbols, this third interpretation combines the symbols and applies them to both.

Baptism, the New Testament and the Church, JSNTSup 171, eds. S. E. Porter and A. R. Cross (Sheffield: Sheffield Academic Press, 1999), 71; Craig S. Keener, *A Commentary on the Gospel of Matthew* (Grand Rapids: Eerdmans, 1999), 128; Gary T. Cage, *The Holy Spirit: A Sourcebook with Commentary* (Reno: Charlotte House, 1995), 374–77.

8. Taylor, *The Immerser*, 138–43; Floyd V. Filson, *The Gospel According to St. Matthew* (London: A&C Black, 1975), 66; Herman Ridderbos, *Matthew*, trans. R. Togtman (Grand Rapids: Zondervan, 1987), 54–57; Geerhardus Vos, *Redemptive History and Biblical Interpretation*, ed. Richard B. Gaffin (Phillipsburg: Presbyterian & Reformed, 1980), 300–01; W. H. Brownlee "John the Baptist in the Light of Ancient Scrolls," in *The Scrolls and the New Testament*, eds. Krister Stendahl and James H. Charlesworth (New York: Crossroad, 1992), 43; Luz, *Matthew*, 1.171–72; Charles H. H. Scobie, *John the Baptist* (London: SCM Press, 1964), 70–71.

9. Dunn, "Spirit-and-Fire Baptism," 86.

10. George R. Beasley-Murray, *Baptism in the New Testament* (Grand Rapids: Eerdmans, 1962), 37–39, William D. Davies and Dale C. Allison Jr., *Matthew I–VII*, ICC (Edinburgh: T&T Clark, 1988), 316–17; Warren Carter, *Matthew and the Margins: A Sociopolitical and Religious Reading* (Maryknoll: Orbis, 2005), 100; Hagner, *Matthew 1-13*, 52; Brian C. Dennert, *John the Baptist and the Jewish Setting of Matthew*, WUNT 403 (Tübingen: Mohr Siebeck, 2015), 159.

The result is still largely the same, the repentant will be purified and the wicked will be consumed in fire. All pass through the same judgment, but the results will vary depending upon the status of the individual (i.e., the righteous or the wicked).

Evaluation of Category #1

There is no question that category #1 provides an interpretation of Holy Spirit and fire which has numerous parallel passages in the OT, NT, and DSS (Joel 2:28; Ezek 36:25–27; 39:29; Zech 13:9; Mal 3:2; Acts 1:8; 2:4; Rom 15:16; 1 Cor. 3:13; Titus 3:5; 1 QS 4.20ff.). Also attractive is the possibility of the fulfillment of John's preaching at Pentecost (Acts 2). Furthermore, this pre-Pentecost announcement could offer useful corroborating information concerning the role of the Holy Spirit, particularly with respect to sanctification (Rom 15:16; Eph 1:13–14; Titus 3:5).

The greatest difficulty is the contextual indicators within the pericope. If we are to assume that purification is the intended meaning of the fire imagery in v. 11, it would be strange that vv. 10 and 12 present the same image as destructive. It is not that the baptism in the Holy Spirit and fire merely refines and purifies the recipients, it destroys and consumes them.[11] Without exception, the meaning of πυρί is negative in Matthew's Gospel.[12] If a purification interpretation is adopted, this would be the only place in Matthew's Gospel where fire is not destructive, eschatologically, or otherwise.

Evaluation of Category #2

The second category fares somewhat better contextually, as it accounts for two categories of people (believing and unbelieving) listening to John. This interpretation rightly understands πυρί in light of its bracketing verses. Akin to the first interpretation and in agreement with other NT passages (John 14:26; 15:26; 16:13; Acts 15:18; Rom 5:5; 8:2–27; 15:16; 2 Cor 13:14; Eph 1:13), this second category also understands the work of πνεύματι ἁγίῳ to be generally positive. Notwithstanding these aspects, there are several difficulties which suggest a different meaning.

First, the Matthean context does not suggest that John is addressing two different groups of people in v. 11. Those arguing for this category could view vv. 11–12 as an insertion of a separate discourse, or John may have "turned" from the religious leaders to the crowds in his address, but there are no textual indicators to suggest a shift in audience. The second difficulty is the distinction made between the

---

11. Cf. πνεῦμα: Eze 37:14; Jub. 1.23; 4 Esr. 6.26; T. Jud 24.3; 1QS 4.20–21; 1QH 16.11–12; 1 Cor 2:13; Rom 8:12–14; John 3:3–5; 4:23–25; Acts 10:38–45; 11:15–16; πυρί: Deut 4:24; 9:3; Isa 6:6–7; 10:17; 33:14; Zech 13:9; Mal 3:3; 1 Pet 1:7.

12. Matt 3:10–12; 5:22; 7:19; 13:40; 13:42; 13:50; 17:15; 18:8; 18:9; 25:41.

baptism(s) in πνεύματι ἁγίῳ and πυρί, as already indicated above.[13] Matthew has combined πνεύματι ἁγίῳ and πυρί and sees them as descriptive of a unified event.

Evaluation of Category #3

The benefit of category 3 is that it avoids the separation of πνεύματι ἁγίῳ and πυρί while retaining the dual outcomes of the baptism. The difficulty is the Matthean context. Specifically, to whom is John speaking? Is it to a mixed group of people (such as in Luke 3:7)? To the religious leaders (Matt 3:7)? A combination of the two? This question directly affects whether or not something positive, negative, or a combination of the two is in view.

Matthew's shaping of the text has not deterred scholars from looking for an original (i.e., unmodified) address delivered to a mixed crowd.[14] This concern is understandably influenced by a comparison with Luke and the parallelism, especially of the pronoun ὑμᾶς.[15] Because ὑμᾶς is thought to be representative of the repentant and unrepentant, commentators have sought to find something positive in 3:11.[16] One solution has been to understand the combination of Spirit and fire as constituting a form of purification. Evans admits that an attempt to anchor fire to OT purification only yields a couple of results.[17] Second Temple literature could also support an explanation of the Holy Spirit and fire as refinement/purification.[18] As advantageous as these backgrounds are, it is difficult to see how an announcement of purification fits within the context. Outside of v. 11, there is nothing in the immediate context that suggests refinement or purification.[19] Removal of the fruitless trees and chaff is different than refinement of the fruit-bearing trees and wheat. What is the nature of the refinement? With few exceptions, this question is usually not addressed. [20]

---

13. Cf. ch. 2.

14. Davies and Allison *Matthew*, vol. 1, 317; Hagner, *Matthew* 1.52.

15. Cf. Dunn, "Spirit-and-Fire Baptism," 86.

16. Some are still content to hypothesize that Q could have read: αὐτὸς ὑμᾶς βαπτίσει ἐν πυρί. W. Barnes Tatum, *John the Baptist and Jesus: A Report of the Jesus Seminar* (Sonoma: Polebridge Press, 1994), 130–31.

17. Evans lists only two passages (Num 31:23; Isa 4:4). Christopher F. Evans, *Saint Luke*, TPINTC (London: SCM, 1990), 243.

18. Daniel J. Harrington, *The Gospel of Matthew*, SPS 1 (Collegeville: The Liturgical Press, 1991), 59; Davies and Allison, *Matthew*, 1.317; France, *Matthew*, 93; Hagner, *Matthew*, 1.52; Hill, *Matthew*, 94–95.

19. Unlike Josephus (*Ant.* 18.117), the gospels nowhere attribute a purification function to John's baptism.

20. Geldenhuys postulates that both sin and the sinner clinging to sin will be consumed in the refinement process. Norval Geldenhuys, *The Gospel of Luke*, NICNT (Grand Rapids: Eerdmans, 1979), 140.

According to Davies and Allison, "He (John) proclaimed that at the boundary of the new age, all would pass through the fiery *rûah* of God, a stream which would purify the righteous and destroy the unrighteous."[21] This is the case for 4 Ezra 13.8–11, but it is not clear that this is what Matthew is intending. The axe and the fire do not suggest a refinement that cleanses the individual, but a judgment that destroys the wicked (3:10–12). This is an important clarification: if all experience the Spirit/fire baptism, then 3:10 and 3:12 are out of place, for *there the wheat and fruit trees are spared the fire*. If the Matthean context does not indicate the dual function of destroying/purging the wicked *and* refining/purifying the righteous in vv. 10 and 12, why should v. 11 be an exception? Apart from importing a notion of refinement and purification into πνεύματι ἁγίῳ, the Baptist's preaching is, by and large, *curse-laden*. As Hagner observed, any blessing here is indirect.[22]

Eschatological Judgment against Israel

The interpretation offered here agrees with that of category 3. Baptism in the Holy Spirit and fire is the removal of the wicked. What we do not find is a notion of future cleansing, unless one understands the removal of the wicked to be a cleansing of Israel. We can also agree with the second interpretation that the fire of v. 11 is not for the repentant. But the differences are greater than the similarities and for this reason a fourth category of interpretation is offered. John is not announcing a baptism of Spirit/fire that cleanses the righteous, or has a dual outcome for the righteous and the wicked. The Matthean usage and placement of the baptism in the Holy Spirit and fire is eschatological judgment upon Israel for national disobedience and unbelief.[23] Again, our specific focus is to explain the meaning and the function of the logion as it appears in Matthew. The emphases and implications of the other synoptic accounts (as well as John and Acts) are not necessarily those of Matthew.[24]

This interpretation of eschatological judgment against Israel also shares certain affinities with the analysis of Goguel, nearly a hundred years ago.[25] Goguel understood that the meaning of John's prophecy is best explained by v. 12. The "stronger one" with his winnowing basket in hand will clean the threshing floor, putting the grain in the granary and burning the bundle of chaff with unquenchable fire.[26] "This latter comment *fixes the meaning* of the prophecy which relates to

---

21. Davies and Allison, *Matthew*, 1.317.

22. Hagner, *Matthew*, 1.52.

23. Detailed reasons for the judgment will be treated in chs. 7, 8, and 10.

24. Neither do we believe that Matthew's accentuation of the judgment is entirely missing in his synoptic counterparts.

25. Maurice Goguel, *Au seuil de l'évangile Jean-Baptiste* (Paris: Payot, 1928).

26. Goguel, *Au seuil de l'évangile*, 39.

the 'stronger one.'"[27] Goguel thought that John was referring either to God or to an Apocalyptic Messiah who would discriminate between the just destined to salvation and the evil doomed to annihilation.[28] The messianic judgment is expressed by two images—by that of baptism of fire and by that of the harvest.[29] "It is a judgment which will be realized by the Spirit, that is to say, by the power of God and by the fire."[30] He goes on to show how John's announcement is "at home" in Judeo-Christian apocalyptic.[31]

In his study of John the Baptist, Goguel offered his interpretation in a cursory manner, with little exegetical argumentation to support his analysis. His synoptic approach is supplemented here with exegetical and grammatical arguments that demonstrate that the Matthean meaning of the Holy Spirit and fire is eschatological judgment and that the recipient of that judgment is national Israel.

The Grammatical Structure of the Logion

The paratactic structure of v. 11 with its correlative conjunctions μὲν … δέ strengthens the contrast between the respective baptisms and baptizers and is set forth in a chiastic configuration:[32]

A Ἐγὼ μὲν ὑμᾶς βαπτίζω εἰς μετάνοιαν,
   B ἐρχόμενος ἰσχυρότερός
   B¹ οὐκ εἰμὶ ἱκανὸς
A¹ αὐτὸς ὑμᾶς βαπτίσει ἐν πνεύματι ἁγίῳ καὶ πυρί÷

The juxtaposing of the baptismal clauses helps to accentuate the degree of the contrast, with the parenthetical center stressing the superior/inferior qualities of the baptizers. The chiastic structure with its repetition of ὑμᾶς provides a clue as to the recipients of the baptism in Spirit/fire. Is John addressing the crowds, the Pharisees and Sadducees, or a combination of the two? In the case of Mark, it is clear that the crowds are in view. Mentioning no other observers, the recipients of John's baptism are by default his listeners. Luke's account is also directed to the multitudes (Luke 3:7, 15–16). The ethical imperatives following the crowd's response to John's γεννήματα ἐχιδνῶν are unique to Luke. The crowds receive the rebuke (3:7–9) as well as the news of the coming baptism in the Holy Spirit and fire (vv. 16–17).

---

27. Ibid., emphasis mine.
28. Ibid.
29. Ibid.
30. Ibid., 39–40.
31. Ibid., 40.
32. Harrington, *Matthew*, 58.

It is at this point that Matthew differs from his synoptic counterparts. He inverts Mark's order, inserting the coming of the crowds for baptism (Mark 1:1–5; Luke 3:7) between the comparison of Elijah and John the Baptist on the one hand (Mark 1:6; missing in Luke), and the comparison of John and the Coming One on the other (Mark 1:7–8; Luke 3:16).[33] Matthew ends the crowd's response to John by introducing a second group: the Pharisees and Sadducees. From a grammatical and narrative perspective, 3:7–12 is a unit, despite the original context of the saying. Matthew introduces the change by inserting the coordinating conjunction δέ:

The crowds: Τότε ἐξεπορεύετο πρὸς αὐτὸν (3:5)

The religious leaders: Ἰδὼν δὲ πολλοὺς τῶν Φαρισαίων καὶ Σαδδουκαίων ἐρχομέν ους ἐπὶ τὸ βάπτισμα αὐτοῦ (3:7)

Jesus: Τότε παραγίνεται ὁ Ἰησοῦς . . . πρὸς τὸν Ἰωάννην τοῦ βαπτισθῆναι ὑπ᾽ αὐτοῦ. (3:13–17).

Unlike Mark and Luke, Matthew directs John's scathing rebuke (vv. 7–12) to one group of people *within* the crowds that have come out to receive his baptism. A number of scholars maintain that John's invective is unlikely to be leveled at the crowds, as the address is ill-suited for those coming in sincerity for baptism.[34] On the other hand, such a derisive censure would fit if those addressed were religious opponents. The phrase "we have Abraham as our father" suggests that they were not intending to be baptized, but were instead counting on their birth status. Goulder surmises that Luke is "generalizing."[35] According to Witherington, the Baptist's "Who warned you to flee?" indicates that John is surprised to find the Pharisees and Sadducees coming for baptism in order to flee from the wrath to come, whereas this was surely not his reaction to all those who came.[36] He would not have been generally surprised to see the crowds coming out to him because he was the one who called them.[37] Such observations have not gone unchallenged.[38]

---

33. Robert H. Gundry, *Matthew: A Commentary on His Literary and Theological Art* (Grand Rapids: Eerdmans, 1982), 45.

34. Michael D. Goulder, *Luke: A New Paradigm*, JSNTSup 20 (Sheffield: Sheffield Academic Press, 1989), 273; Ben Witherington III, "Jesus and the Baptist—Two of a Kind," *Society of Biblical Literature 1988 Seminar Papers*, SBLSP 27 (Atlanta: Scholars Press, 1988), 230; Joseph A. Fitzmyer, *The Gospel According to Luke 1–9*, AYBC (New York: Doubleday, 1995), 467; E. Earle Ellis, *The Gospel of Luke*, NCBC (Grand Rapids: Eerdmans, 1987), 89. Webb, *John the Baptizer and Prophet*, 175–78.

35. Goulder, *Luke: A New Paradigm*, 273. Cf. Ellis, *The Gospel of Luke*, 89.

36. Witherington was preceded by Tasker. R. V. G. Tasker, *Matthew* (Leicester: IVP, 1976), 48. Others believe that it is not *surprise* but *sarcasm* coming from the lips of John. So Blomberg, *Matthew*, 78; Carson, *Matthew*, 1.103; Gundry, *Matthew*, 46.

37. Ben Witherington III, "Jesus and the Baptist," *DJG*, 230.

38. The unlikely alliance of "Pharisees and Sadducees," so David Catchpole, *The Quest for Q* (Edinburgh: T&T Clark, 1993), 9–10.

In the end, whether the crowd's questions and John's ethical responses were omitted by Matthew or added by Luke remains unresolved.[39]

Despite Matthew's grammatical signal (Ἰδὼν δέ) of a transition to the Pharisees and Sadducees, some commentators view the ὑμᾶς of v. 11 to be an indication that Matthew has returned to the crowds, making vv. 11–12 a new paragraph.[40] Yet, if ὑμᾶς refers to the repentant crowd, one can only wonder why Matthew structured John's proclamation against the religious leaders the way that he did.[41]

On this reading of judgment against Israel, how might ὑμᾶς be understood? In the first place, Matthew's fondness of parallelism can scarcely be missed (Matt 5:39–40; 6:19–21, 22–23; 7:13–14, 24–27; 10:24–25, 32–33; 12:35; 18:8–9; 23:12) and has been duly noted by others.[42] Ἐγὼ μὲν ὑμᾶς βαπτίζω . . . αὐτὸς ὑμᾶς βαπτίσει is part of the parallelism. Secondly, the baptism that John performs is a national sign for Israel and is not individualistic by design. As we will go on to show, John is performing a sign-act before Israel and the sign is one of judgment. So understood, the sign performed for Israel (ὑμᾶς) balances the Spirit/fire judgment that will be carried out against Israel (ὑμᾶς). Thirdly, upon closer inspection the pronoun serves Matthew's polemical interests as he accentuates the comparison of the baptisms to make certain the judgment applies to the nation. As a national sign, John's rhetorical question, "Who warned you to flee?" (v. 7) is decidedly answered: they will *not* escape τῆς μελλούσης ὀργῆς. The nation of Israel is represented by their (religious) leaders. Even though John baptizes the crowds, the specter of judgment was only suspended, not withdrawn. To side with their leaders (21:24–26) would ultimately mean to share in the same fate. Matthew will go on to show that those who truly heed John's warning are the ones who believe and obey Jesus. By heeding the words of Jesus, especially those of the Olivet Discourse (on which see ch. 12), one could escape the coming wrath upon Jerusalem.

The combination of narrative markers on both sides of the discourse (3:7, 13a) and Matthew's overarching polemic against the religious leaders make it difficult to exegete v. 11 as a gracious promise, either explicitly or implicitly. The purview of 3:7–12 does not suggest that those addressed in v. 11 have two choices before them: refinement or wrath. Neither does the pericope suggest a division of vv. 7–10 from 11–12.[43] Matthew provides one continuous address that begins in

---

39. "The proof is not forthcoming." Davies and Allison, *Matthew*, 1.311.

40. Jeffery A. Gibbs, *Matthew 1:1-11:1* (Saint Louis: Concordia, 2006), 172.

41. Matthew could have prefaced v. 11 with, καὶ εἶπεν τοῖς ὄχλοις.

42. Davies and Allison, *Matthew*; 1.94–95; Lawerence M. Wills, "Scribal Methods in Matthew and Mishnah Abot," in *Biblical Interpretations in Early Christian Gospels*, vol. 2, LNTS 310, ed. Thomas R. Hatina (Edinburgh: T&T Clark, 2008), 183–97; Rainer Riesner, *Jesus als Lehrer: Eine Untersuchung zum Ursprung der Evangelien-Überlieferung*, WUNT 2 (Tübingen: Mohr Siebeck, 1981), 392–93; Gary Yamasaki, "Broken Parallelism in Matthew's Parable of the Two Builders," *Direction* 13.2 (2004): 143–49.

43. Hill, *Matthew*, 94; Carter, *Matthew and the Margins*, 99; Herman Ridderbos, *Matthew*, trans. R. Togtman (Grand Rapids: Zondervan, 1987), 54; Davies and Allison, *Matthew*, 1.312.

v. 7 and ends in v. 12. The emphasis, then, is judgment upon Israel, as represented by their leaders. Matthew goes to great lengths to demonstrate that the religious leaders are the enemies of Yahweh because they oppose God's son. This is a point that Matthew does not grow tired of repeating (5:20; 7:29; 9:3,11,32–34; 10:25; 12:1–8,9–15; 15:1–11; 16:21; 19:3–9; 20:17–19; 21:15–17; 22:15–22, etc.). When readers come to the passion of Jesus, there is little doubt of Matthew's view of the religious leaders and the culpability of the nation that cries out, καὶ ἀποκριθεὶς πᾶς ὁ λαὸς εἶπεν· τὸ αἷμα αὐτοῦ ἐφ᾽ ἡμᾶς καὶ ἐπὶ τὰ τέκνα ἡμῶν (27:25, note the qualification πᾶς ὁ λαὸς).

By following Matthew's narrative cues, one can discover the meaning to be the judgment of Israel. As the remaining chapters will seek to demonstrate, Matthew's prologue functions as a preview of the judgment against Jesus (2:13; 3:16), the religious leaders (2:4–6; 3:7–12), and the people of Israel (2:3–4).[44] With regard to the religious leaders, 2:1–3:12 introduces Matthew's audience to Jesus's enemies and raises the expectation that Jesus will be opposed.

Conclusion

We have surveyed alternative understandings of the Spirit/fire baptism and have indicated their strengths as well as weaknesses. First, the Matthean context provides an indispensable key for the correct understanding of v. 11. The objects of John's rebuke are the narratively intractable religious leaders. Any notions of blessing and purification of these enemies of Jesus are foreign to Matthew's Gospel. Secondly, the difficulty of fire as purification is made acute by Matthew's consistent usage throughout his gospel and the immediate context (vv. 10 and 12). Relying upon Matthew's shaping of the text as a requisite key for understanding the unique Matthean meaning, the baptism in the Spirit of fire is not easily understood as something that will ultimately purify some and destroy others. It was, instead, an approaching event that promised to destroy all who experienced it. The indication that some trees and wheat would remain was not because the Spirit/fire ultimately purified them, but rather, it was because they were spared from the messianic judgment of the kingdom of heaven. The cumulative effect of the grammar (previous chapter), context, and negative outlook of the religious leaders throughout the gospel provides a stable confirmation of the interpretation offered here. The baptism in the Holy Spirit and fire serves Matthew's narrative purposes as a descriptive preview of the fate of the stewards of the nation and the people they represent.

Matthew 3:11 is a proclamation of impending national doom. The author will carry this threat out to its climax when the religious leaders succeed in putting Jesus to death. Even after the death and resurrection of Jesus, the failure

---

44. For the various judgment "themes" see ch. 12.

of the religious leaders to ποιήσατε οὖν καρπὸν ἄξιον τῆς μετανοίας is stressed (28:11–15). In Matthew's theology, there could be no "purification" of such people and their followers.

In conclusion, John's preaching was a declaration of the day of Yahweh, which would overtake the nation of Israel in eschatological judgment, of which the preaching of John conforms. To this OT backdrop of messianic judgment and the eschatological day of the Lord we now turn.

Chapter 4

ISAIAH 11, THE ROOT OF JESSE—THE DAVIDIC KING

Introduction

Because Matthew's Gospel is replete with OT quotations and allusions we will have to be selective in our survey and narrow our focus to three texts that have greater prominence to the theme of the judgment preached and symbolized by John the Baptist and undertaken and experienced by Jesus of Nazareth. We will look closely at Isa 11, Mal 3–4, and Dan 7 in the next three chapters for the following reasons. Isaiah 11 deals with the rise of a kingly ruler and the return from exile. Malachi 3–4 contains a prophecy of the coming of Elijah and the day of the Lord. Daniel 7 provides a preview of the coming of one who is described as a "Son of Man," and the judgment upon kings/nations. Matthew makes use of these OT themes as John the Baptist comes as the promised Elijah, preparing the people for the day of the Lord that will be carried out by an unnamed kingly figure in judgment upon his enemies and in redemption of his people.

Matthew has more than a passing interest in Isaiah, whose name appears six times in his gospel (Matt 3:3; 4:14; 8:17; 12:17; 13:14; 15:17), along with an additional seventy-five (potential) allusions to the OT book.[1] Not only does Matt 3 contain a citation from Isaiah (Matt 3:3), it also conveys an eschatological outlook similar to Isa 11. Like Isa 11, Matthew describes a king who would arise, having been anointed with the Spirit and endowed with the power and authority of heaven to: usher in the kingdom, destroy the ungodly, and make a way for a new exodus. The themes contained in this Isaianic prophecy (fire of judgment, Spirit/breath, and second exodus) are similar to those found in Matt 3 and will be explored. We will also consider how subsequent religious texts have interpreted the shoot/branch of Jesse as a messianic figure, after which we will highlight the nature of this messianic figure's rule, the people under his rule and finally, how Matthew shapes his messianic material.

---

1. This calculated number is based upon the NA[27] reference list. Barbara Aland et al., eds., *Novum Testamentum Graece*, Nestle-Aland, 27th ed. (Stuttgart: Deutsche Bibelgesellschaft, 2001), 79–95.

The question of whether or not Isa 11 is a redactional insertion into the first main section of the book need not deter us. Whether written as a prophecy concerning the destruction and reestablishment of Jerusalem, or assigned to the aftermath of the judgments upon Judah, Isa 11 holds out hope that a righteous king will come to deliver his people and establish the Davidic throne for the age to come.[2]

The chapter breaks down into two main sections: vv. 1–9 address the inaugurated rule of the root of David, with v. 10 functioning as the bridge to the second section; and vv. 12–16, which elaborates upon the return of the people from exile.[3] As we will see, vv. 10–11 are also important for linking the signal of the return of the exiles to the Davidic kingship of v.1. Put another way, the first half (vv. 1–9) has to do with the nature of the messianic rule and the paradise that results from his reign, while the second half (vv. 12–16) gives a picture of the dispersed people who will be gathered under his rule.[4]

Messianic Descendant of Jesse

The chapter opens in the wake of the overthrow of Judah, having been reduced to that of a stump. Childs comments:

> Chapter 11 has been editorially positioned to form the culmination of a theological direction that commenced at chapter 6, moved through the promise of a coming messianic ruler in chapter 7, and emerged in chapter 9 with the portrayal of a righteous messianic king upon the throne of David. Chapter 11 offers both a correction and an exposition of the messianic reign . . . chapter 11 begins with the end of the old. The Davidic dynasty had been cut off to only a stump. Not only did God fell the mighty power of arrogant Assyria (10:33ff.), but also the proud and corrupt house of David.[5]

The appearance of the stump links ch. 11 with 10:33–34, where the Assyrian invaders have become the recipients of God's axe.[6] In a similar fashion, Israel has fallen under the judgment of Yahweh and has become what was predicted in 6:13.[7]

---

2. George Buchannan Gray, *A Critical and Exegetical Commentary on the Book of Isaiah 1-27*, ICC (Edinburgh: T&T Clark, 1911), 213–14; Otto Kaiser, *Isaiah 1-12*, 2nd ed., trans. John Bowden (Philadelphia: Westminster, 1972), 163–64; Ronald Clements, *Isaiah 1-39* (Grand Rapids: Eerdmans, 1980), 121–22.

3. Hans Wildberger, *Isaiah 1-12*, trans. T. H. Trapp (Minneapolis: Fortress, 1991), 467.

4. Alec Motyer, *The Prophecy of Isaiah* (Downers Grove: IVP, 1993), 120.

5. Brevard Childs, *Isaiah* (Louisville: Westminster John Knox Press, 2001), 102.

6. The scrolls maintain the deforesting motif but apply it instead to the *Kittim*.

7. And though a tenth remain in it, it will be burned again, like a terebinth or an oak, whose stump remains when it is felled. The holy seed is its stump.

But unlike the end of the proud Assyrian king, from the stump of Jesse comes a shoot and branch for Israel (11:1). The beginning of new growth points beyond the Assyrian threat and is more than simply a resumption of the Davidic dynasty: Isa 11 is looking to the fulfillment of the promise to David in the coming eschatological, messianic king.[8] This king, quite unlike the others, will be full of the Spirit (v. 2) and will render just verdicts for the poor and the meek (vv. 3–4). This is especially so in light of the failures of previous kings (cf. especially Isa 7:13). The ushering in of peace (vv. 9, 12–13) and Eden-like results of his reign (vv. 6–9) are eschatological realities that remind readers of what life would be like without sin and corruption. The earlier chapters of Isaiah reveal the need and set the stage, as it were, for a faithful king of Judah.

Isaiah 11 orients readers to look beyond the temporal monarchical failure to the eschatological king, and with him, the kingdom of peace. This messianic nuance of Isa 11 was the perspective of the DSS, Paul, and the Isaiah targums.

Qumran

Isaiah 11 was a particularly important text for the Qumran community.[9] The pesher of Isa 11 underscores the community's messianic understanding.

> *18* [The interpretation of the word concerns the shoot] of David which will sprout in the fi[nal days, since] *19* [with the breath of his lips he will execute] his [ene]my and God will support him with [the spirit of c]ourage [. . .] *20* [. . . thro]ne of glory, h[oly] crown and multi-colour[ed] vestments *21* [. . .] in his hand. He will rule over all the pe[ople]s and Magog *22* [. . .] his sword will judge [al]l the peoples. And as for what he says: «He will not *23* [judge by appearances] or give verdicts on hearsay.[10] (4Q16)

4QIsaiah describes a messianic ruler who would arise in the last days and be endued with the spirit of discretion, wisdom, advice, and knowledge of Yahweh

---

8. For a temporal, non-eschatological fulfillment see John D. Watts, *Isaiah 1-33*, WBC 24, rev. ed. (Nashville: Thomas Nelson, 2005), 209, 212; Willem A. M. Beuken, "The Emergence of the Shoot of Jesse: An Eschatological or a Now Event?" *CTJ* 39 (2004): 88–108; Raija Sollamo, "Messianism and the 'Branch of David,'" in *The Septuagint and Messianism*, BETL 195, ed. M. A. Knibb (Leuven: Leuven University Press, 2004), 366; Kaiser, *Isaiah 1-12*, 1974, 153–55, 157.

9. Isaiah 11, Gen 49:10, and Num 24:17 play "an important, generative role" in shaping the messianic patterns; Craig Evans, "Messianism," *DNTB*, 699–700. See 4Q252 5:1–7; 4QpIsaa frags. 7–10 iii 25, (possibly) T. Jud. 1:6; CD 7:20; 1QSb 5:27–28; 1QM 11:4–9; T. Levi 18:3. T. Jud. 24:1–16.

10. Cf. 4252 5:1–7, 4QFlor (1:10–13, 4Q161 8-10:18–25, and 4Q285 5:1–6), 4 Ezra (7:28f.; 11:37–12:1; 12:31–34; 13:3–13; 13:25–52), and 2 Bar. (29–30, chs. 36–42 and chs. 72–74).

(*Frags.* 8–10 col. iii 11–13). While Isa 10 spoke of the threat and downfall of Assyria (as does *Frags.* 2–6 col. II 9; 4QIsaiah Pesher *Frags.* 2–3 1), this messianic ruler will also do battle with (and presumably defeat) the *Kittim* (*Frags.* 8–10 col. III 10; *Kittim* = the Romans) which would result in his rule over all peoples. This shoot of David conforms to what is found in Isa 11. He is a militaristic leader, endowed with the spiritual gifts necessary for ruling all peoples and judging the wicked.

4Q285 5:1–6 contains a future messianic shoot from the stump of Jesse, the branch of David (צמח דויד), who marches out into battle.

> *1* [. . . as] the Prophet Isaiah [said] *Isa 10:34*: « And [they] shall cut [the most massive of the] *2* [forest with iron and Lebanon, with its magnificence, will] fall. A shoot will emerge from the stump of Jesse [. . .] *3* [. . .] the bud of David. And they will go into battle *Blank* with [. . .] *4* [. . .] and the Prince of the Congregation will kill him, the bu[d of David . . .] *5* [. . .] and with wounds. And [the High] Priest will command [. . .] *6* [. . . the s]lai[n of the] Kitti[m . . .] (4Q285 (4QSM) *Frag.* 5 = 11Q14 1 i)

This particular text was thought by Eisman to be speaking of a slain messiah, but has been shown otherwise.[11] The slain is not the messianic shoot from the stump of Jesse, but is most probably the *Kittim* who oppose God's people. This fragment corresponds to the Isaiah pesher by providing an eschatological and messianic interpretation of the king who comes from Jesse's line to deliver his people and execute his enemies.

Finally, themes from Isa 11 are found in *The Rule of Blessing*:

> *24* May you be [. . .] with the power of your [mouth.] With your sceptre may you lay waste the earth. With the breath of your lips *25* may you kill the wicked. May he give [you a spirit of coun]sel and of everlasting fortitude, a spirit of knowledge and of fear of God. May *26* justice be the belt of [your loins, and loyalt]y the belt of your hips. May he make your horns of iron and your hoofs of bronze. *27* May you gore like a bu[ll . . . and may you trample the nation]s like mud of the streets. For God has raised you to a sceptre *28* for the rulers be[fore you . . . all the na]tions will serve you, and he will make you strong by his holy Name, *29* so that you will be like a li[on . . .] your the prey, with no-one to give it [back]. (1Q28b [1QSb] 5:24–29)

Though no specific mention is made of the root or branch issuing from Jesse, the scepter, destruction of wicked by the breath of his lips, endowment of the spirit and the mention of the belt of justice are Isaianic allusions. It is doubtful

---

11. Geza Vermes, "The Oxford Forum for Qumran Research Seminar on the Rule of War from Cave 4 (4Q285)," *JJS* 43 (1992): 85–90; Markus Bockmuehl, "A 'Slain Messiah' in 4Q Serekh Milhamah (4Q285)?" *TynBul* 43 (1992): 155–69; Martin G. Abegg Jr., "Messianic Hope and 4Q285: A Reassessment," *JBL* 113.1 (1994): 81–91.

that this document would be interpreted by the community as anything less than the eschatological victory of the messiah. This eschatological outlook is broadly consonant with John the Baptist's expectations in Matt 3. John's preaching of judgment is not only understandable against the backdrop of the OT and the interpretive work of Qumran, but both Matthew and the Qumran community have a shared interest, namely, their denunciation against the priests. There will be no mercy for the arrogant men of Jerusalem (4Q Isaiah Pesher[b]) (4Q162 [4QpIs[b]]). They are a culpable (Matt 2:4) brood of vipers (Matt 3:7), who are ripe for messianic judgment in the fiery judgment of the Spirit (Matt 3:7–12).

Romans 15:12

The NT more generally, and Paul specifically, provides messianic interpretations of Isa 11. Paul's apostolic blessing hinges upon Jesus's work as the Christ for both the Jew and the Gentile (Rom 15:5–6). He describes Jesus's relationship to the circumcised as that of the βεβαιῶσαι τὰς ἐπαγγελίας τῶν πατέρων (15:8). He then goes on to cite Isa 11:10 (LXX) to accentuate Jesus's messianic relationship to the nations, "And again Isaiah says, 'The "root of Jesse" will come, even he who arises to rule the Gentiles; in him will the Gentiles hope'" (15:12). In the Pauline context, this OT citation is being used for different purposes than that of the DSS. Paul's selection of the root of Jesse is in keeping with the soteric and promissory aspects of the work of the messiah for the *benefit* of the nations. For the DSS, Isa 11 was useful in showing the root of Jesse as the messianic king who *fights* and *conquers* the nations. These differing accents are not to suggest that either Paul or the covenanters would have read Isa 11 as one or the other (i.e., either judgment or salvation). It is more likely that they would affirm both aspects of the messianic work of Jesse's root. It is a difference of emphasis then, not of substance.

Romans 15:12 is the conclusion of a pastiche of OT citations from the Law (15:10), the prophets (15:9,12), and the writings (15:11). The Isaianic quotation supports Paul's contention that the twofold promises to both Jew and Gentile are brought together in Jesus, who is the expected root of Jesse. Paul is not the only one to draw such conclusions. The messianic reading of Isa 11 and its applications to the work of Jesus are also affirmed in several places in the NT (Matt 3:16; John 7:24; 2 Thess 2:18; 1 Pet 4:14; Rev 5:5; 19:15, 21; 22:16).[12]

Paul's appeal to the Davidic messiah as a blessing to the nations is a theme shared by Matthew. The genealogy with its references to certain gentiles (Matt 1:3, 5–6), the wise men from the east (Matt 2:1–12), and John the Baptist's declaration, "from these stones, God can raise up children for Abraham" (Matt 3:9) make the point that just as there will be a repentant remnant of Israelites within the nation

---

12. For a list of early Christian and apocryphal handlings of Isa 11 cf. Evans, "Messianism," 700.

of Israel (3:5–6), there will also be a remnant within the gentile nations who will come to embrace the Son of David. The motif that begins suggestively (Matt 1:1) ends explicitly (Matt 28:19).[13]

The Isaiah Targum

Like the DSS and Paul, the Isaiah Targum provides a one-to-one correspondence between the shoot of Jesse and the messianic deliverer of Israel. "And a king shall come forth from the sons of Jesse, and the Messiah shall be exalted from the sons of his sons" (11.1). After striking down the sinners with the command of his mouth, it reads, "In the days of the Messiah of Israel shall peace increase in the land" (11.6).[14] The latter half of the targum retains the Isaianic emphases of the return of Israel and the reunification of the tribes of Israel (11:10–14).

The matrix of the root of Jesse's work is that of judgment against the wicked sinners and the unification and peaceful coexistence between Judah and Ephraim. Whereas Paul sees the arrival of the root of Jesse as the expected sign of the gentiles' hope and future, the DSS and targum lay greater stress upon his role as the judge of the gentiles and locate his aid and comfort within the faithful community (so Qumran) or Israel (targum). For Matthew, the Messiah's role in judgment and salvation is not an exodus that ends in a return to Jerusalem, but it is an exodus out of Jerusalem which ends in judgment on it. The experience of Jesus in infancy (Matt 2:13–15) takes place symbolically with the peoples from Jerusalem and all Judea and all the region about the Jordan going out to John in the wilderness (Matt 3:5), and is gravely underscored by Jesus's words in Matt 24.

What all three selections have in common is a messianic interpretation of the root of Jesse. Each of the aforementioned samples bring out their own interpretive contours of the messiah's role. This small sample shows that messianic readings of Isaiah belong in the Second Temple period, the NT, and beyond. There is good evidence for an interpretive tradition extending back to at least the postexilic period, which viewed Isa 11 as messianic in character. With this development of a messianic, promissory understanding in view, we can now turn to the characteristics of the eschatological king as well as the nature of his rule, after which we will show the themes that likely aided Matthew in developing his portrait of the one announced by John the Baptist.

13. Jesus is *the* son of Abraham. Implied in this status is the promise, "In you (in your offspring) shall all the nations of the world shall be blessed" (Gen 12:2–3; 15; 22:18).

14. The "wicked" is preceded by "Romulus" which is a cipher for Rome. Bruce D. Chilton, *The Isaiah Targum: Introduction, Translation, Apparatus and Notes*, TAV 11 (Wilmington: Michael Glazier, 1987), 28.

The Nature of the Messianic Rule, vv. 1–9[15]

There are three terms in v. 1 which are used to describe the successor of Jesse as a messianic leader: There shall come forth a shoot (חטר) from the stump of Jesse, and a branch (נצר) from his roots (שרש) shall bear fruit (Isa 11:1).

"Branch and shoot" are parallel expressions that overlap with "roots," as v. 10 reintroduces.[16] חטר is a rare word, occurring here and in Prov 14:3 as an instrument of judgment. While "branch" (צמח) develops a messianic connotation elsewhere (Jer 23:5; 33:15; Zech 3:8; 6:12; 4Q252 5:3; 4Q285 f7:3–4; 11Q14 f1i:11–13), its parallel term (נצר) does not seem to be used outside of Isa 11 with a messianic nuance, but rather is a symbol for Israel's future prosperity. Similar terms describing royalty can be found outside of the OT. "Branch" is used of Essarhddon "the precious branch of Baltil, and enduring shoot."[17]

The branch that issues forth from Jesse's roots (שרש) indicates that Jesse is the source.[18] The root of Jesse is a metaphorical expression for a human relationship, namely Jesse's son. Motyer observes that in the OT, Davidic kings are often assessed by their resemblance or lack thereof to David, but he finds that none but David are ever called "son of Jesse" (1 Sam 20:27–33; 1 Kgs 12:16).[19] There is a subtle difference in the choice of words.[20] It may be that a preexisting character is hinted at by the reintroduction of שרש instead of the expected נצר. The ambiguity is likely deliberate. The root of Jesse, or perhaps the "source" of Jesse, becomes the offspring of Jesse.[21]

15. For the messianic elements of Isaiah see Paul D. Wegner, *An Examination of Kingship and Messianic Expectation in Isaiah 1-35* (Lewiston: The Edwin Mellen Press, 1992), 217–74, esp. 253–61.

16. R. Laird Harris, Gleason L. Archer Jr., Bruce K. Waltke, "נצר," in *TWOT*. Bibleworks Software 4.

17. Gary V. Smith, *Isaiah 1-39*, NAC 15a (Nashville: B&H, 2007), 271 n. 415.

18. If the שרש of Israel becomes rotten the blossoms will be dust (5:24), but God is also able to cause the house of Judah to take שרש, put forth shoots, and fill the earth (27:6). From the serpent's שרש comes the adder (14:29). God kills Philistia's root with famine (14:30). In 40:24 the theme of God's judgment is again likened to the wind that withers the שרש. Finally, the servant of the Lord is likened to a שרש out of the dry ground (53:2).

19. Motyer, *The Prophecy*, 121. Ridderbos understands the significance of the name, root of Jesse, to turn in the opposite direction. It is the root of Jesse, not David, because the Davidic dynasty has lost its splendor "and has sunk back to the obscurity and insignificance of its origin." Jan Ridderbos, *Isaiah*, trans. John Vriend (Grand Rapids: Zondervan, 1985), 130.

20. Wildberger, *Isaiah 1-12*, 482.

21. Motyer, *The Prophecy*, 121.

According to von Rad, Isa 11:1 is not merely a continuation of the line of David, but a "total new reestablishment of it."[22] There is both continuity and discontinuity as a messianic and kingly figure emerges from the stump of Jesse. Though the throne has been cut off, a stump remains. Just as the believing remnant of the nation were the stump (Isa 6:13), so also the royal line. The latter half of v. 1 speaks either of the branch issuing from the stump or פרה conveys the idea of (metaphorical) fruitfulness. The former interpretation would be somewhat repetitious, while the concept of fruitfulness makes better sense in light of what follows. Not only will this future king have a hereditary connection to the royal line, he will also be endowed with the Spirit to secure God's righteous rule in the world through this new son of Jesse.

Messianic Virtues

> And the Spirit of the LORD shall rest upon him, the Spirit of wisdom and understanding, the Spirit of counsel and might, the Spirit of knowledge and the fear of the LORD. (Isa 11:2)

The three sets of dual characteristics are the signs of the Spirit upon him, "resting upon him."[23] Taken together, these sets of ideal characteristics emphasize the ideal king. The cumulative effect of the word pairing supports the conclusion that this king's rule is harmonious with Yahweh's rule.

Not surprisingly, various proposals have been suggested for the triadic descriptors. Wisdom and understanding belong to intellectual life, counsel and might to practical life, and knowledge and fear of the Lord to the direct relation to God.[24] Clements likens the Spirit of knowledge to insight and discernment, counsel and might to firmness in negotiations, and the fear of the Lord to reverent humility.[25]

While the potential meanings could be expanded if one were to go to other OT passages, yet within the book of Isaiah, these six virtues indicate that this is the Lord's redress of the problems caused by former kings and nations, remedied by the messianic king. The king of Assyria boasted in his wisdom and understanding (10:13). The culpability of fallen Israel is also due to their lack of knowledge and a failure to fear the Lord (8:12–13).[26] Not surprisingly the messianic king will have them in their divinely intended fullness. He will use the divinely endowed gifts to reverse the misfortunes of the poor and needy among Israel. Because oppression of the weak and the poor were the outcomes of the policies of the monarchy

---

22. Gerhard von Rad, *Theology of the Old Testament*, vol. 2, trans. D. M. G. Stalker (London: Oliver and Boyd, 1965), 170.

23. Dumbrell, *Search for Order*, 91.

24. Franz Delitzsch, *Biblical Commentary on the Prophecies of Isaiah*, vol. 1, trans. James Martin (Edinburgh: T&T Clark, 1886), 282.

25. Clements, *Isaiah 1-39*, 123.

26. John Goldingay, *Isaiah*, NIBC (Peabody: Hendrickson, 2001), 84.

(3:5,14–15; 10:2), the root of Jesse will judge (11:3) with righteousness for the poor and humble (11:4).[27]

Messianic Judgment

The theme of judgment so-pictured in the stump reemerges in 11:4. If the global work of the messiah is cast in terms of equity for the meek of the earth, then the consequence is judgment for the oppressors, "And he shall strike the earth with the rod of his mouth, and with the breath of his lips he shall kill the wicked" (Isa 11:4).

The use of the rod in a judicial setting (v. 3) is hardly surprising (Ps 2:9). Assyria was described as the rod of the Lord's anger in Isa 10:5, 15, 24. The strike against the earth is closely associated with the execution of the wicked, the instrument being the רוח of his lips. The point seems to be that the entire world can only be transformed by the messianic reign (vv. 6–9) after undergoing the judicial (v. 3) and retributive aspects (v. 4) of the rule of the eschatological Davidic figure. Once all wrongs have been righted, the judgments of vv. 3–4 can give way to the idyllic scenes of vv. 6–9. These concluding scenes of the first half of the chapter reveal the sensational after-effect of the Messiah's presence in the world.

Messianic Outcome

> *The wolf shall dwell with the lamb, and the leopard shall lie down with the young goat, and the calf and the lion and the fattened calf together; and a little child shall lead them. The cow and the bear shall graze; their young shall lie down together; and the lion shall eat straw like the ox. The nursing child shall play over the hole of the cobra, and the weaned child shall put his hand on the adder's den. (Isa 11:6–10)*

From here the prophet turns to the results of the messianic reign. It is a picture of peace in a restored world where not only the human realm but also the animal kingdom will no longer threaten and be in dread of one another. The future harmonious relations of the predators and their prey, intermingled with the children playing among them (v. 6), show that "hostilities on every level and in every dimension of creation will be overcome."[28] It is the restoration of creation by a new act of God through the vehicle of a righteous ruler.[29] The result of the reign of the messiah is that the world is "Edenized," or what Vos called "the supernaturalizing of the entire state of existence."[30] Others have suggested that the

---

27. Goldingay, *Isaiah*, 83–85; Clements, *Isaiah 1–39*, 123.

28. Walter Brueggemann, *Theology of the Old Testament: Testimony, Dispute, Advocacy* (Minneapolis: Fortress, 1997), 549.

29. Childs, *Isaiah*, 105.

30. Geerhardus Vos, *Biblical Theology: Old and New Testaments* (Carlisle: The Banner of Truth Trust, 1996), 295.

predators of vv. 6–11 are symbols representing the nations.[31] Assyria was called a lion in 5:29. The Syrians and Philistines, like predators, devour with open mouths (9:12; MT 9:11). People devour one another like meat (9:20). Even the nation of Israel plays the part of the animal. The widows and fatherless have become the prey (10:2), but God issues the warning that he will strike his people with the rod of the king of Assyria (10:5), who is himself described as one that gathers the people like eggs from a nest (10:14). Read in this way, the hostilities of the nations will come to an end and the whole earth will be filled with the knowledge of God, "They shall not hurt or destroy in all my holy mountain; for the earth shall be full of the knowledge of the LORD as the waters cover the sea" (Isa 11:9).

As a summary statement, v. 9 supports such a reading. In Isaiah, the problem is not that animals hurt (רעע) and destroy (שחת), but people do. In the second half of the chapter there will be a cessation of aggression, particularly between Ephraim and Judah. The repetition of 11:9 in 65:25 confirms that it is the destructive behavior of God's people that will be remedied and come to an end in the new heavens and earth (65:17). Verse 9 is, then, a fitting conclusion to the first half of the oracle tying together both the nature of the messianic reign and the impact of his reign. As Motyer observed, "the Spirit of knowledge and of the fear of the Lord in the Messiah becomes, under his reign, the knowledge of the Lord (9) filling the whole earth."[32] The entire earth becomes the sacred mountain of God.[33] Precisely because the entire world is destined to become a sacred space, the identity of those who would occupy it brings ch. 11 to a close.

The People under the Messianic King

The bridge between the first and second halves of the prophecy is v. 10. "In that day the root of Jesse, who shall stand as a signal for the peoples—of him shall the nations inquire, and his resting place shall be glorious."

The relationship between vv. 1 and 10 is evident by the future orientation of both verses and by the repetition of the words "Jesse" (ישי) and "root" (שרש), which stand near the beginning of both sets of poems. What proceeds from Jesse in v. 1 is the *shoot* (חטר). In v. 10 the imagery provocatively shifts and instead of the expected shoot extending from the stump in the ground, it is the root of Jesse that stands as the signal for the nations. The shoot of Jesse and the root of Jesse refer to the same individual or entity. The former (חטר) is a rare word occurring here and in Prov 14:3 where it is an instrument of judgment. שרש has a semantic range that includes nature, metaphorical uses in relation to people, groups of people, and nations and can be used to indicate the source or foundation of something.[34] As Isa

---

31. Christopher R. Seitz, *Isaiah 1-39* (Louisville: Westminster John Knox Press, 1993), 106–07; Patricia K. Tull, *Isaiah 1-39* (Macon: Smyth & Helwys Publishing, 2010), 231.

32. Motyer, *The Prophecy*, 120.

33. Clements, *Isaiah 1-39*, 124.

34. "שרש," *HALOT*, Accordance Bible Software 11.1.6.

11:1 was understood to be a metaphorical usage describing a person (though a number of scholars have sought to read the root of Jesse as a group of people, namely, postexilic Israel), the root of Jesse in v. 10 is best understood as describing the messiah.[35]

Behind the root of Jesse is the God who has raised him up. Yahweh has appointed a particular person for a particular moment in time. The well-known prophetic utterance, "in/on that day" prefaces the eschatological announcement. In this bridging verse the eschatological formula followed by the messianic root of Jesse has a people. He will not be a localized leader to a particular people. Isaiah 2:1–4 spoke of a time when the nations would go up to the mountain of the Lord. In Isa 11:10 they gathered around the root of Jesse. The signal (נס) that was once raised to summon the nations to rise up against his people (5:12) is now the נס for the nations to come to his resting place (11:10).

In keeping with the themes of the messiah's wisdom (v. 2) and just judgments (vv. 3–4), it is not at all extraordinary that the nations are depicted as inquiring of Jesse's son (cf. the similar usage of דרש in Isa 34:16; Amos 5:14; Ecc 1:13). At the dawning of the eschatological age, the nations will be positive benefactors of the king's wisdom and work.

A Second Exodus

Once more, the eschatological phrase "in/on that day" is repeated (v. 11), but the focus narrows from the gathering of the nations generally to the return of God's outcast people, Israel. "In that day the Lord will extend his hand yet a second time to recover the remnant that remains of his people. . ." (Isa 11:11). The meaning of the return of Judah and Ephraim (vv. 12-13) is summarized for the reader in v. 16, "And there will be a highway from Assyria for the remnant that remains of his people, as there was for Israel when they came up from the land of Egypt."

In the first exodus, it is Moses who gathers the people; in the second, it is the Davidic king. Mention is made in both passages of Yahweh's outstretched hand (Exod 15:12; Isa 11:11, 15).[36] The waters are made ready for the people of God, being pushed back by the wind/רוח (Exod 14:21; 15:9–10; Isa 11:15). Edom and Moab will experience the dread of the released captives (Exod 15:14; Isa 11:14). Finally, the goal of both exoduses is to arrive safely at God's mountain (Exod 15:17; 11:9). But unlike the first exodus, Isaiah's new exodus envisions only the return of a remnant.

The cosmological victory over the sea is a stock theme in the OT. Within the Psalms, Yahweh's battle with the waters (and its monsters) is sometimes associated

---

35. For a discussion of the singular and collective interpretations see Jacob Stromberg, "The 'Root of Jesse' in Isaiah 11:10: Postexilic Judah, or Postexilic Davidic King?" *JBL* 127.4 (2008): 656–57.

36. The differing Hebrew verbs, Exod 15:12 = נטה, Isa 11:11 = יוסיף, do not detract from the fact that it is the raised hand of Yahweh in the deliverance of his people.

with his work of creation (Pss 74:12–14; 89:11; 104:6–9).[37] Isaiah 11 uses the ideological founding of the nation, from exile to freedom, to project a new exodus from captivity, which will conclude with nothing short of a new creation.[38] The recasting of Israel's redemption is decidedly transformed by the prophet. It is not a return to life once lived, or even a new start with the potential of repeating the past. It is the end of old hostilities (11:6–9, 12–13), the transformation of a creation gone wrong (v. 9), which inspires the rejoicing of Isa 12.

Conclusion

God's judgments against his people were poignantly stated near the end of the nation's covenant document, "'I will cut them to pieces; I will wipe them from human memory,'. . . . For they are a nation void of counsel, and there is no understanding in them. If they were wise, they would understand this; they would discern their latter end!" (Deut 32:26, 28–29). Israel will barely be spared; only an exiled remnant will survive. The covenant curses will fell the tree, reducing the towering Davidic dynasty to that of a stump. Were it not for the fixed promises of God's covenant commitment, their end would be in their captivity (Deut 30:1–6).

Israel did return without a king from the line of David and without a messiah. The homecoming to Canaan left the Deuteronomic promises largely unfulfilled (Deut 30:6). To this testimony the prophetic voice added its own nuance, rather than something altogether new. The exile could not come to an end until the raising of God's signal (Isa 11:10–11). Therefore, Israel's return to the land, the infighting among the people, and the subjugation to Rome left much to be desired.

Isaiah, the gospels, and the writings of Qumran indicate that a belief in the coming king of David/shoot of Jesse was still a future prospect. What Israel's leaders do not appear to expect is that the nation itself would also endure the striking of the rod and the slaying with the breath/spirit of his lips. Israel would, once again, undergo another exile and only a remnant would be gathered around the messiah/Jesus.

Qumran saw the messiah as a threatening reality for the largely wicked Israelites. They read texts like Isaiah and withdrew into the wilderness, striving for purity and awaiting the inbreaking of the messiah to exact vengeance upon Rome and uproot the entrenched religious leaders of the compromised nation. The Qumran community believed that they would be the victors marching out with the messiah against Jew and Gentile alike.

But in Matthew, it is Jesus who will undergo the exile (1:17; 2:13–15; 4:1–11; 27:45, 50–53) and will slay the wicked with the breath/spirit of his mouth. This will be their baptism in the Holy Spirit and fire. The imagery is Isaianic: "Even now the

---

37. Michael Fishbane, *Text and Texture: Close Readings of Selected Biblical Texts* (New York: Schocken Books, 1979), 126–28.

38. Childs, *Isaiah*, 105.

axe is laid to the root of the trees. Every tree therefore that does not bear good fruit is cut down and thrown into the fire" (Matt 3:10).

The finality of this messianic work grows out of the prophetic soil of the OT. The only hope for Israel is to submit to Jesus as the Old Covenant passed away. Matthew advances the eschatological crisis by leveraging a theme from Israel's past and reapplying it in a new way. The axe is not laid at the trunk, but at the very root itself, which indicates a final, eschatological end even as the image of gathering the wheat into the barn (Isa 11:10–16; Matt 3:12) and burning of the chaff with unquenchable fire makes certain. The rising of the shoot from the stump is the signal for Israel's return and restoration of prominence in the DSS and the targum. In Matthew, the coming of Jesus is the signal of the end of not only the religious leaders of Israel, but also Jerusalem, as the center to which the nations will be gathered (Isa 11:9). Matthew has reworked this theme. The center to which Jew and Gentile alike must arrive is faith in Jesus who is the true embodiment of faithful Israel even as he gathers the true Israel of God (Jews and Gentiles) around himself and prepares to judge national Israel for their persistent rejection of David's heir, the righteous branch.

Jesus will gather his people into his kingdom rather Jerusalem, and he will judge his enemies (Jew and Gentile alike) with the Holy Spirit and fire. But for Matthew, this can only take place because Jesus himself voluntarily goes to the cross, undergoing the judgment, being made like the stump of Jesse, to rise in resurrection life and through his apostles, to call Israel and the nations to repentance and faith in Christ, the son of David (Matt 28:19).

Chapter 5

MALACHI 3–4, ELIJAH, AND THE DAY OF THE LORD

Introduction

In Matthew's Gospel, Malachi's prophecy of the arrival of Elijah is fulfilled in John the Baptist who is Ἠλίας ὁ μέλλων ἔρχεσθαι (Mal 3:23 MT, [4:5]; Matt 11:14). Fulfillment of Malachi's prophecy can be seen in John's identity, in his message of crisis, and in his demand for repentance before the coming of the Lord. We will begin with the charge that forms the basis for the day of the Lord, and then analyze its usage in Malachi and show how the day of the Lord coheres with the new exodus. The fate of the wicked, the destiny of the righteous, and the one who would come announcing this great event will also be discussed. We will then conclude with an application of our findings for Matt 3.

The Charge

The book of Malachi is comprised of six disputations between Yahweh and his people.[1] It begins with a declaration of the love of God (1:2), but concludes with a portentous threat of impending curse (3:24/4:6). The conflict between the great King (1:17) and Israel builds to the culmination of a familiar theme found throughout the Book of the Twelve, namely, the day of the Lord.[2]

---

1. Raymond B. Dillard and Tremper Longman III, *An Introduction to the Old Testament* (Grand Rapids: Zondervan, 1994), 439–40.

    1. God's love for his people (1:1–5)
    2. Priestly contempt toward God (1:6–2:9)
    3. Israel's covenant breaking (2:10–16)
    4. God's justice and honor (2:17–3:5)
    5. Repentance and return to the Lord (3:6–12)
    6. Harsh words spoken against the Lord (3:13–4:3 [MT 3:13–21])

2. "Book of the Twelve" as a title for the Minor Prophets is drawn from early sources that appear to indicate that the collection was thought of as a literary whole. Cf. Sir 49:10

The form of the final disputation follows the previous patterns. Once again, the Lord brings his complaint to substantiate the charge: "Your words have been hard against me, says the LORD. But you say, 'How have we spoken against you?' You have said, 'It is vain to serve God. What is the profit of our keeping his charge or of walking as in mourning before the LORD of hosts? And now we call the arrogant blessed. Evildoers not only prosper but they put God to the test and they escape'" (Mal 3:13–15).

Yahweh begins by declaring that Israel's adversarial words have been "severe" against him.[3] In the HB חזק occurs in contexts of conflict and conveys the idea of strength needed to prevail over someone or something (1 Sam 17:50; 2 Sam 10:11; 13:14; 1 Kgs 20:23–25; 2 Sam 24:4). Additionally, the phrase, "Your words . . . against me" (עלי דבריכם) occurs in only one other place in the HB, Eze 35:13, where Yahweh contends with Edom because the nation spoke against him. Interestingly, Malachi has made reference to Edom in the opening of his book (1:3–5). The similarities between Edom and Israel are not inconsequential. Both speak words against Yahweh and both are heard (שמע) (1:4; 2:17; 3:13–14, 16). The descendants of Esau are the "wicked" (רשע) country (Mal 1:4), and the Israelites complain that their "wicked" (רשע) countrymen prosper and escape (Mal 3:15).[4] Edom could (arrogantly) claim that they can rebuild the ruins following God's judgments (Mal 1:4), and Israel complains that the arrogant are blessed (3:15). The Lord who promised to tear down wicked Edom (1:4) issues a severe threat to Israel: he will uproot the evil (3:19).

Edom functions as a mirror on Israel. In Matthew, one finds an Edomite on the throne, a messenger who speaks of the coming wrath, and the inability of the

and 4 Ezra 14:41 and Origen (taken from Eusebius, Ecclesiastical History vi 25). Marvin A. Sweeney, Jerome T. Walsh, and Chris Franke, *The Twelve Prophets: Hosea, Joel, Amos, Obadiah, Jonah*, vol. 1 (Collegeville: The Liturgical Press, 2000), xv.

3. R. Laird Harris, Gleason L. Archer Jr., Bruce K. Waltke, "חזק," in *TWOT*. Bibleworks Software 4.

4. While it is possible that the statements concerning the wicked in 2:17 and 3:14–15 refer more generally to the gentile nations, the apostatizing Israelites are more likely the referent. It would make very little sense to say that the nations were putting Israel's God to the test when they neither knew him, nor his requirements. As Verhoef pointed out,

> The zēḏîm of v. 15a are characterized in v. 15b as "evildoers," and in v. 19 these categories are identified as one and the same. It is evident from Malachi's prophecy concerning the Day of the Lord (3:1–5; 3:19) that it presupposes an innerjudische situation. The "arrogant" therefore were either the covenant people as such, or else those members of the nation who had already inwardly and publicly broken with the faith of the fathers, the agnostics, and the skeptics.

Peter A. Verhoef, *The Books of Haggai and Malachi* (Grand Rapids: Eerdmans, 1987), 318. Cf. Andrew E. Hill, *Malachi: A New Translation with Introduction and Commentary* (New York: Doubleday, 1998), 341; Beth Glazier-McDonald, *Malachi: The Divine Messenger*, SBL 98 (Atlanta: Scholars Press, 1987), 215–17.

unrighteous to escape. Those who saw no reason to walk before the Lord of hosts in mourning (Mal 3:14), understood by some as a gesture of repentance,[5] are confronted with an Elijah-like individual with a threatening proclamation (Matt 3:7–12), prefaced with the word, "repent!" (Matt 3:2).

The Day of the Lord

For behold, the day is coming, burning like an oven, when all the arrogant and all evildoers will be stubble. The day that is coming shall set them ablaze, says the LORD *of hosts, so that it will leave them neither root nor branch.* (Mal 3:19/4:1)

Whether one views the Minor Prophets as a collection of books, or a literary whole, the day of the Lord motif is a dominant theme.[6] The day of the Lord is indicated by a variety of expressions in the Book of the Twelve: "the day" (Mal 3:2), "the day of the wrath of Yahweh" (Zech 2:2–3), "the great and terrible day" (Joel 3:3–5) and especially "that day."[7] Such diverse phrases are also present in Malachi (3:2, 19, 23).

The day of the Lord cannot simply be equated with a single, final judgment found in later apocalyptic writings.[8] In Malachi, the day of Yahweh is predominantly God's visitation and temporal judgment of Israel. Even though Malachi makes no explicit statements of Yahweh judging the world and bringing a definitive end to all opposition to his rule, the day of the Lord is eschatological in orientation, and

5. So John Goldingay and Pamela J. Scalise, *Minor Prophets II*, NIBCOT (Peabody: Hendrickson, 2009), 357. This OT *hapax* could also be a reference to walking in penitence, so David L. Petersen, *Zechariah 9–14 and Malachi* (Louisville: Westminster John Knox, 1995), 221. Cf. 1 Clement 9:1; Jos. *Ant.* 7, 361.

6. Mark Leuchter, "Another Look at the Hosea/Malachi Framework in the Twelve," *VT* 64 (2014): 249–65; Jason T. LeCureux, *The Thematic Unity of the Book of the Twelve* (Sheffield: Sheffield Phoenix Press, 2012), 224–31; James D. Nogalski, "Recurring Themes in the Book of the Twelve: Creating Points of Contact for a Theological Reading," *Int* 127 (2007): 125–36; *Thematic Threads in the Book of the Twelve*, BZAW 325, eds. P. L. Redditt and A. Schart (New York: W. de Gruyter, 2003).

7. "The day of the Lord" (and variations) occurs 175 times in the former and latter prophets. James D. Nogalski, "The Day(s) of YHWH in the Book of the Twelve," in *Thematic Threads in the Book of the Twelve*, 193–95. Cf. A. Joseph Everson, "The Days of Yahweh," *JBL* 93 (1974): 329–37; Yair Hoffmann, "The Day of the Lord as a Concept and a Term in the Prophetic Literature," *ZAW* 93.1 (1981): 37–50.

8. Nogalski, "Recurring Themes," 126; David L. Petersen, *The Prophetic Literature: An Introduction* (Louisville: Westminster John Knox, 2002), 211. Elsewhere in the Twelve, the day of the Lord can be the occasion for blessing and restoration (cf. Joel 3:18; Zeph 3:11–17; Zech 14:4–12).

ushers in a new, yet anticipated era of God's rule.[9] The reason for the day of the Lord is due to Israel's rebellion. Israel's return from exile and rebuilding of the temple did not produce the desired effect upon the people (Isa 35:10; 51:11). Instead, Israel's attitude largely became one of indifference toward the Lord, his Law, and cultic practice. In response, Malachi announces the day of the Lord to the postexilic community.

We will now review the character of Malachi's day of the Lord as a day of eschatological judgment against Israel. As we proceed, we will also make a case that (in Malachi) the day of the Lord can and should be understood as the start of the new exodus. After showing the lexical and thematic correlations of the day of the Lord and new exodus in Malachi, we will apply our findings to Matthew and the eschatological arrival and announcement of John the Baptist. We will then have opportunity to consider how such implications illuminate certain aspects of the ministry of John the Baptist as the herald of a new exodus, which ironically comes on the day of the Lord. This OT backdrop of the coming of Elijah before the day of the new exodus points readers in the direction of eschatological judgment for Israel, by means of the fire of the Spirit.

But before we go on to make our case for the coming of the Lord as the day of the new exodus, we must first ask whether or not it is valid to use "day" language for the exodus. The exodus did not begin ביום (by day) but הלילה (by night) (Exod 12:42). The answer lies in the variegated uses of "day" in the OT. ביום can be vague ("time"), or specific (successions of time, Exod 18:13; Gen 43:16, etc.), or general ("in the time of").[10] As a moment, definite time, or near future, "The emphasis in such expressions rests not on the basic meaning of *day* as a period of daylight, but rather on the close connection of events within a time frame determined by the context."[11] This latter point well-expresses the meaning of the exodus in terms of time. Though Israel leaves Egypt at night, the exodus event is repeatedly called "the day/that day" (Exod 12:17, 41, 51; 13:13; Deut 16:3; Jer 7:22; 31:32; Hos 2:15). Though the exodus was referred to as, "that day," it does not necessarily require that the future day is by default the new exodus. The flexibility of "that day": eschatological and non-eschatological, salvation and judgment, means that contextual themes and lexical repetition are necessary to confirm such a conclusion. With these caveats in place, we now can turn to the character of Malachi's day of the Lord.

God's Response to the Righteous and the Wicked

The day (of the Lord) is found three times in the sixth disputation, essentially bracketing the response of God to the arrogant (3:13–15) and penitent (3:16). It

---

9. Hugo Gressmann, *Der Messias*, FRLANT 26 (Göttingen: Vandenhoeck & Ruprecht, 1929), 75–77.

10. R. Laird Harris, Gleason L. Archer Jr., Bruce K. Waltke, "ביום," in *TWOT*. Bibleworks Software 4.

11. Ellen Robbins, "Day, OT," *NIDB*, 2.48. Emphasis is that of Robbins.

also appears in the second appendix ("the great and awesome day of the Lord," cf. Joel 2:31). In Mal 3:17 Yahweh declares his ownership of those who fear him, "They shall be mine." The variation of והיו לי indicates possession and according to Hill is an adapted covenantal formula. God's relationship to Israel is cast in absolute terms: Israel will be the covenant people of his possession, or the objects of his wrath.

Positively, והיו לי appears in contexts of God gathering his people from the nations (the new exodus): "Therefore say, 'Thus says the Lord God: I will gather you from the peoples and assemble you out of the countries where you have been scattered, and I will give you the land of Israel'. . . that they may walk in my statutes and keep my rules and obey them. And they shall be [to me] (והיו לי) my people, and I will be their God" (Ezek 11:17, 20; cf. 37:21–23; Zech 2:6–7,11; 8:6–8; Jer 24:6–7; 32:37–38).

The new exodus reverses the curses of the covenant and the restored relationship is underscored when the covenantal formula is announced, והיו לי.[12] The old declaration lies behind the new covenantal declaration, "Behold, I have taken the Levites from among the people of Israel instead of every firstborn who opens the womb among the people of Israel. The Levites shall be mine" (והיו לי הלוים, Num 3:12). The formula is then repeated and linked to the exodus, "for all the firstborn are mine. On the day that I struck down all the firstborn in the land of Egypt, I consecrated for my own all the firstborn in Israel, both of man and of beast. They shall be mine (לי יהיו): I am the Lord" (Num 3:13).

Significantly, in all but one exception (Ezek 14:11), the formula לי יהיו on the lips of Yahweh has to do with God bringing his people out of exile. This nearly monolithic character of the new exodus accomplishing the cherished status, והיו לי, raises a presumption that Malachi is likely using it in a similar way.

To elaborate further, Israel is described as "my treasured possession" (סגלה). This designation has its roots in the exodus from Egypt: "You yourselves have seen what I did to the Egyptians, and how I bore you on eagles' wings and brought you to myself. Now therefore, if you will indeed obey my voice and keep my covenant, you shall be my treasured possession (סגלה) among all peoples, for all the earth is mine" (Exod 19:4–5; cf. Deut 7:6; 14:2; 26:18; Ps 135:4).

While the term is not always linked to the exodus (though see Deut 7:8; Ps 135:8–9), its origination is in Israel's founding moment when the people were taken by God out of the nation of Egypt and assembled at the foot of mount Sinai. Exodus 19:5 is the source of Malachi's (סגלה) "citation."[13] As Glazier-McDonald observed, Malachi's unique contribution is to connect סגלה with the יום יהוה.[14] This original move by Malachi is also a logical one: the day of the Lord is the day of the new exodus of the people of God.

Clearly, this special status was not due to Israel's virtuosity. Israel would again be Yahweh's treasured possession, not by any merit of their own, but because the

12. Hill, *Malachi*, 341.

13. Ibid., 361.

14. Glazier-McDonald, *Malachi*, 225; Hill, *Malachi*, 361.

Lord promised to pity them. The final clause of v. 17 confirms this analysis and is, therefore epexegetical, "and I will spare them as a man spares his son who serves him" (חמלתי עליהם כאשר יחמל איש על בנו העבד אתו). The people who had complained of the vanity of serving (עבד) God (3:14) would experience "the day" quite differently. In the first exodus all the Israelites were spared/brought out of Egypt and סגלה was descriptive of the entire nation, upon condition of obedience (Exod 19:5). The future day would not simply be Israel distinguished from the gentile nations; a deeper distinction would occur *within* the nation itself. Only a repentant remnant would be spared and so designated סגלה.[15]

Malachi 3:18 is the bridge transitioning readers to the fate of those who refuse to take Yahweh's admonition to heart, "Then once more you shall see the distinction between the righteous and the wicked, between one who serves God and one who does not serve him." The day of Yahweh's coming will create a distinction between the righteous and the wicked, between those who serve God and those who do not serve God. It is a distinction that the Bible repeatedly uses and it is a distinction that is characteristic of the exodus and new exodus.

On the day of Israel's exodus the Lord made a distinction between the land and livestock of Israel and Egypt (Exod 8:22; 9:44). The firstborn of the Egyptians would die so "that you may know that the LORD makes a distinction between Egypt and Israel" (Exod 11:7). In Malachi the distinction between the righteous and the wicked is that of faithful service to God, or disobedience, either by abstention (possibly implied in 3:7, 15) or ritual perversion (1:7–8, 13–14; 3:8–10). The distinction between Israel and Egypt was because of Israel's sonship. Sonship and service were the key reasons of the first exodus, "and I say to you, 'Let my *son* go that he may *serve* me'" (Exod 4:23). These twin themes are also the basis for which the future distinction will be made. Yahweh will have compassion and spare his *son* who *serves* him, distinguishing the son as his special possession (Mal 3:17–18).

In summary, the themes of Malachi echo the first exodus, the "day" of God's deliverance. The first exodus is utilized by Malachi to forecast a day of the new exodus. If one considered the data in isolation, there would be no reason to deduce a new exodus motif. However, when considered collectively, the thematic and verbal allusions—God making a distinction between the righteous and the wicked, a son who serves (his father), and a people as a treasured possession are all exodus themes *reintroduced under the rubric of the day* (of the Lord). If Yahweh will again distinguish and spare his God-fearing remnant, those not spared would presumably share a fate similar to that of Egypt, which is precisely the direction Mal 3:19 takes.

The Fate of the Wicked

Malachi 3:19 graphically shows that those who practice evil and test God will not escape (3:15). The adverbial clause כי הנה has been understood as disjunctive or

---

15. It is also possible that the exodus citation is a further indictment against the previously mentioned Levitical priesthood (Mal 2:1–9). Cf. Hill, *Malachi*, 361.

conveying a logical and/or emphatic force.[16] "For behold the day is coming," (cf. 3:1–2) is eschatological and ominous.[17] The content of the day elaborates upon what it means not to be God's special possession/the righteous. As the day of the Lord is so often characterized as wrath, so here the flames of fire consume all the evildoers (כל עשה רשעה). The priests, too, had been promised that they would experience the fire on God's day, though not all priests would be destroyed. Some would experience the flame for purificatory purposes (Mal 3:2–3). For the wicked there will be no purification and no escape. The arrogant and the wicked will instead be like stubble for the fire (כל עשה רשעה קש, 3:19). Malachi's choice of "set ablaze" (להט) is probably taken from Joel 2:3 and is almost everywhere used to describe the fate of God's enemies (Deut 32:22; Job 41:21; Pss 83:14; 97:3; 106:18; Isa 42:25; Joel 1:19). Unlike Edom who had the opportunity to rebuild, even if only to be frustrated (1:4), the wicked within Israel will have neither root nor branch, an idiomatic way of saying total annihilation will take place on "that day."

The day of the Lord "burning" (בער) is unique to Malachi, though the concept of Yahweh's burning anger is well known in the OT (Gen 19:24–28; Num 11:1; Pss 2:12; 89:47 [46]; 106:8; Isa 9:17; 10:17; 30:27; Jer 4:4; 21:12; Amos 1:4,7,10,12,14; 2:2, 5; Zeph 1:18; 3:8) and destruction by fire is a type of covenant curse (Deut 28:24; 32:22).[18] "Burning like an oven" (תנור) is a rare but significant description of Yahweh's arrival (Ps 21:8–10). The promise of a special nation coming from Abraham was made by a theophanic appearance of Yahweh "on that day" (Gen 15:18; ביום ההוא) and in the form of a "smoking fire pot" (תנור עשן) passing through the severed animals of the enacted covenant (Gen 15:17–18). God's arrival and covenant-making concerned the promise to give Abraham an offspring (Gen 15:4–5, 18). The specifics of the covenant detailed the giving of a land to Abraham's descendants that would extend from the river of Egypt to the Euphrates. The nations mentioned in Gen 15:19–21 were to be removed to make way for the children of Abraham. In Malachi's eschatological oracle the situation is reversed. The wicked have returned to the land, but will be uprooted by the same God who first appeared to their patriarchal head in תנור עשן. Yahweh will return to Abraham's descendants "burning like an oven" (Mal 3:19; בער כתנור), but this visitation will carry out the curses of the covenant. Instead of expanding Abraham's biological descendants, God promises to reduce them. Instead of distinguishing them from the nations, some will be treated as the nations Yahweh destroyed. Instead of

---

16. Petersen, *Zechariah and Malachi*, 224.

17. Meyers and Meyers point out that in Malachi this announcement formula nearly always introduces punitive action on the part of Yahweh. Cited in Hill, *Malachi*, 345.

18. Verhoef, *Haggai and Malachi*, 325; Glazier-McDonald, *Malachi*, 230–31; Douglas Stuart, *Malachi*, in *The Minor Prophets*, 3 vols., ed. Thomas E. McComiskey (Grand Rapids: Baker, 2003), 3.1386.

tenure in the land, some will be permanently removed.[19] In short, when God returns, he will reduce the nation to a remnant.[20]

The eschatological judgment by fire will not be temporal, such as that of Edom (Mal 1:4). In "that day," the fires of God's judgment will so annihilate the wicked that it will leave them "neither root nor branch." This merism "highlights the totality of the coming destruction, with its completeness made more evident through the burning even of the roots, which ordinarily do not succumb to a flash fire, being protected by the earth. New life can shoot up from a remaining root (Job 14:8–9; Isa 11:1; 37:31). On that coming day, the people who asked for justice (2:17) will see it, and it will befall them."[21]

It is not difficult to see the return of the great king (1:14), coming on his day to destroy those who refuse him through pretension (or possibly abstention). Neither is it too difficult to see in this announcement of a fiery appearance of God to judge his enemies a correlation to the preaching of John the Baptist. Yet as in the days of John the Baptist, so also in the time of the postexilic community, hope remained for those who demonstrated the fruits of repentance (Matt 3:8; Mal 3:14). The negative aspect of "the day" is counterbalanced by its positive pronouncement that the day brings with it deliverance for the righteous, whose experiences resemble that of a new exodus.

The Destiny of the Righteous: The New Exodus

> But for you who fear my name, the sun of righteousness shall rise with healing in its wings. You shall go out leaping like calves from the stall. And you shall tread down the wicked, for they will be ashes under the soles of your feet, on the day when I act, says the LORD of hosts. (Mal 3:20–21)

The destiny of the righteous is explained by three images: healing, liberation, and triumph over enemies.

Healing

The reference to God as a sun of righteousness rising is found only here in Malachi. The phrase שמש צדקה could either be an attributive genitive, "the righteous sun," or an epexegetical genitive (of association) "righteousness like the sun."[22] It is probably the case that the latter is the correct reading. Yahweh has been accused of unrighteous favoring of the wicked (2:17; 3:14–15). In response, the Lord promised

---

19. This is the perspective of Ps 21:8–10, though in this psalm the enemies who plan evil (v. 11) are the nations. If Malachi is borrowing the imagery from Ps 21 his purpose would dovetail with the argument presented here, that Israel becomes like the nations God judged.

20. Hill, *Malachi*, 347; Stuart, *Malachi*, 1386.

21. David W. Baker, *Joel, Obadiah, Malachi*, NIVAC (Grand Rapids: Zondervan, 2006), 297.

22. Hill, *Malachi*, 349.

that his vindication would be seen by all (3:18).[23] In either case, precedence can be found for both readings. Astronomical signs of Yahweh's approach are pervasive throughout the OT (Exod 19:16–20; 24:10; Pss 68:7–8; 77:16–18; 104:3; Ezek 1:4; Joel 3:15; Zech 9:14).

The description of God's ascent among his people is next described as bringing "healing in its wings." The shadow of God's wing is a pictorial expression of safety, particularly in the Psalms (17:8; 18:11[10]; 36:8 [7]; 57:2 [1]; 61:5 [4]; 63:8 [7]; 91:4).[24] The first direct connection between God and כנף is in the exodus, "You yourselves have seen what I did to the Egyptians, and how I bore you on eagles' wings and brought you to myself" (Exod 19:4). This idea is next repeated in the Song of Moses (Deut 32:11). The language, according to Craigie, "alludes to God's care for his people in Egypt, his bringing them out of that land, and the guidance and provision that he grants them during their travels."[25]

The care of Yahweh bearing up Israel under his wings, bringing them out of their affliction and leading them to the promised land, appears to be the motifs Malachi draws upon. The arrival of God on his day provides wings of healing for his people, resulting in their "going out," ויצאתם ופשתם כעגלי מרבק. Given the eschatological context, Hill wonders if Zech 14:3 has influenced Malachi or vice versa.[26] In Zechariah it is the Lord who goes out to fight, but in Malachi it is the departure of God's people. The first exodus is described by the Hiphil of יצא "you brought them out" (Deut 4:20, 37; 5:15; 6:21; Jer 32:21; Ezek 20:10), as are the announcements of the new exodus, "I will bring them out" (Ezek 20:34; 34:13). The survivors of the day of the Lord will also "go out" and with all that we have argued for, the new exodus connections would naturally lead to such a response. Additionally, the image of the calf leaping upon its release looks similar to the exuberance of the people of the new exodus in Jer 30–31, "They will go out rejoicing," and in Isa 48:20–21 "with a shout of joy the people are summoned to 'go out from Babylon.'"[27] The similarities between God's protective wing and the exodus from Egypt looks to be an even stronger connection, especially in light of the next statement that this is a release from captivity.

There are few occurrences of the עגלי מרבק (1 Sam 28:24; Jer 46:21; Amos 6:4) and the great majority of English translations render it "calf from the stall" (ESV, NASB, KJV, NET, ASV, RSV), with the NIV opting for "fattened calf." The LXX translates מרבק as δεσμός: καὶ ἐξελεύσεσθε καὶ σκιρτήσετε ὡς μοσχάρια ἐκ δεσμῶν ἀνειμένα (4:20 LXX), "and you will go out and leap exuberantly like calves released,

---

23. Note also that the issue is the difference between the righteous and the wicked (3:18).

24. Hill, Malachi, 352.

25. Peter C. Craigie, The Book of Deuteronomy, NICOT (Grand Rapids: Eerdmans, 1976), 380; see the similar remarks in Meredith G. Kline, Treaty of the Great King: The Covenant Structure of Deuteronomy (Eugene: Wipf & Stock, n.d.), 141.

26. Hill, Malachi, 352.

27. Isaiah 55:12–13 is another possible illustration, though there is no verbal link to the new exodus.

loosed from (their) bonds." The LXX shows an affinity to the new exodus by way of verbal repetition (δεσμός, ἐξέρχομαι). In Hos 11:4 Yahweh draws Israel with bonds of love: ἐξέτεινα αὐτοὺς ἐν δεσμοῖς ἀγαπήσεώς μου. Isaiah 42:7 describes Israel's release as ἐξαγαγεῖν ἐκ δεσμῶν δεδεμένους. A new exodus motif is also likely in Isa 49:9, λέγοντα τοῖς ἐν δεσμοῖς Ἐξέλθατε. The released captives will neither hunger nor thirst as the Lord levels the mountains making a way for his people πᾶν ὄρος εἰς ὁδόν (Isa 49:11). Finally, Jer 37:8 [30:8] is prefaced by "that great day" (ὅτι μεγάλη ἡ ἡμέρα ἐκείνη, Jer 37:7) *and* the new exodus (37:3). On this fierce, eschatological day, Israel will be saved/καὶ ἀπὸ τούτου σωθήσεται, and ἐν τῇ ἡμέρᾳ ἐκείνῃ the Lord will shatter the yoke from their necks and destroy their bonds τοὺς δεσμούς (Jer 37:8 LXX). The result will be that the people serve the Lord/καὶ ἐργῶνται τῷ κυρίῳ θεῷ αὐτῶν (Jer 37:9 LXX).

The LXX of Malachi declares that on the day of the Lord, Israel will be released from its bonds like a calf, exuberantly frolicking in its new-found freedom. The parallels to the bursting of Israel's bonds in Isaiah and Jeremiah and eschatological release to serve the Lord suggest that the arrival of the Lord on "his day" is the new exodus. The question is where or "whom" is Israel leaving when the Lord removes the bonds of his people and they go out as God's special treasure? For John the Baptist it will be an exodus out of Israel (Matt 3:3,5). The new exodus will be a departure of true Israel, from the compromised nation of Israel upon the day of the Lord.

The day of the Lord is the day of wrath and salvation. The wicked are judged and become as ash under the feet of those released people who experience a new exodus. Malachi's second appendix identifies the herald of this day of the exodus.

The Herald of the New Exodus

> Behold, I will send you Elijah the prophet before the great and awesome day of the Lord comes. 6 And he will turn the hearts of fathers to their children and the hearts of children to their fathers, lest I come and strike the land with a decree of utter destruction. (Mal 3:23–24)

The eschatological identity of Elijah is adapted for the eschatological event that awaited God's people. According to Childs,

> The use of the eschatological vocabulary of Joel 3.4 (ET 2.31) removes any ambiguity as to what day is meant. Elijah's task is to restore the spiritual unity of God's people in preparation for the coming of God to establish justice. . . . Like Malachi, Elijah addressed "all Israel" (1 Kings 18.20). The people of Israel were severely fragmented by indecision of faith (18.21). A curse had fallen on the land (18.1 // Mal. 3.24, EVV 4.6). Elijah challenged all Israel to respond to God by forcing a decision between the right and the wrong (// Mal. 3.3) and fire which fell from heaven (// Mal. 3.3, 19). Of course Elijah could return because he had not died, but had been taken alive into heaven.[28]

---

28. Brevard S. Childs, *Introduction to the Old Testament as Scripture* (Minneapolis: Fortress, 1979), 495–96.

This day of the Lord underscores the destructive overthrow God intended to bring, but the identity of a messenger who prepares that way provides a second layer of meaning by way of intertextual interpretation. The interpretive outlook of Malachi is that Elijah will be sent before the coming of the Lord on his day of the new exodus.

"Behold, I send my messenger, and he will prepare the way before me" (Mal 3:1). This eschatological passage is based on Isa 40:3–5.[29] "The combination of (Piel imperative) *pnh* + *derek* occurs three times in Second Isaiah (40:3; 57:14; and 62:10), and," says Hill, "in each case the context of the phrase is an oracle of salvation and restoration addressed to Israel."[30]

Malachi appears to be adapting Isaiah's consolation to prepare the way of the Lord to his subject of the wrathful day of the Lord. But as Malachi later elaborates, the preparation of the Lord's way is not only the day of wrath—it is also the day of the deliverance. The function of the Elijah-messenger in Mal 3:24 reinforces the hope for those who will heed the message. Because there is a day of wrath coming for the wicked, there is likewise a new exodus hope. Malachi's oracles of salvation (new exodus) and retribution (day of the Lord) are twin aspects of the same eschatological coming of God. He may have borrowed such an idea from Ezekiel who also combines the two:

> As I live, declares the LORD GOD, surely with a mighty hand and an outstretched arm and with wrath poured out I will be king over you. I will bring you out from the peoples and gather you out of the countries where you are scattered, with a mighty hand and an outstretched arm, and with wrath poured out. And I will bring you into the wilderness of the peoples, and there I will enter into judgment with you face to face. As I entered into judgment with your fathers in the wilderness of the land of Egypt, so I will enter into judgment with you, declares the LORD GOD. I will make you pass under the rod, and I will bring you into the bond of the covenant. I will purge out the rebels from among you, and those who transgress against me. I will bring them out of the land where they sojourn, but they shall not enter the land of Israel. Then you will know that I am the LORD. (Ezek 20:33–38)

The time of the new exodus will be a time of "wrath poured out" (v. 33): the Lord will bring his people out of their exile only to enter into judgment with them (v. 35). What the exodus was for the first generation, so it will be in the future (v. 36). Like in Malachi's day of the Lord, this new exodus entails a distinction between the righteous and the wicked. Though the rebels are brought out with the remnant, they will be purged and will not share in the inheritance of the land of Israel.[31]

---

29. Ralph L. Smith, *Micah–Malachi*, WBC 32 (Grand Rapids: Zondervan, 1984), 328. Goldingay and Scalise, *Minor*, 349; Richard A. Taylor and E. Ray Clendenen, *Haggai, Malachi*, NAC 21a (Nashville: Broadman & Holman, 2004), 384–85. Glazier-McDonald, *Malachi*, 136–38; Hill, *Malachi*, 266.

30. Hill, *Malachi*, 266.

31. For the rhetorical affect of Ezekiel's use of Exod 6:6–8 see Michael Fishbane, *Biblical Text and Texture: A Literary Reading of Selected Texts* (Oxford: Oneworld Publications, 1998), 131–32.

Jeremiah also could speak of the day of the Lord as if it were the new exodus. Jeremiah 30–31 contains the twin themes of Malachi: "I have loved you" (Jer 31:3; Mal 1:1) and God's people going out dancing and leaping (Jer 31:4; Mal 3:20). The situation Jer 30 (and 31) describes is the new exodus, "For behold, days are coming, declares the LORD, when I will restore the fortunes of my people, Israel and Judah, says the LORD, and I will bring them back to the land that I gave to their fathers, and they shall take possession of it" (Jer 30:3). But Jer 30:7–8 combines the day of the Lord with the new exodus: "Alas! That day is so great there is none like it; it is a time of distress for Jacob; yet he shall be saved out of it. 'And it shall come to pass in that day, declares the LORD of hosts, that I will break his yoke from off your neck, and I will burst your bonds, and foreigners shall no more make a servant of him.'"

"The day" is like that spoken of in Joel and Malachi. It is the "great day" of "distress" for Israel. And yet, Jeremiah insists that "in that day" (ביום ההוא) Israel will be freed (30:8). Israel's freedom is their return from exile, "I will save you from far away, and your offspring from the land of their captivity. Jacob shall return and have quiet and ease, and none shall make him afraid" (v. 10), and it is a restoration of fortunes (v. 18) which results in songs of celebration (v. 19). On "that day" Israel will be assured of its covenant status, "And you shall be my people, and I will be your God" (והייתם לי לעם) (30:22; 31:1).

Both Ezekiel and Jeremiah blend "the day" and new exodus into one coming of Yahweh. When the day arrives it will be woe for those who remain hardened against him. They will be judged and the exiled penitent will be set free. What they describe is something that transcends the historical horizon—it is an eschatological description.

Summary

The book of Malachi is a postexilic address to a compromised nation, no longer serving the Lord according to his Law. Though the problem is national in scope (2:10–17; 3:6–15), Yahweh singles out Israel's leaders (the priests) for rebuke (1:6–2:9; 3:3). After responding to Israel's complaints (the disputations), Yahweh ends by issuing an ultimatum. If national Israel will not turn from their wickedness they will face the day of the Lord.

We have argued that the language selected to describe the day of the Lord does double duty in that it also can describe Israel's exodus from Egypt. The book of Malachi shows lexical and thematic signs that the future day of the Lord is paradoxically a new exodus. On "that day" Israel will experience a judgment that completely destroys the wicked (3:19), but as Yahweh overthrows the apostate, he will also spare those who fear him and submit to his authority (3:16) and he will lead them out, freed like a calf from the stall (3:20). We have also argued that the new exodus of Malachi is a departure out of rebellious, national Israel. Like in Isa 11, those who are delivered will tread down the wicked on "that day" that the Lord leads them out (3:21; cf. Isa 11:13–16).

As Moses was sent with words of judgment for Egypt and deliverance for Israel, another messenger is promised to arrive before the appearance of "that day." Elijah will come. His presence is the signal that the day of the Lord is about the arrive (3:1) and should he not be successful in turning Israel back, God will strike the land with a decree of utter destruction (3:24).

Conclusion

Turning to the Gospel of Matthew, we find that the author has done much the same thing with the timing of the arrival of the Lord in judgment and the coterminous new exodus. In Matt 3:3 he cites Isa 40:3 to describe John the Baptist, and the retrospective summary of John and his ministry is captured by citing Mal 3:1 (Matt 11:10; cf. Mark 1:2–3). The one coming of God is both the new exodus and the day of the Lord. As the day of the Lord can be for mercy (Joel 2:32; Mal 3:17–18), so also can the new exodus be for judgment (Mal 3:21; cf. Ezek 20:33–38). As a herald of the day of the new exodus, this wilderness prophet also offered the people a way of escape, "μετανοεῖτε" (Matt 3:2). He announced the nearness of the kingdom of heaven, using a formula describing the nearness of the day of the Lord:

ἤγγικεν γὰρ ἡ βασιλεία τῶν οὐρανῶν (Matt 3:2)
διότι ἐγγὺς ἡμέρα Κυρίου (Obad 1:15)
Ὅτι ἐγγὺς ἡμέρα Κυρίου ἡ μεγάλη (Zeph 1:14)
ὅτι ἐγγὺς ἡμέρα Κυρίου (Joel 1:15)
ὅτι ἐγγὺς ἡμέρα Κυρίου (Joel 3:14)

The arrival of the king will be against the wicked leaders (3:7–12), which is a perspective of the religious establishment not unlike that of Malachi's day (Mal 2:1–9). In classic form, fire is the means by which the wicked will be extirpated. It will consume those who perform their duties without the fruit of repentance (Matt 3:8). It is an eschatological judgment that will leave no trace of the wicked. John proclaimed that the axe was already laid at the exposed root/ῥίζαν (Matt 3:10), leaving it exposed to the day of the Lord, and Malachi warned "that day" would not leave for the wicked ῥίζα οὐδὲ κλῆμα (Mal 3:19).

It was at the same time an exodus. The need to return from exile is indicated by the genealogical story of their ancestors (Matt 1:1–17), with ch. 2 functioning as a retelling of Israel's exile and exodus (Matt 2:15). How the people would experience that day of the exodus would depend upon their response to the forerunner. Those who went out into the wilderness and heeded the voice crying there could seek the Lord's solution to all that was wrong with Israel by following Jesus. Submitting to God's judgments and seeking his favor in the Son of his pleasure (Matt 3:16) was the new exodus out of a nation on the brink of eschatological judgment in the Spirit and fire. John assured his listeners that the repentant would be spared like the wheat gathered in the barn while the chaff experienced the eternal flame (Matt 3:12). In requiring baptism, John was preparing the people for the day of God's visitation in judgment. The only way to escape it was to follow Jesus in faith, leading a new people into the day of the new exodus.

For Matthew, the great judgment and salvation themes of the prophets are once more paradigmatic for the future of the nation. The recasting of these themes is the concern of ch. 7, as Matthew retells the story of Israel in preparation for the warning of the Elijah-to-come (Matt 3:1–4).

Chapter 6

DANIEL 7, THE ONE TO COME: JUDGMENT AND SALVATION

Introduction

Although the specific term "Son of Man" is not found in Matt 3, the themes of John the Baptist are reduplicated and reinserted into the Matthean Son of Man sayings. The one announced by John and the Son of Man are apocalyptic figures who come (ἐρχόμενος: 3:11; 16:27; 24:27, 30) to bring eschatological wrath upon Israel (3:7; 24:36–44). The chaff/weeds will be gathered and burned (3:12; 13:40–42), a distinction will be made between good and bad trees (3:10; 12:32,33), and the identity and fate of the Pharisees is described with the epitaph: "brood of vipers" (3:7; 12:34). For these reasons, Dan 7 is included in this study as an interpretive lens upon John's unnamed figure whom Matthew shows to be Jesus, the Son of Man. For Matthew, this Son of Man is the one who baptizes his enemies in the Holy Spirit and fire.

We will first look at the literary features of Daniel's vision and then compare Daniel's Son of Man with 1 Enoch and 4 Ezra. Finally, we will show that these extra-canonical authors molded Daniel's unnamed Son of Man into an apocalyptic judge and that this provides further illumination of the saying of John: "He who comes after me is more powerful than I . . . he will baptize you with the Holy Spirit and fire" (Matt 3:11).

Daniel's Apocalyptic Vision

The book of Daniel is an important work in Jewish and Christian traditions. The apocalypses, 1 Enoch, 4 Ezra, and DSS make use of the imagery, themes, and persons found in Daniel. NA[27] lists thirty-one Danielic citations/allusions in the NT and the Son of Man title occurs more than seventy times in the NT.[1] Starting

---

1. Adela Y. Collins and John J. Collins, *King and Messiah as Son of God* (Grand Rapids: Eerdmans, 2008), 75. Proceeding on the assumption that "Son of Man" is a title in Matthew, we will refer to the Son of Man using capitalization. For the proposals of the Son of Man's identity and therefore appropriateness of the title, see nn. 22–25.

in ch. 5, Matthew makes use of the title twenty-eight times.[2] The themes of God's kingdom, an eschatological king, a fiery judgment, final salvation, and the inauguration of an eternal kingdom coalesce in the Son of Man. Matthew's awareness of Daniel's Son of Man, his leveraging of apocalyptic images in ch. 3 and particularly in ch. 24 with the added Son of Man designation, makes Dan 7 a suitable OT background.

The structure of Daniel's nocturnal vision consists of five scenes. Scene one (vv. 2–8): the kings/kingdoms that emerge from the sea, concluding with the horn that speaks "great things"; scene two (vv. 9–10): the throne room judgment; scene three (vv. 11–12): the judgment against the fourth kingdom; scene four (13–14): the Son of Man; scene five (vv. 15–28): the interpretation of the dream(s) and conclusion.[3] The chapter scenes are introduced by the repetition of the variable, but formulaic expression וארו חיוה, "and behold."[4]

In the vision, Daniel sees four beasts rising out of the sea, having been stirred up by the four winds of heaven (cf. Ezek 47:9; Dan 8:8; 11:4; 1 En. 18:2; 4 Ezra 13:5). This motif of God's power and sovereign control over the sea is a common one (Gen 1:2; 7:8; Job 38:8–11; Pss 29:3–4, 10; 74:12–17), as is his authority over the mythological creatures that inhabit it (Job 40:25–32; Ps 104; Isa 27:1; Ezek 37:9; Rev 13).[5] The four winds which stir up the sea and the four creatures symbolically convey the notion of worldwide hostility.[6] It is the domain of all that is opposed to God (cf. Pss 89:9; 93:3–4; Isa 27:1; 51:9–11).[7]

The animal imagery in Dan 7 has a parallel in 1 Enoch:

> Dan 7 has clear links outside the actual OT with 1 Enoch. The animal allegory in chaps. 85–90 also features predators symbolizing rulers or kingdoms, an animal transformed into a man, animals with horns of extraordinary size, a throne set up for God to sit in judgment as books are opened before him, and animals being destroyed by fire. In chap. 14, Enoch is carried by winds and clouds into

2. Matthew's usage might be more in line with Ezekiel's than with Daniel's, but nearly half of the occurrences have an eschatological orientation (10:23; 11:19; 13:41; 16:27–28; 19:28; 24:27,30,37,39; 25:32; 26:64).

3. Structurally, vv. 1–2 introduce the content and v. 28 brings the content to its conclusion.

4. The phrases occur in vv. 2,5,6,7,8 ("I considered . . . and behold"), 9,11 ("I watched . . ."), 13 ("I watched . . . and behold").

5. John D. Levenson, *Creation and the Persistence of Evil: The Jewish Drama of Divine Omnipotence* (Princeton: Princeton University Press, 1996), 54–55. For an analysis of Akkadian influence (*Enuma Elish* 1.105–110) on Dan 7 see John H. Walton, "The ANZU Myth as Relevant Background for Daniel 7?" in *The Book of Daniel: Composition and Reception*, 2 vols., eds. John J. Collins and Peter W. Flint (Leiden: Brill, 2001), 1.69–90.

6. John E. Goldingay, *Daniel*, WBC 30 (Nashville: Thomas Nelson, 1989), 160.

7. Maurice Casey, *Son of Man: The Interpretation and Influence of Daniel 7* (London: SPCK, 1979), 18.

heaven, where he sees a throne from which flaming fire issues and on which God sits in a gown whiter than snow, surrounded by myriad upon myriad of attendants. There are also parallels in chaps. 46–48 and 71 with the throne scene and the humanlike figure in Dan 7. There is disagreement over whether different parallels suggest Dan 7 is dependent on 1 Enoch.[8]

Animal imagery is also found in Hos 13:7–8 where God is described as being fierce as a lion, bear, and leopard.[9] The symbolic meaning of the beasts of Dan 7 parallels ch. 2.[10] Both chapters contain dreams (2:1,28; 7:1), interpretations (2:36–45; 7:23–27), and the images in both represent four emerging kingdoms (2:37–40; 7:17). God changes times and seasons (2:21), and the evil one tries to change the times and the laws (7:25). God establishes the eternal kingdom in the days of the kings (2:44), and while further detail is given in ch. 7, the eternal kingdom will be given to the saints of the Most High (7:27).[11] Finally, both chapters underscore that the kingdom of God and the kingdom of the world (in this case Babylon) are in conflict with one another, with ch. 7 showing the triumph of the former over the latter.

Broadly speaking, the four beasts correspond to Babylonian, Median, Persian and Grecian empires and/or Rome. It might also be that the four kings/kingdoms are a representative number corresponding to the "four winds of heaven" (7:2).[12] The threat to God's people escalates as the dream progresses. The lion appears neutral (7:4). The bear with the ribs between its teeth devoured much flesh (7:5). The leopard was given dominion (7:6). The fourth is not comparable to any animal but is described as "terrifying," "dreadful," and "exceedingly strong." The fourth beast had ten horns, the horn being a symbol of power, and in this case, a symbol of kingship.[13] The mention of iron teeth also recalls the fourth kingdom of 2:40 and the violent language of devouring and stamping out everything that remains. This captures the fierceness of this beast.[14] It is a picture of upheaval and total domination, "The fourth kingdom . . . shall devour the whole earth, and trample it down, and break it to pieces." (7:23)

8. Goldingay, *Daniel*, 150.

9. John J. Collins, *Daniel: A Commentary on the Book of Daniel*, Hermeneia (Minneapolis: Fortress, 1993), 295.

10. Moses Stuart, *A Commentary on the Book of Daniel* (Boston: Crocker & Brewster, 1850), 173–84. Childs, *Introduction*, 616–17.

11. Childs, *Introduction*, 617.

12. Cf. the four horns and the four winds of heaven in Dan 8:8; 11:1–3.

13. 2 Chron 18:10; Pss 18:2; 75:4–5, 10; 89:17, 24; 92:10; 132:17–18; Jer 48:25; Dan 2:37–45. Cf. Goldingay, *Daniel*, 173.

14. Collins, *Daniel*, 299.

The Ancient of Days

In the vision, the final horn (king) fights against the saints and prevails over them (7:20–21).[15] Like the beasts, the precise identity of the "saints" is not given. The persecuting king will appear unstoppable as he tramples upon the world and the saints of God, but the Ancient of Days brings the turmoil into sharp relief. Like the previous chapters, the main emphasis in Dan 7 is that Yahweh rules (4:32, "heaven rules"), brings judgments upon the kingdoms of this world, and delivers his people. Surrounded by thrones and heavenly attendants, the refulgent description of the Ancient of Days (his clothing appears white as snow, 7:9; cf. Ps 51:7; Isa 1:18; 1 En. 14:20; 3 En. 28:7) is intensified by fire imagery: "His throne was fiery flames; its wheels were burning fire. A stream of fire issued and came out from before him; a thousand thousands served him, and ten thousand times ten thousand stood before him; the court sat in judgment, and the books were opened" (7:9c–10).[16]

Fire is a common attendant in theophanies (Gen 15:17; Exod 3:2; 13:22; 19:18; 24:17; Num 14:14; Deut 4:12, 15, 33; Judg 6:21; 13:20; 2 Kgs 2:11; Isa 4:5; Ezek 1:27). So close was the relationship that Yahweh could be described as a devouring fire (Deut 4:24; 9:3; Isa 33:14) while also being distinguished from it (1 Kgs 19:11–12; Ps 50:3 [LXX 49:3]; 104:4 [103:4]). In Isaiah and Ezekiel, fire is a symbol of Yahweh's holiness and glory (Isa 6:1–4; Ezek 1:27–28). It became an expectation of the latter prophets that the day of Lord would arrive in fire (Joel 2:7, 30; Mal 3:19) with the enemies of Yahweh being destroyed by the same (Isa 47:14; 66:15–16; Ezek 38:22; 39:6; Mal 4:1). Fire is a common image for the final judgment and everlasting punishment in the OT and Second Temple texts (Isa 50:11; 66:24; 1 En. 14:9–22; 91:9; 100:9; 102:1; 2 Bar. 37.1; 44.15; 48.39; 2 Esd 7:38; 13:10–11; 1QpHab. 10.5; 1QS II, 7–8; IV, 12–13). Both aspects are brought together in Dan 7:9–10. The stream of fire that flows from Yahweh's burning throne is a manifestation of his glory and fire is the instrument of his judgment, silencing the boasting of the little horn: "I looked then because of the sound of the great words that the horn was speaking. And as I looked, the beast was killed, and its body destroyed and given over to be burned with fire" (7:11).

After the seating of the court in judgment (7:10), the beast is slain with no mention of the one who carried out the execution (7:11).[17] "The burning of a corpse in the OT was a punishment reserved for those guilty of particularly heinous crimes (cf. Lev 20:14; 21:9; Jos 7:25). Although two different words are used for 'fire' in the section (Aram. *nûr*, v. 9; *'eššā'*, v. 11), the point is the utter

---

15. *Ant.* 10.276. Commentators have generally interpreted the fourth horn as Antiochus Epiphanes IV. For the mythological overtones of the beast and Antiochus's devotion to Baal Shamem/Zeus Olympius see John J. Collins, *Seers, Sibyls and Sages in Hellenistic-Roman Judaism* (Leiden: Brill, 1997), 150–52.

16. The following references to fire are taken from "πῦρ" *NIDNTTE*, Accordance Bible Software 11.1.6.

17. This observation will become important when we compare Daniel's Son of Man to 1 En. and 4 Ezra.

destruction of the fourth beast or earthly kingdom and its arrogant ruler."[18] Yahweh's enthronement upon flames of fire with streams of fire flowing from it is the reverse of the river of life.[19]

Where this judgment takes place is not specifically stated. It might be that the judgment takes place in "mythic space."[20] Fire and angelic attendants occur in descriptions of heaven (cf. Job 1:6; 2:1; 1 Kgs 22:19; Isa 6:1; Pss 83; 103:21) and, if such were the case here, it would suggest that the one like the Son of Man approaches heaven rather than earth (Dan 7:13). On the other hand, Daniel's perspective is that of an onlooker to the events of earth. Beasley-Murray makes the added observation that the Ancient of Days "came" (7:22).[21] The placing of the thrones in v. 9 could also suggest an earthly orientation (Jer 1:15). Apocalyptic images and locations can be more fluid than fixed, which cautions against emphasizing one particular visionary aspect of the narrative at the expense of the other.

The eschatological scenario of Dan 7 can be summarized as a great upheaval (7:7, 23), persecution (7:21, 25), the coming of God and his hosts (7:9–10), judgment upon his enemies (7:11–12), final deliverance for the saints (7:22, 27) and the enthronement of a king, the enigmatic Son of Man (7:13–14).

Son of Man

The scene shifts as Daniel sees one like a Son of Man coming with the clouds to the Ancient of Days. The interpretations of the Son of Man typically fall under three categories: angelic,[22] symbolic,[23] and eschatological or messianic

---

18. Andrew E. Hill, "Daniel," in *Daniel – Malachi*, EBC 8, rev. ed., eds. Tremper Longman III and David E. Garland (Grand Rapids: Zondervan, 2008), 138.

19. Cf. Charles Briggs, *Messianic Prophecy: The Prediction of the Fulfillment of Redemption through the Messiah* (New York: Scribner's, 1886; repr., Peabody: Hendrickson, 1988), 420.

20. Collins, *Daniel*, 303.

21. George R. Beasley-Murray, "The Interpretation of Daniel 7," *CBQ* 45 (1983): 49, presumably not to his throne but to earth. In the book of Ezekiel, the prophet sees Yahweh come to earth (Ezek 1–2).

22. Nathaniel Schmidt, "The 'Son of Man' in the Book of Daniel," *JBL* 19 (1900): 22–28; cited by Ziony Zevit, "The Structure and Individual Elements of Daniel 7," *ZAW* 80 (1968): 394-95; John J. Collins, *The Apocalyptic Vision of the Book of Daniel*, HSM (Missoula: Scholars Press, 1977), 14; C. Rowland, *The Open Heaven: A Study of Apocalyptic in Judaism and Early Christianity* (New York: Crossroad, 1982), 182; John Day, *God's Conflict with the Dragon and the Sea: Echoes of a Canaanite Myth in the Old Testament* (Cambridge: Cambridge University Press, 1985), 169. Within the book of Daniel, not only do angels appear as humans, they are also called holy ones (3:25; 8:15; 9:21; 10:5,18).

23. J. Drummond, *The Jewish Messiah* (London: Longmans, Green, 1877), 226–41; S. R. Driver, *Daniel* (Cambridge: Cambridge University Press, 1936), 88, 102–10 understands the Son of Man to be "the ideal and glorified people of Israel." R. H. Charles, *A Critical and*

king.[24] Understandably, the debates are complex and ongoing.[25] As it relates to Matthew's Gospel, there is no question that Jesus is the Son of Man (Matt 8:20; 9:6; 10:23; 11:19; 12:8, 32, 40; 13:37, 41; 16:13, 27–28; 17:9, 12, 22; 19:28; 20:18, 28; 24:27, 30, 37, 39, 44; 25:31; 26:2, 24, 45, 64). Our inquiry will proceed upon the premise of the messianic interpretations of the Son of Man as espoused by Matthew.

In contrast to the winds that stir up the sea (7:2), the Son of Man comes with the clouds which resembles the theophanic coming of God on the clouds as king and warrior (Exod 13:21–22; Deut 33:26; Job 22:14; 26:9; 37:15–16; 36:29; Pss 18:9–15; 68:4; 97:2; 104:1–4; Isa 19:1; Jer 4:13–18; Nah 1:3).[26] His rule is cast in transcendent terms: "everlasting," "unable to pass away," "never to be destroyed" (7:14). Although not so-named, the unending character of his throne points in one of two possible directions: either to God or to David (Ps 89:20–23, 29–37). The hope for a righteous ruler of David upon an eternal throne came to be a messianic hope (Pss 2, 110 and especially 61:6–7), both before and especially after the exile.[27]

Exegetical Commentary on the Book of Daniel (Oxford: Clarendon Press, 1929), 187. James A. Montgomery, *A Critical and Exegetical Commentary on the Book of Daniel*, ICC (Edinburgh: T&T Clark, 1927), 319–20. Sigmund Mowinckel, *He That Cometh: The Messiah Concept in the Old Testament and Later Judaism*, trans. G. W. Anderson (Nashville: Abingdon Press, 1956; repr., Grand Rapids: Eerdmans, 2005), 350; Geza Vermes, "The Use of בר נש / בר נשא in Jewish Aramaic," in *Post-Biblical Jewish Studies*, ed. Geza Vermes (Leiden: Brill, 1975), 147–65; Joachim Becker, *Messianic Expectation in the Old Testament*, trans. D. Green (Minneapolis: Fortress, 1977), 79, n 1; L. F. Hartman and A. A. Di Lella, *The Book of Daniel*, AB 23 (New York: Doubleday, 1978), 218–19; Maurice Casey, *The Solution to the 'Son of Man' Problem* (Edinburgh: T&T Clark, 2009); Douglas R. A. Hare, *The Son of Man Tradition* (Minneapolis: Fortress, 1990).

24. 1 En. 37–71; cf. 4 Ezra 13; Justin Martyr, *Dialogue with Trypho*, 31–32. Cf. Irenaeus, *Against Heresies* 4.20.11; Hippolytus, *Treatise on Christ and Antichrist*; Tertullian, *Against Marcion* 4.10; Cyril of Alexandria (*PG* 70:1461). Ernst W. Hengstenberg, *Christology of the Old Testament*, 2nd ed., trans. J. Martin (Edinburgh: T&T Clark, 1864), 82–92; Carl F. Keil, *Daniel*, trans. M. G. Easton (Edinburgh: T&T Clark, 1866–91; repr., Peabody: Hendrickson, 2001); 646; Beasley-Murray, "The Interpretation of Daniel 7," 44–58; Seyoon Kim, *The Son of Man as Son of God* (Grand Rapids: Eerdmans, 1985); Chrys C. Caragounis, *The Son of Man*, WUNT 38 (Tübingen: J. C. B. Mohr, 1986); Ernsest C. Lucas, *Daniel*, AOTC (Downers Grove: IVP, 2002), 185.

25. For a survey of the nineteenth- to twentieth-century perspectives on the Son of Man and eleven scholarly proposals of background influences, see Jürg Eggler, *Influences and Traditions Underlying the Vision of Daniel 7:2-14*, OBO 177 (Göttingen: Vandenhoeck & Ruprecht, 2000), 55–87; Mogens Muller, *The Expression "Son of Man" and the Development of Christology: A History of Interpretation* (London: Equinox, 2008).

26. Cf. Tremper Longman III and Daniel G. Reid, *God Is a Warrior* (Grand Rapids: Zondervan, 1995), 63–69.

27. Marvin Tate, *Psalms 51-100*, WBC 20 (Grand Rapids: Zondervan, 1990), 261; Damuel Terrien, *The Psalms: Strophic Structure and Theological Commentary*

The Rabbis came to see in the Son of Man an enthroned Davidic king (*b. Hag. 14a; b. Sanh. 38b*).

From the apocalyptic perspective of Daniel, the Son of Man arrives after a period of intense persecution for the people of God and is given universal dominion in a kingdom that will never be supplanted or pass away (7:14). What is not stated is whether or not this Son of Man plays a part in the judgment against the kings of vv. 11–12. If we are to view 7:13–14 as recapitulating the conclusion to the crisis (vv. 2–8), then vv. 9–12 and vv. 13–14 could be understood as a dual perspective on the resolution from differing vantage points. If this is the case, then it is equally possible that the Son of Man is the one who carried out the judgment of the heavenly court (v. 10). His presentation before the Ancient of Days would be that of a successful warrior presented to a king after a military victory.[28] The heavenly court announces the verdict of the persecuting kings/kingdoms and the heavenly Son of Man carries out the judgment and returns victorious from his conquest to receive a universal rule. Again, we note that the *agent(s)* of the acts of judgment (slaying, burning, removal of dominion, etc.) are left unspecified. The coming of the Son of Man to receive a throne and everlasting dominion suggests that he was the one who delivered his people by executing their oppressor. Such a perspective fills in the remaining details of vv. 11–12.

Though such a reading is plausible, like any other interpretation it can only be inferred that the Son of Man was the agent carrying out the decree of heaven. But what can only be inferred here is made explicit in the works of 1 Enoch, 4 Ezra, and the Gospel of Matthew.

1 Enoch

While the dating of the *Similitudes* has been disputed, the majority consensus is a date prior to or within the first century CE.[29] Whether or not it predates Matthew, the *Similitude* is dependent upon the Danielic Son of Man.[30] The heavenly being is described as a "righteous one," "anointed one," "chosen one," and "Son of Man."[31]

(Grand Rapids: Eerdmans, 2003), 455; Frank-Lothar Hossfeld and Erich Zenger, *Psalms 2: A Commentary on Psalms 51-100* (Minneapolis: Fortress, 2005), 107.

28. Note the suggestion of Lacocque, "That is why the scene of judgment in Daniel 7 is also a scene of war. The judge is also the Great Warrior, and he vindicates the righteous." He later surmises, "Dominion is given to the 'Son of Man,' who is logically to be credited with the victory or, rather, with the execution of the Evil power." André Lacocque, "Allusions to Creation in Daniel 7," in *The Book of Daniel: Composition and Reception*, 1.117, 130.

29. Darrell L. Bock, "Dating the *Parables of Enoch*: A *Forschungsbericht*," in *Parables of Enoch: A Paradigm Shift*, eds. James H. Charlesworth and Darrell L. Block (London: Bloomsbury, 2013), 58-113; Collins, *The Scepter*, 177.

30. Collins, *The Scepter*, 177.

31. Adela Y. Collins, "Son of Man," *NIDB*, 5.343.

In 1 En. 48 the Son of Man (48:2) is called the chosen one (48:6) and messiah (48:10). Drawing upon Dan 7, the function of the Son of Man (note his relationship to the Lord of Spirits who is described like Daniel's Ancient of Days) is that of a judge:

> At that place, I saw the One to whom belongs the time before time. And his head was white like wool, and there was with him another individual, whose face was like that of a human being. His countenance was full of grace like that of one among the holy angels. And I asked the one—from among the angels—who was going with me, and who had revealed to me all the secrets regarding the One who was born of human beings, "Who is this, and from whence is he who is going as the prototype of the Before-Time?" And he answered me and said to me, "This is the Son of Man to whom belongs righteousness and with whom righteousness dwells. And he will open all the hidden storerooms; for the Lord of the Spirits has chosen him, and he is destined to be victorious before the Lord of the Spirits in eternal uprightness. *This Son of Man whom you have seen is the One who would remove the kings and the mighty ones from their comfortable seats and the strong ones from their thrones. He shall loosen the reins of the strong and crush the teeth of the sinners. He shall depose the kings from their thrones and kingdoms.* For they do not extol and glorify him, and neither do they obey him, the source of their kingship. The faces of the strong will be slapped and be filled with shame and gloom. Their dwelling places and their beds will be worms. They shall have no hope to rise from their beds, for they do not extol the name of the Lord of the Spirits." (1 En 46:1–6; emphasis mine)

In this parable, the Son of Man performs the work of judgment implied in Dan 7. He removes kings and crushes the teeth of sinners. This judgment ends with the kings dwelling in death: "Their beds will be worms." The reason given for the Son of Man's judgment is twice mentioned: "they do not extol and glorify him" (the Son of Man) and "they do not extol the name of the Lord of Spirits" (God). The account of the kings likely builds upon the little horn who speaks against the Most High (Dan 7:25). These kings "raise their hands (to reach) the Most High while walking upon the earth and dwelling in her. They manifest all their deeds in oppression; all their deeds are oppression" (1 En. 46:7). A paradoxical statement follows which describes these kings as also congregating with the people of the Lord of the Spirits, "in his houses" (1 En. 46:8). However this is to be understood, what is made clear is that their persecution of the righteous (1 En. 47:1; 48:8, "in those days") ends with the Son of Man's judgment followed by his receiving the worship of the peoples. "All those who dwell upon the earth shall fall and worship before him [the Son of Man, cf. 48:2–5]; they shall glorify, bless, and sing the name of the Lord of the Spirits" (48.5).

In 1 En. 62, there is a fusion of biblical imagery drawn from Dan 7 and Isa 11:2, 4 depicting the slaying of the wicked by the Son of Man:

> Thus the Lord commanded the kings, the governors, the high officials, and the landlords and said, "Open your eyes and lift up your eyebrows—if you are able

to recognize the Elect One!" The Lord of the Spirits has sat down on the throne of his glory, and the spirit of righteousness has been poured out upon him. The word of his mouth will do the sinners in; and all the oppressors shall be eliminated from before his face. On the day of judgment all the kings, the governors, the high officials, and the landlords shall see and recognize him—how he sits on the throne of his glory, and righteousness is judged before him, and that no nonsensical talk shall be uttered in his presence. Then pain shall come upon them as on a woman in travail with birth pangs—when she is giving birth (the child) enters the mouth of the womb and she suffers from childbearing. One half portion of them shall glance at the other half; they shall be terrified and dejected; and pain shall seize them when they see that Son of Man sitting on the throne of his glory. (1 En. 62:1–5)

Of particular significance is that the eschatological event occurs on the day of judgment (1 En. 62:3). Elsewhere, when the day of judgment arrives, books are opened and angels cast the wicked into the eternal fires to be tormented (1 En. 54:6; 67:12–13; 90:22–25). In ch. 61 this day of judgment is also called "the day of the elect One" (61:5) and on this day, he also judges the works of the "holy ones of heaven" (61:8).

Once more, the elect one/Son of Man judges (cf. 38:3; 45:6) and destroys the wicked kings. This time the Parable elaborates upon the method of execution by the word of his mouth (62:2). The combination of pouring the Spirit upon him and the word of his mouth killing sinners is taken from Isa 11:2,4.[32] The rulers are then delivered "to the angels for punishments in order that vengeance shall be executed on them—oppressors of his children and his elect ones" (62:11).[33] Their fate is sharply contrasted with those they persecuted: "The righteous and elect ones shall be saved on that day; and from thenceforth they shall never see the faces of the sinners and the oppressors. The Lord of the Spirits will abide over them; they shall eat and rest and rise with that Son of Man forever and ever" (62:13–14). As in Dan 7, so also in 1 Enoch the people who belong to the Son of Man will, in the end, enjoy the eternal benefits of his kingdom. His role in their deliverance, suggested in Dan 7, is made plain in 1 Enoch.

The Danielic Son of Man has undergone transformation in the *Similitude*. The Son of Man, who is seated upon the throne of glory, is the deliverer of his people and judge of the wicked, all of which takes place on the day of judgment. A further expansion is seen in the transformation of the fire that burns the body of the slain horn of Dan 7, which in Enoch becomes a place of eternal torment. Although it is the Son of Man who slays his enemies, it is the function of the angels to take the

---

32. Collins, *The Scepter*, 182.

33. "After that, their faces shall be filled with shame before that Son of Man; and from before his face they shall be driven out. And the sword shall abide in their midst, before his face" (1 En. 63:11). In 1 En. 53 and 54 chains are prepared for the kings of the earth and the angels are depicted as casting the enemies of God into a valley burning with fire (53:3–5; 54:1–2).

judged kings and throw them into the fire (1 En. 53–54, 62). As we will see below, these apocalyptic roles of the Son of Man and the angels are part of the eschatological scenario repeatedly described in Matthew.

4 Ezra

4 Ezra is an apocalyptic work that is dated near the end of the first century CE.[34] Though not an antecedent to Matthew, it does provide evidence of a broader, Jewish apocalyptic development of the Son of Man as an expected messianic judge. The vision of 4 Ezra 13 contains the churning of the sea, as does Dan 7. But unlike the beasts that arise from the sea, the visionary sees the Son of Man coming out of it:

> And I looked, and behold, this wind made something like the figure of a man come up out of the heart of the sea. And I looked, and behold, that man flew with the clouds of heaven; and wherever he turned his face to look, everything under his gaze trembled, and whenever his voice issued from his mouth, all who heard his voice melted as wax melts when it feels the fire. (4 Ezra 13:3–4)

The confusion over the Son of Man's origin is given voice in 13:51, "I said, 'O sovereign Lord, explain this to me: Why did I see the man coming up from the heart of the sea?'" (13:51). Ezra knows that the sea is a place of hostility and opposition to God (4 Ezra 11:1). The enigmatic answer is given in 13:52, "He said to me, 'Just as no one can explore or know what is in the depths of the sea, so no one on earth can see my Son or those who are with him, except in the time of his day.'"[35] However we are to understand this strange start, the Son of Man does fly upon the clouds and is appointed to judge his enemies:

> After this I looked, and behold, an innumerable multitude of men were gathered together from the four winds of heaven to make war against the man who came up out of the sea. . . . And behold, when he saw the onrush of the approaching multitude, he neither lifted his hand nor held a spear or any weapon of war; but I saw only how he sent forth from his mouth as it were a stream of fire, and from

---

34. Marius Reiser, *Jesus and Judgment: The Eschatological Proclamation in Its Jewish Context*, trans. Linda M. Maloney (Minneapolis: Fortress, 1997), 111.

35. Beale proposes that a typological reversal of Dan 7 for polemical purposes "may be present" in the depiction of the Son of Man coming from the sea, "Specifically, the prediction in Daniel 7 of the cosmic foe's emergence from the sea, which marks the beginning of his attempt to defeat the saints, is seen by the writer as containing an ironic typological pattern of the beginning of this same foe's ultimate defeat by the Messiah. The same way in which the enemy will try to subdue God will be used by God Himself to subdue this enemy in the end." Gregory K. Beale, "The Problem of the Man from the Sea in 4 Ezra 13 and Its Relation to the Messianic Concept in John's Apocalypse," *NovT* 25.2 (1983): 185–86.

his lips a flaming breath, and from his tongue he shot forth a storm of sparks. All these were mingled together, the stream of fire and the flaming breath and the great storm, and fell on the onrushing multitude which was prepared to fight, and burned them all up, so that suddenly nothing was seen of the innumerable multitude but only the dust of ashes and the smell of smoke. When I saw it, I was amazed. (4 Ezra 13:5, 9–11)

In 4 Ezra there is no mention of the Ancient of Days or heavenly attendants accompanying the Son of Man. He appears alone against a vast army. The scene is reminiscent of Rev 20:7–10 where the devil gathers an army like the sand of the sea and from the four corners of the earth, but is destroyed by fire that falls from heaven. The fiery blast of the Son of Man also parallels OT descriptions of Yahweh destroying armies with the blast of his nose/mouth (Exod 15:8; Isa 30:28; likewise the messianic Son of Jesse in Isa 11:4).[36] Despite the oddity of the Son of Man coming out of the sea, the further description of his flying on the clouds of heaven illustrates 4 Ezra's dependence upon Dan 7. We also note that 4 Ezra's Son of Man rides with the clouds as he goes out to war, whereas in Daniel he approaches the Ancient of Days (possibly after the war has been concluded). Finally, the most obvious development and expansion beyond both the *Similitude* and Dan 7 is the graphic description of the Son of Man's judgment as flaming breath and streams of fire proceeding from his mouth and destroying the army (cf. 2 Thess 2:8).

Summary

The later eschatological scenarios of the Son of Man are dependent upon Dan 7 and are examples of a further development of the Son of Man's eschatological role. As the enthroned king, he is also a savior figure sent out to rescue his people and a judge who destroys their persecutors. He shares certain traits with the divine: a throne of glory, riding upon the clouds, executing his enemies with fire and having authority over the angels. Daniel's Son of Man was interpreted messianically before and during the Christian era and such interpretations have numerous parallels to Matthew's Gospel. If the previously mentioned works are representative of a Jewish outlook, and if they are representative of broader apocalyptic interpretations of the end of the age, then such a matrix could have informed Matthew's version of John the Baptist's apocalyptic eschatological perspective.

"Son of Man" was but one designation used to describe a kingly figure who would perform such mighty works. In the Psalms of Solomon, the psalmist prays that the Lord would raise up another son of David (17:21). This eschatological king's task is similar to previous perspectives:

36. The interpretation given to Ezra is "The fire that proceeds from the mouth of the Son of man is both a symbol of the law and a sign of the torment of the wicked by which they will be tortured" (4 Ezra 13:38).

And gird him with strength, that he may shatter unrighteous rulers, and that he may purge Jerusalem from gentiles who trample (her) down to destruction. Wisely, righteously he shall thrust out sinners from (the) inheritance; he shall destroy the arrogance of the sinner as a potter's jar. With a rod of iron he shall shatter all their substance; he shall destroy the godless nations with the word of his mouth. At his rebuke nations shall flee before him, and he shall reprove sinners for the thoughts of their heart. And he shall gather together a holy people, whom he shall lead in righteousness, and he shall judge the tribes of the people who have been made holy by the Lord his God. (Pss. Sol. 17:22–26)

Other texts could be added (1Q28b, 4Q246, and 4Q521) which show that the early Christian communities were not the only ones looking for God to act on behalf of his people through an anointed figure who would come bringing both salvation and judgment.[37] The preaching of John the Baptist fits into an apocalyptic eschatological mold.

Conclusion

In the Gospel of Matthew, John the Baptist prepares people for the coming of the Lord (Matt 3:3). Yet John's description of the one who brings in the eschatological kingdom is described by the opaque ὁ δὲ ὀπίσω μου. He, like the Son of Man, has the power of God to destroy his enemies with fire (Matt 3:10–12). This "Coming One" is like a man (3:11, ὑποδήματα). The eschatological kingdom is likewise "front and center" both in Daniel (Dan 7:14) and Matthew (Matt 3:1), while the saints are the recipients of the kingdom.[38] Both Daniel and Matthew portray the enemies of God (and his people) with the imagery of deadly animals (Dan 7:1–8; Matt 3:7). The glory and honor that belong to this king is aptly summarized in John's declaration that he is unworthy to carry his sandals (Matt 3:11).

It is to be expected that there will be certain differences also. Daniel sees an apocalyptic vision of catastrophic proportions (Dan 7:19, 23), while John the Baptist calls for national repentance and an ethical change in light of the apocalyptic dawning. By comparison, the feature that is most striking is the way in which Matthew has labeled the enemies. They are largely the Jewish-religious leaders of the people of Israel and as Matthew will go on to show, the vipers do persecute God's people and put the Son of Man to death (Matt 23:32–36). No mention is made of a formal judicial process in Matthew. Instead, the impression is the nearness of the heavenly verdict which is about to be rendered. The possible *implication* of Dan 7 is that the beasts' destruction is the result of the Son of Man, but in Matthew the one to come is like the Son of Man of the *Similitudes* and 4 Ezra, executing judgment upon the wicked in a baptism of Spirit/fire (Matt 3:11).

---

37. Cf. Evans, "Messianism," 698.
38. Implied in Matt 3:6, 8, 12.

While no mention is made of a Son of Man in Matt 3, Matthew does make use of the enigmatic figure elsewhere. The Son of Man will send his angels and they will gather out of his kingdom all causes of sin and all law-breakers (13:41). The Son of Man will come with his angels in the glory of his Father, then he will repay each person according to what he has done (16:27). For Matthew, it is more than a crushing defeat of Jesus's enemies which secures the kingdom for his disciples—it will take nothing less than the Son of Man's dying and rising from the dead (17:29). Such a work secures the blessings described by the *Similitudes* in 62:13–14. In Matthew, it is described as "the new world" where "the Son of Man will sit on his glorious throne and you who have followed me will also sit on twelve thrones, judging the twelve tribes of Israel" (Matt 19:28). Like in the deliverance brought by the Son of Man in 1 Enoch (and inferentially in Daniel), the opposite side of the eschatological reality is the reverse of salvation: the day of judgment. The tribes will mourn when the Son of Man comes on the clouds of heaven with power and great glory (24:30). When the Son of Man comes in his glory, and all the angels with him, then he will sit on his glorious throne (25:31), gathering his sheep into his kingdom (25:34) and sending away the goats into the eternal fire (25:41, 46).

In all, Matthew's rendition of the coming judge finds much in common with Daniel, 1 Enoch, and 4 Ezra. The imminence of the kingdom of heaven means an end of the oppressors (3:7; 12:14; 23:31, 37; 26:4) and the ingathering of the saints of the Most High (Matt 3:12). Matthew does not speak of the Son of Man in Matt 3, but the themes and content of John's preaching are later repeated by Jesus (3:7; 12:34; 23:33) and applied to Jesus as the Son of Man (3:11–12; 13:41–42; 16:27). Hagner's comments on Matt 3:1–12 are on target, "The background of the passage is to be found in the expectation of Jewish apocalyptic (cf. Dan 2:44; 7:14–27)."[39]

---

39. Hagner, *Matthew 1-13*, 46. Cf. Scott M. Lewis, *What Are They Saying about New Testament Apocalyptic?* (Mahwah: Paulist Press, 2004), 31.

Chapter 7

MATTHEW'S TYPOLOGICAL STORY

Introduction

The escape from the baptism in the Holy Spirit and fire required repentance and returning to the Lord. The prophetic summons was not issued from within the city of Jerusalem, but rather from the wilderness of Judea. Matthew sums up John the Baptist in terms of Isa 40:3 (Matt 3:3). Such a text was thought to be a summons to a new exodus.[1] It is a text that commences with comfort (Isa 40:1) and good news for Israel. How then is the positive Isaianic declaration to be understood within the framework of John's thundering denunciation of Israel and his sign of judgment?

In this chapter we will focus upon Matthew's use of the OT quotations in his opening chapters (Matt 1–3) to tell his story. We will discover, not surprisingly, that John's preaching against the nation was conceived by Matthew as a call out of Israel and is in keeping with the narrative emphases of judgment.

Matthew's Typology

If there is a salvation to take place (Matt 1:21) and an expectation of a judgment soon to arrive (Matt 3:2, 7–12), it should come as no surprise that a way of escape would also be provided (3:7; τίς ὑπέδειξεν ὑμῖν φυγεῖν ἀπὸ τῆς μελλούσης ὀργῆς). The direction of escape and how one escapes are the important factors to evaluate. By OT allusions and citations, Matthew shows that Jesus undergoes an exodus out of national Israel.

---

1. The Qumran community viewed itself as the fulfillment of Isa 40:3. 1QS 8.12–16; 1QS 9.19–20; 1QS 4.1–2. Craig L. Blomberg, "Matthew," in *Commentary on the New Testament Use of the Old Testament*, eds. G. K. Beale and D. A. Carson (Grand Rapids: Baker, 2007), 12–13.

Matthew's interest in exile and exodus is found throughout the genealogy. The fourteenth generation, though numerically short, connects Jesus to the deportation and to its end (Matt 1:17; καὶ ἀπὸ τῆς μετοικεσίας Βαβυλῶνος ἕως τοῦ Χριστοῦ γενεαὶ δεκατέσσαρες). Matthew's interest in the deportation and return is by no means exhausted in the genealogy. It is a theme he goes on to explore through the life of Jesus, making connections to it from the events of Jesus's birth and the coming of John the Baptist. Bethlehem in 2:6 is the birthplace of David (1:1, 6) and is the main location for the story of Ruth (1:5). Ramah was the place of Rachel's weeping over her slaughtered children, the survivors being deported to Babylon (1:11–12; 2:17–18). Kingship plays an important role in the story of Jesus (1:6; 2:2). Herod's question concerns the birthplace of ὁ χριστὸς (2:4), a title already introduced at the conclusion of the genealogy (1:16). The end of the exile is encapsulated in Matthew's citation of Isaiah 40:3 (Matt 3:3); the one whose way is prepared is the one who experiences the exile and brings it to an end (Matt 1:17; 2:15, 18).[2] Interwoven through ch. 2, in particular, is the imprint of an exodus/ Moses typology.[3] In sum, Matthew gives an encapsulated history of Israel, in miniature, through the life of Jesus.

Given the preponderance of Matthew's formula citations in these early chapters, we want to discover how the citations illuminate the narratives' meanings. This same method will then be applied to Matthew's citation of Isa 40:3. Though not a formula quotation, it serves a similar narrative function by explaining the significance of the circumstances unfolded in the story. The OT citations and the exodus typology are, then, only one aspect of this survey. Important are the questions: Who are "his people" (Matt 1:21)? Where are they to go (seeing that they are already in the land)? What does Jesus and the things he experienced mean for Israel? To these issues and questions we now turn.

Immanuel, God with Us

Matthew's first OT citation is drawn from Isaiah. Before Jesus's birth, Joseph is told that the child will save his people from their sins (Matt 1:21). Matthew inserts that

---

2. See further, Joel Kennedy, *The Recapitulation of Israel: Use of Israel's History in Matthew 1:1-4:11*, WUNT 257 (Tübingen: Mohr Siebeck, 2008), 106–108.

3. Dale C. Allison Jr., *The New Moses: A Matthean Typology* (Minneapolis: Fortress, 1993); Raymond E. Brown, *Birth of the Messiah: A Commentary on the Infancy Narratives of Matthew and Luke*, rev. ed. (New York: Doubleday, 1993), 110–99, 600; David E. Garland, *Reading Matthew: A Literary and Theological Commentary* (Macon: Smyth & Helwys Publishing, 2001), 29; Davies and Allison, *Matthew I-VII*, 192–95; "The reader is invited to recognize in Herod and Jesus a counterpart to Pharaoh and Moses." Hagner, *Matthew 1-13*, 34, Ulrich Luz, *The Theology of the Gospel of Matthew*, trans. J. B. Robinson (Cambridge: Cambridge University Press, 2003), 24–25; R. T. France, *The Gospel According to Matthew*, NICNT (Grand Rapids: Eerdmans, 2007), 63.

this time of the Holy Spirit's visitation (Matt 1:20) is the time of Immanuel, God with us (Matt 1:23). "God with us" frames the beginning and conclusion of Matthew's Gospel:

Beginning	Conclusion
Genealogy: gentile inclusion	"Go and make disciples of all nations."
(e.g., Rahab, Ruth, 1:1–17)	(28:18–19)
Immanuel, God with us (1:22–23)	"I am with you always" (28:20)

Μεθ᾽ ἡμῶν ὁ θεός has been understood as God in the midst of his people through Christ;[4] or as a statement asserting Jesus's deity.[5] The meaning for Jesus, while important, is not the point under consideration. What the promise and fulfillment means for Israel is our objective. What does Immanuel, "God with us," mean for Israel in Matthew's Gospel? In brief, while understood by many to be a sign of hope,[6] the child-sign has been interpreted by others as a promise of judgment.[7]

The Immanuel announcement comes within a context of near thorough unbelief and rejection of God. Isaiah's vision concerned Judah and Jerusalem (Isa 1:1); the "faithful city has become a whore" (Isa 1:21). Isaiah's commission was to announce that Judah's cities will be laid waste, the houses will be without people and the land will be desolate καὶ ἡ γῆ καταλειφθήσεται ἔρημος (Isa 6:11). The Lord will remove the people far away and the land will be forsaken (Isa 6:12). Immediately after Isaiah receives this news, he is called to go to Ahaz (Isa 7:1) and assure him that the kings of Syria and Israel will not overtake Judah and replace the king (Isa 7:4–9). Ahaz must not depend upon the Assyrian king for protection, but should instead trust Yahweh for deliverance. The king is then commanded to seek a sign from the Lord. In keeping with the evaluation of the abysmal spiritual state of Judah (Isa 1–6) the king refuses (Isa 7:11–12). A sign will be given anyway: a child, Immanuel (Isa 7:14; 8:8; Matt 1:23), God with us (Isa 8:10; Matt 1:23). The sign would not necessarily be welcome news. Though in one sense the child ensures

---

4. Hill, *Matthew*, 1981, 79–80.

5. Hagner, *Matthew*, 1.21.

6. John Nolland, *The Gospel of Matthew*, NIGTC (Grand Rapids: Eerdmans, 2005), 101–02; David L. Turner, *Matthew*, BECNT (Grand Rapid, MI: Baker Academic, 2008), 72–73; Hagner, *Matthew*, 1.20–21; Robert H. Gundry, *Matthew* (Grand Rapids: Eerdmans, 1982), 25; Fredrick D. Bruner, *The Christbook: Matthew 1-12*, vol. 1 (Grand Rapids: Eerdmans, 2004), 34–37; David D. Kupp, *Matthew's Emmanuel: Divine Presence and God's People in the First Gospel* (Cambridge: Cambridge University Press, 1996), 164.

7. Warren Carter, "Evoking Isaiah: Matthean Soteriology and an Intertextual Reading of Isaiah 7–9 and Matthew 1:23 and 4:15–16," *JBL* 119.3 (2000): 503–20. See also Rikk E. Watts, "Immanuel: Virgin Birth Proof Text or Programmatic Warning of Things to Come (Isa 7:14 in Matt 1:23)?" in *From Prophecy to Testament: The Function of the Old Testament in the New*, ed. Craig A. Evans (Peabody: Hendrickson, 2004), 92–113.

that the Davidic line will not end,[8] it also was a prophetic sign that paralleled the prophetic call of Isaiah to announce the approaching doom and resulting desolation. In this case, it is a deportation and barrenness at the hand of the king of Assyria. Like flies that cover everything, this king will come into Israel's land (Isa 7:18–19), and it will be depopulated and ruined (Isa 7:20, 23–24).

The direct address to Ahaz, "The Lord will bring upon you . . . the king of Assyria" (Isa 7:17), indicates that Judah is primarily the object of the Assyrian king's aggression. The Isaianic announcement continues:

> Therefore, behold, the Lord is bringing up against *them* the waters of the River, mighty and many, the king of Assyria and all his glory. And it will rise over all its channels and go over all its banks, and it will sweep on *into Judah*, it will overflow and pass on, reaching even to the neck, and its outspread wings will fill the breadth of *your land, O Immanuel*. Be broken, you peoples, and be shattered; give ear, all you far countries; strap on your armor and be shattered; strap on your armor and be shattered. Take counsel together, but it will come to nothing; speak a word, but it will not stand, for God is with us. (Isa 8:7–10, emphasis mine)

Whoever Immanuel was, he was a sign against Israel for their treachery, and moreover, he was a sign that the Davidic dynasty would continue despite the judgment coming upon Ahaz. Immanuel was a double-edged sign. In the face of Ahaz's rejection of God's request, "Immanuel, God with us" becomes a liability. God with his people can mean salvation (Ps 48:8,12; 2 Sam 7:3; Amos 5:14 and Zeph 3:15), but for Ahaz who is neither faithful nor repentant, God's presence would have devastating consequences (Num 14, 16; 1 Sam 4:3–5, 10–11, 18–22; Mic 3:11; Mal 3:1–5 [4:1–6]).[9] The names given to children were often expressions of God's actions or attitudes on behalf of or against his people (cf. Hos 1).

What significance does Matthew find in Jesus's name, Immanuel? Threatened by the Syrian-Israelite coalition, Ahaz turned to his own resources (Assyria) rather than submitting and trusting in the Lord. Ironically, Immanuel was the sign of deliverance as well as of his destruction (Isa 8:16–17). This is the question for readers familiar with the Isaianic backstory: Is the birth of Jesus and his designation, "Immanuel," "God with us," good or bad news for Israel? Will Israel repent and be saved, or will they respond in unbelief like Ahaz? "The liberation Jesus offers will not be acceptable to most of the people of Israel. The people who actually accept Jesus's saving act, *his* people, will be the group Jesus calls, "*my* church" (Matt 16:18)."[10] This is already hinted at when the angel tells Joseph, αὐτὸς γὰρ σώσει τὸν λαὸν αὐτοῦ (1:21). λαός reoccurs in the next pericope, but there it modifies the

---

8. Carter, "Evoking," 510.

9. Watts, "Immanuel," 97.

10. John P. Meier, *Matthew*, NTM (Wilmington: Michael Glazier, 1980), 8. Emphasis is Meier's.

opponents of Jesus (2:4, πάντας τοὺς ἀρχιερεῖς καὶ γραμματεῖς τοῦ λαοῦ).[11] The unbelieving who are soon to appear in Matthew's Gospel will reject the will of God through Jesus, and in so doing, the other side of the sign also aptly fits: he is "Immanuel," "God with us," the judge.[12] The tension has begun.[13]

For Matthew's readers, Jesus-Immanuel is the sign of the Davidic savior. For the disbelieving, the sign recalls the Assyrian invasion which stood as a potent reminder of the consequences of the rejection of God's purposes. Immanuel is a sign of God's salvation and judgment, both of which aptly summarize the ministry of Jesus.

Summary The first words of Matthew's Gospel establish Jesus's importance and relationship to Israel. He is the Christ; he belongs to David and Abraham (Matt 1:1). The significance of Jesus as "God with us," invites informed readers to infer what kind of implication this has for Israel. In ch. 2 Matthew shows how his birth came to be known and the impact it had on Israel. For Brown, "Chapter 2 is the necessary completion of ch. 1 in the sequence of revelation, proclamation and twofold reaction; a sequence that gives to the infancy narrative its status as a gospel in miniature. The gospel is the good news, but the gospel must have a passion and rejection, as well as success."[14]

The Shepherd, the Exodus, and the Weeping (Matt 2)

Matthew has chosen the Immanuel reference to underscore the last hour that has come upon Israel. God, as it were, provides another sign (Isa 7:11); this time a star rises and the gentiles come (Matt 2:1–2).[15] The meaning of their presence is informed by their question. The magi ask, ποῦ ἐστιν ὁ τεχθεὶς βασιλεὺς τῶν Ἰουδαίων (Matt 2:2). This causes Herod to gather together the spiritual leaders of Israel to ask, ποῦ ὁ χριστὸς γεννᾶται (Matt 2:4). This shift recalls the opening of his gospel where Χριστός and kingship are brought together (Matt 1:1, 17). Jesus is the king, but he is born ἐν ἡμέραις Ἡρῴδου τοῦ βασιλέως (2:1). Kingship proves

---

11. From a literary perspective, "Those who comprise the Jewish leaders are the Pharisees, the Sadducees, the chief priests, the elders, and the scribes . . . the rhetorical effect of the way in which these several groups are presented is such as to make of them a monolithic front opposed to Jesus, they can, narrative-critically, be treated as a single character." Jack D. Kingsbury, "The Developing Conflict between Jesus and the Jewish Leaders in Matthew's Gospel," *CBQ* 49 (1987): 57–73, 58.

12. *Pace* Beaton, *Isaiah's Christ*, 96–97.

13. "The contradiction between the divine intention and the human response." Davies and Allison, *Matthew*, 1.240–41.

14. Brown, *Birth*, 183.

15. This is part of the gentile-inclusion theme begun in the genealogy. Brown, *Birth*, 179–82.

to be a central theme for Matthew's Gospel, as does conflict.[16] The story of this conflict takes place in Jerusalem, the city of the king.

The magi come to Jerusalem in response to a guiding light, εἴδομεν γὰρ αὐτοῦ τὸν ἀστέρα ἐν τῇ ἀνατολῇ (2:2).[17] God's angelic hosts resemble the heavenly hosts. צבא השמים is interchangeable with the stars (Deut 4:19; 2 Kgs 17:16; Jer 33:22; Neh 9:6) and the angels (1 Kgs 22:19; Dan 8:10). Angels sometimes have a luminescent appearance (Gen 18:1–2; Num 22:31–35; Josh 5:13–15; Ezek 1:12–14; Dan 10:6; Nah 2:4; 1 En. 18:13–16; 21:3; Luke 10:18; 2 Cor 2:14; Heb 13:2; Rev 4:5).[18] In Matthew angels only appear in the infancy narrative and the resurrection. They give similar commands (1:20 μὴ φοβηθῇς, 28:5 μὴ φοβεῖσθε) and their appearance (after the resurrection) is like lightening and their clothes like snow (Matt 28:3). The role that the angels play might also be compared to the role of angels in the account of Israel's exodus, as the angelic beings instructed and guided God's people.[19]

After being guided to Jerusalem, the magi ask: "ποῦ ἐστιν ὁ τεχθεὶς βασιλεὺς τῶν Ἰουδαίων"; their question is significant for more than just geographical reasons.[20] βασιλεὺς τῶν Ἰουδαίων resurfaces one more time, in the passion narrative (27:11, 37; with the similar expression βασιλεὺς Ἰσραήλ in 27:42). Brown draws the additional conclusion that Matthew is thinking of the passion, perhaps previewing it in the birth story. "In the crucifixion Jesus dies but is brought back to life through the resurrection; in the infancy narrative Jesus is taken away to another land and returns. In each instance God has confounded the kings and rulers who assembled against Him and His Messiah (Ps 2:2, which uses *synagein* as does Matt 2:4)."[21] Jesus's life begins under the threat of death and Jesus returns to life after his exile into death. As we will go on to argue, the preview of the death of Christ is also given in his baptism.

The gentiles coming to worship Jesus are sharply contrasted with Herod's men who are sent to kill him. The reaction of the gentiles (2:10, ἐχάρησαν χαρὰν μεγάλην σφόδρα) is also contrasted with the reaction of Herod and especially Jerusalem (2:3, ἐταράχθη καὶ πᾶσα Ἱεροσόλυμα μετ᾽ αὐτοῦ). Toward the end, the chief priests and elders stir up the crowd to ask Pilate for Jesus's execution (27:20: ἀρχιερεῖς καὶ οἱ πρεσβύτεροι ἔπεισαν τοὺς ὄχλους) and after a short interchange: καὶ ἀποκριθεὶς πᾶς ὁ λαὸς εἶπεν· τὸ αἷμα αὐτοῦ ἐφ᾽ ἡμᾶς καὶ ἐπὶ τὰ τέκνα ἡμῶν (27:25). The opposition to Jesus, that becomes so characteristic of the religious leaders, is made obvious throughout the gospel. The seeds are sown in these early chapters, providing a reason for the need of a new start, a new exodus.

---

16. Jack D. Kingsbury, *Matthew as Story*, 2nd ed. (Philadelphia: Fortress, 1988), 8, 13.

17. The unusual placement of the pronoun before the direct object is probably for emphasis. The star that guides is unique; it is *his* star.

18. Dale C. Allison Jr., *Studies in Matthew* (Grand Rapids: Baker Academic, 2005).

19. Allison, *Studies*, 25–26.

20. Krister Stendahl, "Quis et unde? An Analysis of Matthew 1–2," in *The Interpretation of Matthew*, ed. Graham Stanton (Minneapolis: Fortress, 1983), 56–66.

21. Brown, *Birth*, 183.

The departure to and from Canaan, the threat of death and the appearance of heavenly guides are pieces of Israel's story, retold in the story of Jesus's birth and infancy. A one-to-one typological correspondence is not necessary to establish the validity of a new exodus typology. There is, of course, a difference between repetition and recapitulation and Allison has rightly cautioned against "discrediting a typology by adding up differences between type and antitype."[22]

Micah and 2 Samuel The text form of the religious leaders' answer (Matt 2:5–6) is composed of Mic 5:2 and 2 Sam 5:2. Due to the complexities, a few comments on this interesting text are in order: καὶ σὺ Βηθλέεμ, γῆ Ἰούδα, οὐδαμῶς ἐλαχίστη εἶ ἐν τοῖς ἡγεμόσιν Ἰούδα·ἐκ σοῦ γὰρ ἐξελεύσεται ἡγούμενος, ὅστις ποιμανεῖ τὸν λαόν μου τὸν Ἰσραήλ (Matt 2:6). The selection from 2 Sam 5:2 is virtually word-for-word, while the Micah quotation shares only eight of the twenty-two words found in the LXX. Matthew provides what might better be called "an interpretation."[23] Matthew has inserted Βηθλέεμ, γῆ Ἰούδα for Micah's Βηθλέεμ οἶκος Ἐφράθα. Matthew follows neither the MT's צָעִיר לִהְיוֹת בְּאַלְפֵי יְהוּדָה "too little among the clans" nor the LXX's ὀλιγοστὸς εἶ, also a reference to numerical insufficiency by comparison to Judah. Bethlehem, though incomparably smaller and therefore insignificant in size, is greater, for the ruler-shepherd of God's people comes from this otherwise unimportant city. The last line picks up the declaration of David's leadership of Israel despite Saul's kingship.

The quotation fits the circumstances into which Jesus is born. He is born a king; but in Bethlehem rather than the more important capital of Judah. Saul contested David's rightful rule and sought his life; the murderous king, Herod, also denies Jesus's right to the throne. With the insignificance of Bethlehem and the humble beginnings of David preceding it, readers are enabled to understand better the significance of the lowly birth of Jesus. The modest start of this king is the inbreaking of the end of the age and will conclude with him upon his throne, destroying his enemies (the contrast to Herod's failure to kill Jesus) and shepherding his sheep (in contrast to Israel's spiritual leaders, Matt 2:5--6; 23:13–15).

The broader setting of the Micah quote proves to be relevant to Matt 2. Taking into account the context from which the citation is drawn, one finds several returns from exile in Micah's prophecy.[24] In Mic 4:1 the "latter days" will find the nations coming to the mountain of the Lord (Mic 4:2), followed by a time of peace (Mic 4:3–5). The lame and afflicted will be gathered "on that day" (Mic 4:6). From where

22. Allison, *The New Moses*, 143.

23. Davies and Allison, *Matthew*, 1.242–43. Blomberg, *Matthew*, 64. France, *Matthew*, 73.

24. Gregory K. Beale, "The Use of Hosea 11:1 In Matthew 2:15: One More Time," *JETS* 55:4 (2012): 697. For a fuller description of the issues see also Gregory K. Beale, *Handbook on the New Testament Use of the Old Testament: Exegesis and Interpretation* (Grand Rapids: Baker Academic, 2012), 41–54.

will they be gathered? "You shall go to Babylon. There you shall be rescued; there the LORD will redeem you from the hand of your enemies" (Mic 4:10). Upon their return, Israel finds the nations gathered against them (Mic 4:11–13). Unable to defend himself, the ruler of Israel is struck with the rod (Mic 5:1).[25] The adversative "but you" (ואתה) contrasts Bethlehem with the besieged Jerusalem. From Bethlehem comes the ruler, a messianic king in the likeness of David, which might also indicate a rejection of the reigning Judean king.[26] Such a parallel to Matthew's birth account would be striking. "A legitimate *sensus plenior* is that this Ruler will be a superhuman being associated with God from the beginning of time. Ps 2:7 speaks of the king as the one whom God "sired" (by adoption)."[27] Not only does מקדם מימי עולם seem to echo Ps 2, but also the exaltation and reign of the king is set in the context of the raging of the nations.

Verses 3–4 give the outcome of the Ruler's reign: "Therefore he shall give them up until the time when she who is in labor has given birth; then the rest of his brothers shall return to the people of Israel. And he shall stand and shepherd his flock in the strength of the Lord, in the majesty of the name of the Lord his God. And they shall dwell secure, for now he shall be great to the ends of the earth" (Mic 5:3–4).

The scene reverts back to the decision of Yahweh who gives over his people (cf. 1 Kgs 11:6) until the ruler comes. The Micah citation is both an announcement that the Babylonian captivity will come to an end and that the messianic ruler will come from the house of David, defeat Israel's enemies and reunite God's exiled people. As warrior and shepherd, the Ruler is like David.

Returning to Matthew's citation, and in light of this broader context, one can only surmise from the answer given to Herod that the religious leaders did not believe that such a Davidic correspondence would be found in Bethlehem. The king, leaders, and people of Israel do not gather around the newborn Ruler. When viewed as a monolithic front,[28] the religious leaders refuse to worship him and they refuse to repent at the news that his kingdom has arrived (Matt 3:7–12; 21:25). The citations of Mic 5:2 and 2 Sam 5:2 bring out the broader implications of the prophecy with all its benefits (end of Babylonian exile, defeat of enemies, peace for Israel, a Davidic king who brings peace), in light of the religious leaders' refusal to believe. In the lead up to the next OT citation the situation goes from bad to worse.

---

25. Bruce Waltke, "Micah," in *An Exegetical and Expository Commentary: The Minor Prophets*, vol. 2, ed. Thomas E. McComiskey (Grand Rapids: Baker, 2000), 707.

26. Delbert R. Hillers, *Micah*, Hermeneia (Minneapolis: Fortress, 1984), 66.

27. Francis I. Andersen and David Noel Freedman, *Micah: A New Translation with Introduction and Commentary*, AB 24e (New York: Doubleday, 2000), 468.

28. Kingsbury, "The Developing Conflict," 58.

Hosea 11:1 After the Magi depart, Joseph is warned to flee to Egypt as Herod now seeks to kill the child. Strecker understood Josephus's *Antiquities* (2.205–223) to lie in the *Hintergrund* of Matthew's text and questioned "eine Mose-Christus-Typologie."[29] For others, such as France, the typological connection is warranted:

> The story of Herod's fear for his throne and his ruthless political massacre could hardly fail to remind a Jewish reader of the Pharaoh at the time of Moses' birth whose infanticide threatened to destroy Israel's future deliverer, while Jesus' providential escape to Egypt and subsequent return will echo the story of Moses' escape from slaughter and of his subsequent exile and return when "those who were seeking your life are dead." [Exod 4:19, echoed here in 2:20] Herod's place in the story thus ensures not only a reflection on who is the true "king of the Jews" and on the contrast between Herod's ruthlessly-protected political power and Jesus' different way of being "king," *but also sets up the typological model for the new-born Messiah to play the role of the new Moses, who will also deliver his people* (cf. 1:21) and through whose ministry a new people of God will be constituted just as Israel became God's chosen people through the exodus and the covenant at Sinai under the leadership of Moses.[30]

The placement of the Hos 11:1 citation has been and continues to be debated: "And he rose and took the child and his mother by night and departed to Egypt and remained there until the death of Herod. This was to fulfill what the Lord had spoken by the prophet, 'Out of Egypt I called my son'" (Matt 2:14–15). It has been suggested that the placement ought to have come when Joseph returns with his family from Egypt (2:21). Various proposals have been offered: Matthew's formula quotations are for geographical purposes,[31] or they prepare readers for the transition.[32] It is precisely the placement of the citation that makes Matthew's biblical-theological point so acute.

---

29. George Strecker, *Der Weg der Gerechtigkeit: Untersuchung zur Theologie des Mattäus* (Göttingen: Vandenhoeck & Ruprecht, 1962), 51, n. 5.

30. France, *Matthew*, 63. Emphasis mine. Robin E. Nixon, *The Exodus in the New Testament* (London: Tyndale Press, 1963); Paul J. Kobelski, *The Royal Son of God: The Christology of Matthew 1-2 in the Setting of the Gospel* (Göttingen: Vandenhoeck & Ruprecht, 1979), 34–39; Daniel Patte, *The Gospel According to Matthew: A Structural Commentary on Matthew's Faith* (Minneapolis: Fortress, 1987), 36–40; R. T. France, *Matthew: Evangelist and Teacher* (Downers Grove: IVP, 1989), 186–89; Allison, *The New Moses*; Wayne S. Baxter, "Mosaic Imagery in the Gospel of Matthew," *TJ* 20.1 (1999): 69–83.

31. Stendahl, "Quis et unde?" 71; Joachim Gnilka, *Das Matthäusevangelium*, 2 vols., HTKNT (Freiburg: Herder, 1986), 1.51.

32. Hagner, *Matthew*, 1.36; Garland, *Reading Matthew*, 29; Davies and Allison, *Matthew*, 1.262. Such a reading is rendered difficult if for no other reason that the formula quotations in Chapter 2 follow the scenes, in other words, the OT citations point back to the events just narrated (Kennedy, *Recapitulation*, 134).

Israel's king functions like Egypt's Pharaoh. The Pharaoh and the Egyptians were in dread (קוץ) of Israel (Exod 1:12) and Herod and Jerusalem are troubled (ταράσσω) by the birth of the Jesus (Matt 2:3). The roles have been reversed. Israel has typologically become Egypt.[33] The placement of the formula quotation drives the point painfully home: out of Israel (typological Egypt) God calls his son. Several other contributing factors point in this interpretive direction. Joseph, being warned in a dream, arises and takes his family to Egypt. Their departure is at night. This is yet another parallel to Israel's exodus out of Egypt, also by night.[34] In 2:13 Joseph is told to φεῦγε εἰς Αἴγυπτον as Herod was about to search for Jesus. Likewise, the children of Israel fled from Egypt (Ex 14:5). The return from captivity corresponds to the command given to Moses to return to Egypt, "the divine directive to Joseph in Egypt ('take the child and his mother and go back to the land of Israel, for those who were seeking the child's life are dead') are literally evocative of the divine directive to Moses in Midian when the hostile Pharaoh had died: 'Go to Egypt, for all those who were seeking your life are dead'" (Exod 4:19).[35] Moses returned to the land of Egypt in order to gather up the children of Israel and lead them on their exodus. After Jesus returns to Israel/typological Egypt (and reaches adulthood), he too will lead a new exodus.

This raises the question, "Whom will he lead?" Or as Matthew has it, whom will Jesus save from their sins? Jesus is a sign of the continuation of the Davidic crown, but also of the judgment for disbelief. The birth narrative gives glimpses of the alignments already being made: Herod with Pharaoh, Israel with Egypt. There are contrasts: God's people ("τὸν λαόν μου" Matt 2:6) and the chief priests and scribes of the people ("τοῦ λαοῦ," Matt 2:4). The threat of death for the male infants in Egypt (Exod 1:16) is echoed in the deaths of the male infants in Bethlehem (Matt 2:16). The Israelites fleeing by night out of Egypt is alluded to in the speed of departure by Joseph and his family who also depart by night out of Israel. To these people, places, and activities, Matthew adds to his typological overlay as Jesus departs from Israel: ἐξ Αἰγύπτου ἐκάλεσα τὸν υἱόν μου (Matt 2:15). His work must wait until John the Baptist comes with his ultimatum and summons to prepare for the deliverer.

Jeremiah 31:15 We can note in passing that the result of Jesus's exodus out of typological Egypt is the death of Rachel's sons (Matt 2:16–18). Significantly, Rachel's weeping is set in a context of a new start, a return from exile. Ἐν τῷ χρόνῳ ἐκείνῳ (Jer 31:1, LXX= 37:24) those who survived the sword will find grace in the wilderness (Jer 31:2). Yahweh promises that the exiles would come back (Jer 31:3–14) and though Rachel weeps for the departed (31:15), their end will not be in exile, "your children will come back to their country" (31:17, ושבו בנים לגבולם). In light of the Matthean typology, what country would that be? Is the return to

---

33. Brian M. Nolan, *The Royal Son*, 121, 209; Kennedy, *Recapitulation*, 137–40.
34. Patte, *Matthew*, 37–38; Allison, *New Matthew*, 152; Kennedy, *Recapitulation*, 135.
35. Brown, *Birth*, 107.

the Promised Land? The answer is both yes and no. Rachel's lament is answered—Jesus does return and dwell in Nazareth. But the way will ultimately be out of Israel and into the world (Matt 28:18–20).

Isaiah 40:3 The Isaianic promise of a new start ἐν τῇ ἐρήμῳ begins with the arrival of John ἐν τῇ ἐρήμῳ (Matt 3:1): οὗτος γάρ ἐστιν ὁ ῥηθεὶς διὰ Ἡσαΐου τοῦ προφήτου λέγοντος·φωνὴ βοῶντος ἐν τῇ ἐρήμῳ·ἑτοιμάσατε τὴν ὁδὸν κυρίου, εὐθείας ποιεῖτε τὰς τρίβους αὐτοῦ (Matt 3:3). Matthew's quotation follows the LXX with one minor alteration: he substitutes the pronoun αὐτοῦ (ποιεῖτε τὰς τρίβους αὐτοῦ) for τοῦ θεοῦ ἡμῶν (τὰς τρίβους τοῦ θεοῦ ἡμῶν). It seems probable that this further establishes the coming of Jesus as the fulfillment.[36]

In its original context, the voice cries out to those in Babylonian captivity. Their hard service was now ended and would be relieved by the coming of God to deliver them from their bondage. If Matthew's placement of Hos 1 reinforces that Israel has become like Egypt then the placement of the Isaianic quotation logically follows. John's Isaianic identity and his announcement of the end of the exile/new exodus is another example of Matthew's typological reinterpretation of Israel's past. The voice cries out to prepare the way. While this is news of the end of exile, it is not without judgment, as the way is out of Israel. Those who refuse would be comparable to what is stated next in the OT citation. After announcing the coming of the Lord in the wilderness, the voice again says, "cry" (Isa 40:6). The unidentified listener responds with the question, "What shall I cry?" (Isa 40:6). What follows parallels the preaching of John and the warnings of judgment in the formula quotations and their OT contexts: "All flesh is grass, and all its beauty is like the flower of the field. The grass withers, the flower fades when the breath of the Lord blows on it; surely the people are grass. The grass withers, the flower fades, but the word of our God will stand forever" (Isa 40:6b–8).

The breath of the Lord (רוח יהוה) blows on the grass, the grass being a simile for the people, and withers it. Whether speaking prospectively (to Israel's captors) or retrospectively (of Israel's past judgment) salvation and judgment are the expected and paired themes in the exodus and new exodus announcements of the OT and NT. John's preaching of the blast of messianic judgment in the Spirit and fire is a suitable parallel to the withering of Isaiah's grass. The people must be made ready for the Lord's coming.

Conclusion

In this chapter we have argued that Matthew's story is a typological recasting of Israel. Though Israel is in the land, it is a land like Egypt, which suggests that it too must be vacated. Joseph was commanded to φεῦγε εἰς Αἴγυπτον lest Jesus be destroyed (2:13). John's summons was to φυγεῖν ἀπὸ τῆς μελλούσης ὀργῆς (3:7).

---

36. Gundry, *Matthew*, 45.

John comes with fierce words and a foreboding sign. His invective was leveled against the kingdom that had set itself against Immanuel, the Shepherd-Ruler of God's people. Israel must leave Jerusalem and the surrounding regions for the wilderness. The kingdom was about to arrive.

Like in his Hos 11 citation, Matthew has again added his own biblical-theological description to the typological grid. His description of the response to John's preaching and baptizing follows the exodus pattern of the OT: "Τότε ἐξεπορεύετο πρὸς αὐτὸν Ἰεροσόλυμα καὶ πᾶσα ἡ Ἰουδαία καὶ πᾶσα ἡ περίχωρος τοῦ Ἰορδάνου" (3:5). Their departure looks like a large-scale evacuation, an exodus.[37]

In our survey of Matthew's first two chapters, we have explained how Matthew's typologically driven storyline is reinforced by the formula quotations. Chapter 1 gives the perspective of Israel's past and has connected it to Jesus. The deportation would be reversed. God was raising up his Davidic ruler to shepherd his people. This leader would also be threatened with death and would undergo an exodus. Like Moses, he would also return for his people.

John's Isaianic identity has been crafted by Matthew to serve his typological purposes. It was, on the one hand, to convict Israel of their sin. On the other, it was to call them to prepare for the arrival of their leader and their exodus. John's message was urgent; the kingdom of heaven was about to arrive in judgment. That is the foreground. In the narrative background stood the alarm of the king and people, the indifferent rejection by the religious authorities, the escape under the cover of darkness, and the resulting death of the infant Hebrew males. As Garland put it, "No one sings in Matthew's infancy narrative as they do in Luke's; instead they weep."[38] With the coming of John, Israel now stood at a crossroads: will they believe the messenger sent ahead of the Ruler? Would they believe the final, eschatological sign (baptism) was correct and the judgment was near?

---

37. So Drury, "The reference to 'all' Judea going to John leaves the land empty; Mark is running the nation's history backwards.'" John Drury, "Mark 1.1–15: An Interpretation," in *Alternative Approaches to the New Testament Study*, ed. Anthony E. Harvey (London: SPCK, 1985), 31. Cited in Webb, *John the Baptizer and Prophet*, 364–65 n. 28.

38. Garland, *Reading Matthew*, 30.

Chapter 8

THE TIME, LOCATION, AND IDENTITY OF THE PROPHET

Introduction

Matthew 3 eschatologically orients the reader to understand the significance of John the Baptist and his place in salvation history. For Matthew, John was nothing less than the promised messenger of Isa 40. In this chapter we will argue that Ἐν δὲ ταῖς ἡμέραις ἐκείναις (3:1) is a technical term drawn from the prophets to indicate that the "last days" had arrived, after which we will consider the significance of the place of inauguration ἐν τῇ ἐρήμῳ (Isa 40:3; Matt 3:1, 3). Finally, we will consider John's identity. As a prophet (3:3; 11:13–14), John is an important part of Matthew's salvation-historical schema and he heightens the eschatological scenario. As we will go on to show, John's identity as a prophet illuminates the meaning of his baptism.[1] Put succinctly, Matt 3:1-6 lays out the time ("in those days"), the person (John the Baptist), the location (in the wilderness), the message ("repent") and the sign (baptism) for the purposes of understanding the significance of Jesus as the king of the kingdom and the fulfillment of the Abrahamic and Davidic promises.

These elements of time, place, and person also indicate misfortune for faithless Israel. Unlike Luke's overview of the birth of John the Baptist, Matthew follows Mark by introducing the adult John the Baptist in the wilderness (Mark 1:4; Matt 3:1). Prior to John's arrival, readers are already prepared for John's ultimatum. The declining monarchy and deportation of Israel (Matt 1:1–17), the Pharaoh-like king (Matt 2:16–18), the posture of indifference (if not outright rejection of the infant king) on the part of the chief priests and the scribes (Matt 2:5–6), and the newborn king's escape (Matt 2:13–15) give way to the prophetic messenger, sent to announce the kingdom, issuing fierce words to the Pharisees and the Sadducees.[2] These indicators of national danger are the

---

1. This will be taken up in ch. 10.

2. In these early chapters of Matthew only the Herodians (mentioned once in Matthew's Gospel) are missing from the Jewish opposition to Jesus. The elders of the people are likely a collective term for the various groups. Cf. Kingsbury, "The Developing Conflict," 57–73; Nolland, *Matthew*, 687.

prelude for John's words and activities, and thereby color his prophetic work. The contours and overall direction of the arguments that follow will show that from start to finish, Matt 3 is primarily eschatological. To the time of John's arrival we now turn.

Inauguration of the End of the Age

Ἐν δὲ ταῖς ἡμέραις ἐκείναις παραγίνεται Ἰωάννης ὁ βαπτιστὴς κηρύσσων ἐν τῇ ἐρήμῳ τῆς Ἰουδαίας. (Matt 3:1)

Matthew 3 transitions from the time of the infant Jesus's relocation to Nazareth to the time of the baptism of the adult Jesus in the Jordan. The formulaic transition, Ἐν δὲ ταῖς ἡμέραις ἐκείναις, could refer to an undisclosed period of time, linking chs. 2 and 3 together,[3] or to the time of eschatological arrival.[4] These two interpretive options are not necessarily mutually exclusive. It may be that Ἐν δὲ ταῖς ἡμέραις ἐκείναις does double duty, transitioning the reader to the time of John and raising an eschatological expectation of readers by way of prophetic, OT echoes.

We will begin by looking at its usage primarily in the OT and 1 Enoch, after which we will analyze the syntax and compare it to other passages in Matthew. After surveying the data, we will show how an eschatological connotation is consistent with Matthew's understanding of salvation history and that of OT expectations of an eschatological arrival of the messenger of the Lord.

3. Walter Bauer, *A Greek-English Lexicon of the New Testament and Other Early Christian Literature*, 3rd ed., ed. Frederick William Danker (Chicago: University of Chicago Press, 2000), 302; Francis W. Beare, *The Gospel According to Matthew* (Oxford: Basil Blackwell, 1981), 87; Blomberg, *Matthew*, 72; Carson, *Matthew*, 99; Carter, *Matthew and the Margins*, 92; France, *The Gospel According to Matthew*, 89–90; Michael D. Goulder, *Midrash and Lection in Matthew* (London: SPCK, 1974), 242; Gundry, *Matthew*, 41; Harrington, *Matthew*, 50; Margaret Hannan, *The Nature and Demands of the Sovereign Rule of God in the Gospel of Matthew*, LNTS 308 (London: T&T Clark, 2006), 35; Luz, *Matthew 1–7*, 166; Nolland, *Matthew*, 135; Robert H. Smith, *Matthew*, ACNT (Minneapolis: Augsburg, 1989), 47; Turner, *Matthew*, 105.

4. Garland, *Reading Matthew*, 34; Jack D. Kingsbury, *Matthew: Structure, Christology, Kingdom* (Philadelphia: Fortress, 1975), 28–31. Davies and Allison cautiously observe, "An eschatological connotation is here quite possible." Davies and Allison, *Matthew I-VII*, 288; Meier, *Matthew*, 22; Ben Witherington III, *Matthew* (Macon: Smyth & Helwys, 2006), 78; Hagner, *Matthew 1-13*, 47; Osborne, *Matthew*, 109.

Ἐν δὲ ταῖς ἡμέραις ἐκείναις and OT Examples

In OT narrative, Ἐν δὲ ταῖς ἡμέραις ἐκείναις / בימים ההם often connects and synchronizes chronology (Gen 6:4; Judg 17:6; 18:1; 19:1; 20:28; 21:25; 1 Sam 28:1; 2 Kgs 10:32; 15:37; 20:1; Neh 6:17; 13:15, 23). For example, ἐν δὲ ταῖς ἡμέραις ἐκείναις / בימים ההם is used in Judges as an epigraphical summary, describing the conduct of Israel without a king. With the possible exception of Gen 6:4, ἡμέραις ἐκείναις is used as a transitional statement indicating a particular period of time, especially in the Pentateuch and historical books of the OT.[5] In the OT prophets, the phrase is still used to signal a transition, but the segue is from days of ease to judgment and vice versa.[6] The phrase is used in Jeremiah, Joel, and Zechariah with futuristic import.

Jeremiah   Much of Jeremiah's commission is to indict Israel, God's faithless bride, for whoring after the gods of the nations. Israel will be exiled ἐν ταῖς ἡμέραις ἐκείναις and nearly consumed by Babylonian invaders, leaving only a remnant (Jer 5:18). The calamity of those days is juxtaposed by the restoration and return of God and his people. Ἐν δὲ ταῖς ἡμέραις ἐκείναις Israel will be fruitful and multiply—a thematic complex of creation (Gen 1:22, 28), recreation (Gen 8:17; 9:1; Exod 1:7), and covenant (Gen 17:6; 35:11; Lev 26:9), as the houses of Judah and Israel are united in Jerusalem (Jer 33:15; 31:27), the throne of God (Jer 3:15–18). No longer will individuals suffer for the sins of the nation (Jer 31:29).

Joel   In Joel, ταῖς ἡμέραις ἐκείναις are preceded by apostasy (2:12) and cycles of judgment against Israel. The locusts are sent to destroy (1:1–12); the day of the Lord has drawn near bringing destruction (1:15–20). It is a day of darkness, gloom, and fire (2:2–3). Israel's only hope is to return to the Lord who relents (μετανοέω) from bringing disaster (2:13). After going through the wasting judgments, Israel will finally call upon the Lord (implied in 3:19) and be answered with his aid (3:19–27). Not only the alleviation of need but also the outpouring of the Spirit will take place ἐν ταῖς ἡμέραις ἐκείναις (3:2 LXX). The sun turning to darkness, and the moon to blood are stock apocalyptic themes echoed in Matthew 24:29. The captivity of Judah and Jerusalem will be reversed. The prophet speaks of the time when the people will return to the land (4:1 LXX) and God's judgment will come upon the nations, all of which takes place ἐν ταῖς ἡμέραις ἐκείναις. The resultant change is that strangers will never pass through Jerusalem again because the Lord will inhabit it with his people (3:16–17, 21 ET).

Zechariah   In Zechariah the phrase signals the favor of God (8:6). After scattering his people among the nations (7:14), God will return and dwell in Jerusalem and the city will be populated with old and young alike ἐν ταῖς ἡμέραις ἐκείναις (8:3-5).

---

5. Simon J. Devries, *Yesterday, Today and Tomorrow: Time and History in the Old Testament* (Grand Rapids: Eerdmans, 1975), 52 n. 77.

6. Ezekiel 38:17 excepted.

The exiles will return from among the nations (8:7); the Lord will be their God and they shall be his people (8:8; Lev 26:12; Jer 31:33), dwelling securely in Jerusalem (8:8). The nations will go with the Jews to Jerusalem ἐν ταῖς ἡμέραις ἐκείναις to seek the Lord (8:23).

OT summary In the Pentateuch and historical books ἐν ταῖς ἡμέραις ἐκείναις introduces narrative transitions in the plotline. In Jeremiah, Joel, and Zechariah the transitions are both horizontal and vertical: horizontal, in that exile and earthly tribulations are followed by peace and security; vertical in that there is also a shift in orientation as Yahweh comes down to afflict and restore. The shared characteristics of this prophetic outlook revolve around exile and restoration. But the three prophets do not lay emphasis upon a return from exile into previous conditions that can be forfeited by unbelief. Rather, the accent falls upon ongoing prosperity in an eschatologically energized environment crowned by God's presence with his people.

1 Enoch

The eschatological import of "those days" is also found in the literature of the Second Temple period. In 1 Enoch it is utilized for the purposes of formulaic transition. Frequent examples can be found in the *Similitudes* (chs. 37–71). It is used as a transitional statement to speak of time past (1 En. 39:1–3, 9; 40:10; 47:1–4), or eschatological future (91:8; 94:11; 96:8; 99:3–6; 100:4; Cf. Pss. Sol. 17:44; 18:6; Tob 14:7; 51:1–5).[7] Nickelsburg and VanderKam summarize, "'In those days,' is a frequent introductory phrase in eschatological scenarios but occurs relatively rarely in conjunction with the time of Enoch's visions (39:2, 3, 9; 47:3; 52:1; 61:1; 65:1)."[8] As we will now go on to show, ἐν δὲ ταῖς ἡμέραις likely functions as more than a transition in Matt 3:1.

The Significance of the Sentence Conjunction

Black has conducted several extensive studies of Matthew's narrative syntax analyzing the most common sentence conjunctions, καί and δέ, which make up more than 80 percent of the sentences in Matthew:[9]

---

7. Nickelsburg and VanderKam argue that the threefold repetition "in those days" could be read as occurring in the future or as present imperfect tenses. George W. E. Nickelsburg and James C. Vanderkam, *1 Enoch 2: A Commentary on the Book of 1 Enoch, Chapters 37–82*, 2 vols., Hermeneia, ed. Klaus Baltzer (Minneapolis: Fortress, 2012), 163.

8. Nickelsburg and VanderKam, *1 Enoch*, 226.

9. Stephanie L. Black, "How Matthew Tells the Story: A Linguistic Approach to Matthew's Narrative Syntax," in *Built upon the Rock: Studies in the Gospel of Matthew*, eds. Daniel M. Gutner and John Nolland (Grand Rapids: Eerdmans, 2008), 24–52.

Two-thirds (469/720, 65%) of the narrative sentences in Matthew's Gospel consist either of καί with verb-subject or verb-only constituent order (267 sentences), or δέ with subject-verb constituent order (202 sentences). This basic model, with its single related feature of constituent order, accounts for about eight out of every ten occurrences of the sentence conjunctions καί (267/335, 80%) and δέ (202/257, 79%) in Matthew's narrative framework. We can therefore say these combinations are characteristic of Matthew's narrative syntax.[10]

In unmarked instances of narrative continuity, καί is Matthew's lexical default; δέ is used to signal low to mid-level discontinuity. Examples would include such things as change of time, subject, and (less frequently) place.[11] Following Black's analysis, we note that Matthew's transition from the infant Jesus to the adult John signals: a new time (Ἐν δὲ ταῖς ἡμέραις ἐκείναις), subject (Ἰωάννης ὁ βαπτιστὴς), and place (ἐν τῇ ἐρήμῳ τῆς Ἰουδαίας). Word-order patterns contribute to the "markedness" of the transition; δέ most often occurs with a subject-verb order (202 times).[12] The use of δέ with verb-subject order, as found in Matt 3:1, drops to fifty-four occurrences.[13]

All instances of similar transitions found in Matthew are asyndetic and the time-frame reference is *always* singular.[14] Matthew's decision to underline the transition with a plural time-frame reference might suggest something of particular significance. Finally, Black points out that unlike the analogous constructions found in Matthew, the narrative unit of 3:1–6 contains only present and imperfect tense-form verbs. In Matthew, δέ + an aorist finite verb is the unmarked tense form in Matthew's narrative (213 sentences).[15] By contrast, the number of sentences combining δέ with present finite verbs is eight.[16] Given these syntactical features, the transition of 3:1 is marked. The question now is the significance of the discontinuity.

Ἐν δὲ ταῖς ἡμέραις ἐκείναις as Marking a New Period of Time The sentence conjunction of Matt 3:1 creates mid-level discontinuity in the narrative. Chapter 2 ends with the infant Jesus being taken to Nazareth. Ἐν δὲ ταῖς ἡμέραις ἐκείναις

---

10. Black, "How Matthew Tells the Story," 34–35.

11. Stephanie L. Black, *Sentence Conjunctions in Matthew's Gospel*, JSNTSup 216 (Sheffield: Sheffield Academic Press, 2002), 333.

12. Black, "How Matthew Tells the Story," 35. This total includes the subject as both first in a sentence and occurring later in the sentence.

13. Ibid. It should be noted that the significance of the "markedness" decreases when a new section begins with ἐν + dative since the subject-verb combination is always inverted (Matt 3:1; 11:25; 12:1; 13:1; 14:1; 18:1; 22:23; 26:55).

14. Black, *Sentence Conjunctions*, 207.

15. Matt 11:25; 12:1; 13:1; 14:1; 18:1; 22:23; 26:55—all of which contain singular time-frame references and are followed by Aorist tense forms. Black, *Sentence Conjunctions*, 153–54.

16. Black, *Sentence Conjunctions*, 154.

signals a new period of time. According to Häfner, the referent is to the time of Jesus's residence in Nazareth.[17] Matthew could have chosen a less ambiguous construction such as μετὰ δὲ τὴν μετοικεσίαν Βαβυλῶνος (1:12; cf. 24:29; 25:19; 26:32, 73), but using such a preposition could possibly obscure the path from Nazareth to John in the wilderness (Mark 1:9).[18] Furthermore, the opposition (2:16–18) and potential opposition (2:22) to Jesus, combined with the subsequent relocation to a more remote place, might be themes that help readers to see similarities to John the Baptist who also goes to a remote location where a confrontation with the religious leaders takes place (3:7–12). Nolland has suggested, "Just as the presence of the infant Jesus in Nazareth provides the time reference here for the beginning of the preaching ministry of John, so the arrival of the adult Jesus in Capernaum will provide the time reference for the beginning of the preaching ministry of Jesus."[19]

Ἐν δὲ ταῖς ἡμέραις ἐκείναις *as Eschatological "Time"* This transition has been marked to prepare Matthew's readers to fast forward to a new place and time. But is this all? New pericopes in chs. 1–3 begin with either a circumstantial participle of time or with the adverb τότε.[20] The prepositional phrase used to introduce John the Baptist disrupts the pattern. In 3:13 and 4:1 the pattern resumes.

Kingsbury has also noted that ἐν δὲ ταῖς ἡμέραις ἐκείναις occurs only in Matt 3:1 and ch. 24. "Matthew regularly appropriates it from Mark," but unlike Mark, Matthew consistently uses the demonstrative pronoun in the Olivet Discourse.[21]

Mark	Matthew
13:17 . . . ταῖς θηλαζούσαις ἐν ἐκείναις ταῖς ἡμέραις.	24:19 . . . ταῖς θηλαζούσαις ἐν ἐκείναις ταῖς ἡμέραις.
13:19 . . . ἔσονται γὰρ αἱ ἡμέραι ἐκεῖναι θλῖψις	24:21 . . . ἔσται γὰρ τότε θλῖψις μεγάλη
13:20 . . . εἰ μὴ ἐκολόβωσεν κύριος τὰς ἡμέρας . . . ἀλλὰ διὰ τοὺς ἐκλεκτοὺς οὓς ἐξελέξατο ἐκολόβωσεν τὰς ἡμέρας	24:22 . . . εἰ μὴ ἐκολοβώθησαν αἱ ἡμέραι ἐκεῖναι . . . διὰ δὲ τοὺς ἐκλεκτοὺς κολοβωθήσονται αἱ ἡμέραι ἐκεῖναι.
13:24 . . . Ἀλλ᾽ ἐν ἐκείναις ταῖς ἡμέραις μετὰ τὴν θλῖψιν ἐκείνην	24:29 . . . μετὰ τὴν θλῖψιν τῶν ἡμερῶν ἐκείνων

17. Cited by Luz, *Matthew* 1.134, and Nolland, *Matthew*, 135.

18. Conversely, μετά + accusative would make chronological sense "after those days (the days of Jesus's childhood in Nazareth) John the Baptist came preaching in the wilderness. . ."

19. Nolland, *Matthew*, 135. Cf. Janice C. Anderson, *Matthew's Narrative Web: Over and Over and Over Again*, JSNTSup 91 (Sheffield: Sheffield Academic Press, 1994).

20. Kingsbury, *Matthew: Structure, Christology, Kingdom*, 28.

21. Ibid., 29. Matthew 24:38 is textually uncertain. Nevertheless, the absence of the demonstrative pronoun does not affect Kingsbury's thesis as Matthew is referencing a past event (the flood) rather than a future one (the coming of the son of man).

In Matt 24 Ἐν ἐκείναις ταῖς ἡμέραι refers to the period of time leading up to ἡμέρας ἐκείνης καὶ ὥρας, which will see the coming of the Son of Man (24:39), in the time of θλῖψις. Kingsbury surmises:

> The question is: does Matthew indicate when he believes this eschatological period began? We contend that he does by placing this very phrase at 3:1, which signals the inauguration of the ministry of John the Baptist. The following, then, is the importance of this phrase in the Gospel and why Matthew at 3:1 deliberately alters the manner in which he otherwise begins the pericopes of the first main section of his Gospel: "in those days" designates that eschatological period of time that breaks upon Israel with the public ministry of John the Baptist and will continue until the parousia of Jesus Son of Man.[22]

When Matthew finds the phrase in Mark being used without eschatological meaning, he drops it.[23] Kingsbury concludes, "This phrase is a precise one, and finds its proper place with similar phrases such as the 'end' and the 'consummation of the age.'"[24]

Matthew's narrative asserts that John came as the promised eschatological prophet (11:14; 17:11–13). He appears in the place of eschatological expectation, ἐν τῇ ἐρήμῳ. Matthew describes John for his readers as the Isaianic voice (3:3). Might not ἐν δὲ ταῖς ἡμέραις ἐκείναις signal not only the transition to John, but also the era of eschatological fulfillment? Precisely because Matthew sees John's arrival as a fulfillment of a well-known prophecy, one could ask how else Matthew could draw upon "those days" in a way that lets his readers know that he is referring to the eschatological expectation of the prophets other than to use the phrase itself? The larger thematic pattern of OT rebellion followed by divine retribution is also replayed in ch. 2. In the OT, wholesale refusal of the Lord's right as king met with judgment and exile, as Matthew's genealogy has already intimated. The Lord's response to the rejected son of David, son of Abraham (1:1), is to send his prophet of ultimatum, whose dress, location, and preaching recalls the OT expectations of an unrepeatable time of singular importance.

---

22. Ibid., 30.

23. In the feeding of the four thousand (Mark 8:1), Ἐν δὲ ταῖς ἡμέραις ἐκείναις is a conventional historical expression. Kingsbury thinks that Matthew has dropped the phrase in order to keep with his eschatological meaning.

| Mark 8:1 Ἐν δὲ ταῖς ἡμέραις ἐκείναις ὄχλου ὄντος καὶ μὴ ἐχόντων τί φάγωσιν, προσκαλεσάμενος τοὺς μαθητὰς λέγει αὐτοῖς | Matthew 15:32 Ὁ δὲ Ἰησοῦς προσκαλεσάμενος τοὺς μαθητὰς αὐτοῦ εἶπεν· σπλαγχνίζομαι ἐπὶ τὸν ὄχλον ... |

Kingsbury, *Matthew: Structure, Christology, Kingdom*, 30.

24. Ibid., 31.

Matthew 11:12 There is one other place that suggests that Matthew understands the inauguration of the time of prophetic fulfillment and John's appearance to be intertwined ἐν ταῖς ἡμέραις ἐκείναις. Even though Matt 11:12 is a *crux interpretum*, 11:12–14 lends support for an eschatological interpretation of the phrase in 3:1.[25] After sending the disciples of the imprisoned forerunner back, Jesus begins to speak about John's place and position in redemptive history. He asks the crowds, τί ἐξήλθατε εἰς τὴν ἔρημον θεάσασθαι (11:7)? John was περισσότερον προφήτου (11:9), of him the prophecy says, ἰδοὺ ἐγὼ ἀποστέλλω τὸν ἄγγελόν μου (11:10). While the least in the kingdom of the heaven(s) (ἐν τῇ βασιλείᾳ τῶν οὐρανῶν) is greater than John, none born of women is μείζων Ἰωάννου τοῦ βαπτιστοῦ (11:11). What follows is a cryptic statement: ἀπὸ δὲ τῶν ἡμερῶν Ἰωάννου τοῦ βαπτιστοῦ ἕως ἄρτι ἡ βασιλεία τῶν οὐρανῶν βιάζεται καὶ βιασταὶ ἁρπάζουσιν αὐτήν (11:12).

The difficult interpretive decisions of this text are well known. Osborne provides the following catalogue:

> (1) totally positive ("the kingdom forcefully advances [through God], and forceful people [the disciples] seize it); (2) totally negative ("the kingdom suffers violence [persecution], and violent people [the leaders] plunder it"); (3) negative/positive (the kingdom suffers violence, but forceful people lay hold of it"); (4) positive/negative ("the kingdom is forcefully advancing, but violent people plunder it").[26]

Matthew's use of βιάζεται is contextually different from that of Luke 16:16. Matthew uses a collection of words which are predominantly negative in connotation.[27] To this we add John's imprisonment (11:2), Jesus's caution against taking offense (11:6), rebuke of his generation (11:16–19) and castigation of cities where he had performed miracles (11:20–24). It is difficult to read this passage in the senses of 1 and 4 above. The generation of Jesus and the cities where his ministry was carried out were mostly impervious to his words and deeds. To understand "forceful people laying hold of it" as a metaphorical reference for salvation (or as "discipleship") would be strange.[28] Finally, the picture of a forceful and positive seizing of the kingdom does not fit well with those who are burdened (πεφορτισμένοι) and in need of rest (ἀναπαύσω) (11:28–30), but a kingdom that is

---

25. Ibid., 142. For the history of interpretation, cf. Peter S. Cameron, *Violence and the Kingdom: The Interpretation of Matthew 11:12* (Frankfurt am Main: Peter Lang, 1984).

26. Osborne, *Matthew*, 421–22. Davies and Allison select a sample of seven interpretations. William D. Davies and Dale C. Allison Jr., *Matthew VIII-XVIII*, ICC (Edinburgh: T&T Clark, 1991), 254–55.

27. βιάζεται, βιασταί and ἁρπάζουσιν. While the evidence outside of Matthew is slim (three occurrences), all three instances of βιασταί (a NT *hapax legomenon*) are "in a pejorative sense . . . *violent, impetuous* . . ." Bauer et al., *A Greek-English Lexicon of the New Testament*, 176.

28. Hagner, *Matthew*, 1.307.

being assaulted with violent people plundering it makes for a plausible reading of the text.[29] ἀπὸ δὲ sets up a contrast with verse 11. John the Baptist is great, but he also belongs to a time of suffering. John belonged to the heavenly kingdom, but is himself seized, imprisoned, and executed (14:1–12). The kingdom is plundered as its citizens are violently taken away. ἀπὸ δὲ τῶν ἡμερῶν Ἰωάννου τοῦ βαπτιστοῦ takes readers back to ἡμέραις ἐκείναις (3:1), signaling the time of fulfillment which is likewise a time of conflict. Those that dispute a special usage of the phrase in 3:1 would likely acknowledge that 11:12 signals more than a change of time; it is the inbreaking of the time predicted by the prophets. That ταῖς ἡμέραις ἐκείναις should be understood as a time of prophetic fulfillment is also underscored by what is said next: πάντες γὰρ οἱ προφῆται καὶ ὁ νόμος ἕως Ἰωάννου ἐπροφήτευσαν (11:13). The coordinating conjunction along with πάντες indicates that the time of the end has arrived. There is nothing more to prophesy (in terms of the OT) because the last prophet has come and has prepared the way of the Lord. It might also be a cryptic reference to the death of John, a prophet (11:9), whose prophesying comes to a grizzly end (14:10). The prophets prophesied about the time when prophecy would cease, the Lord would arrive, and the end would be reached. John the Baptist came in "those days," signaling the arrival of the kingdom and the end of the OT prophetic voice. This reading fits within the OT eschatological usage of ταῖς ἡμέραις ἐκείναις.

Summary Considered on its own, "in those days" has little extended referentiality outside of the immediate narrative context. "In those days" would simply refer to the infant Jesus's residence in Nazareth (Matt 2:23), or the days of John the Baptist's proclamation and baptism (Matt 3:1). The Matthean eschatological emphases in chs. 1–2 and the placement of "in those days" for the purpose of introducing the time of John the Baptist invites readers to discover something more. Jesus is the end of the exile (Matt 1:17). He is Immanuel, God with us (Matt 1:22–23), the promised king and ruler of Israel (Matt 2:5–6). Jesus has already undergone an exodus out of Egypt (Matt 2:13–18), and John the Baptist now arrives as the Isaianic voice in the wilderness announcing the coming of the kingdom, declaring the eschatological punishment and the long-anticipated ingathering of the people of God (Matt 3:12). With these OT citations placed throughout chs. 1–3, "in those days" connects thematically and verbally to OT prophetic expectations of which Matthew sees John and Jesus as integrally connected and fulfilling. "Those days" usher in the outpouring of the Spirit (Joel 3:2 [LXX], Matt 3:11), salvation (Zech 8:6–7; Matt 3:12), judgment (Jer 5:15–18; Matt 3:7–12), and ingathering of God's people (Joel 4:1–12; Jer 3:16–18; Matt 3:12), by the coming of God (Joel 2:31–3:2; Matt 3:3), with consuming fire (Jer 5:14; Joel 2:2–3; Matt 3:11), by a righteous king who establishes the kingdom (Jer 33:14–17; Matt 3:2).

---

29. Note the correlative uses of ἁρπάζουσιν: ἢ πῶς δύναταί τις εἰσελθεῖν εἰς τὴν οἰκίαν τοῦ ἰσχυροῦ καὶ τὰ σκεύη αὐτοῦ ἁρπάσαι (Matt 12:29) and ἔρχεται ὁ πονηρὸς καὶ ἁρπάζει τὸ ἐσπαρμένον ἐν τῇ καρδίᾳ αὐτοῦ (Matt 13:19).

The OT and non-canonical eschatological usages of the phrase, combined with the arrival of John the Baptist as the days of prophetic fulfillment and onset of eschatological crisis, indicates that ταῖς ἡμέραις ἐκείναις is being utilized for something more than a narrative transition. The additional plural usage of the phrase and marked grammatical construction alerts the readers that something deeper is being actualized. This importance is further elaborated by the eschatological context (3:3–12) and recurrence in the Olivet Discourse. Finally, that Matthew could have followed Mark's non-eschatological usage but chose not to supports this reading of ταῖς ἡμέραις ἐκείναις as the time of fulfillment, the conclusion of OT prophesying (11:12-13) and the days that would see crisis (3:7–12; 11:12).

The approaching time anticipated by the OT brings with it the anticipated forerunner who announces the way of the Lord. With the eschatological time-frame set, Matthew turns his attention to the one who announces the imminent arrival of the kingdom of God.

John the Baptist as Prophet

It is widely acknowledged that the gospel portraits of John the Baptist depict him as a prophet.[30] With understandable reason, many studies of John the Baptist have

---

30. Carl H. Kraeling, *John the Baptist* (New York: Charles Scribner's Sons, 1951), 30; Flemington, *The New Testament Doctrine*, 13–23; Wolfgang Trilling, "Die Täufertradition bei Matthäus," *BZ* 3 (1959): 271–89; Scobie, *John the Baptist*, 117–30; Walter Wink, *John the Baptist in the Gospel Tradition* (Cambridge: Cambridge University Press, 1968); Ladd, *A Theology of the New Testament*, 35–36; Martin Hengel, *The Charismatic Leader and His Followers*, trans. James Greig (Spring Valley: Crossroad, 1981), 34–37; E. P. Sanders, *Jesus and Judaism* (Minneapolis: Fortress, 1985), 91–92; Vos, *Redemptive History*, 299–300; Davies and Allison, *Matthew* 1.295; John P. Meier, *Mentor, Message, and Miracles*, vol. 2 of *A Marginal Jew: Rethinking the Historical Jesus* (New York: Doubleday, 1994), 21, 29–40; idem., "John the Baptist in Matthew's Gospel," *JBL* 99.3 (1980): 394; Witherington, "John the Baptist," 386; Jürgen Becker, *Jesus von Nazaret* (Berlin: Walter de Gruyter, 1996), 56–58; Reiser, *Jesus and Judgment*, 167, 252; Craig A. Evans, "The Baptism of John in a Typological Context," in *Baptism, the New Testament and the Church*, 45–61; Carter, *Matthew and the Margins*, 91–92; James H. Charlesworth, "John the Baptizer and the Dead Sea Scrolls," in *The Bible and the Dead Sea Scrolls*, vol. 3 of *The Scrolls and Christian Origins*, ed. James H. Charlesworth (Waco: Baylor University Press, 2006), 10; David L. Turner, *Israel's Last Prophet: Jesus and the Jewish Leaders in Matthew 23* (Minneapolis: Fortress, 2015), 129–50; Keener, *A Commentary*, 116–19; Nolland, *Matthew*, 136–37; France, *Matthew*, 97–98; Daniel S. Dapaah, *The Relationship between John the Baptist and Jesus of Nazareth: A Critical Study* (Lanham: University Press of America, 2005), 49; Ben Cooper, *Incorporated Servanthood: Commitment and Discipleship in the Gospel of Matthew* (London: T&T Clark, 2013), 78.

drawn from the literature of the Second Temple period to understand better the "historical John the Baptist." The approach of this chapter is not to engage such lengthy background treatments.[31] Nor will we take up the question of John's relationship to the Qumran community (or Essenes) or the perspective of Josephus.[32] Instead, the limiting approach adopted here is to examine Matthew's usage of προφήτης, found so repeatedly throughout his gospel.

According to Cooper, by presenting John as a "present-day" prophet Matthew implies John's reliability. Cooper, *Incorporated Servanthood*, 78. For Q's evaluation of John as a prophet see John S. Kloppenborg, *The Formation of Q: Trajectories in Ancient Wisdom Collections* (Harrisburg: Trinity Press International, 1987), 105 and Clare K. Rothchild, *Baptist Traditions and Q*, WUNT 190 (Tübingen: Mohr Siebeck, 2005), 34.

31. The literature canvasing the types of prophets in Second Temple Judaism and the early Christian period is enormous. Joseph Blenkinsopp, "Prophecy and Priesthood in Josephus," *JJS* 25.2 (1974): 239–62; Paul Barnett, "The Jewish Sign Prophets—AD 40–70: Their Intentions and Origin," *NTS* 27.5 (1981): 679–97; Morna D. Hooker, *The Signs of a Prophet: The Prophetic Actions of Jesus* (Harrisburg: Trinity Press, 1997); David E. Aune, *Prophecy in Early Christianity and the Ancient Mediterranean World* (Grand Rapids: Eerdmans, 1991); David Hill, "False Prophets and Charismatics: Structure and Interpretation in Matthew 7:15-23," *Biblica* 57.3 (1976): 327–48; Richard A. Horsley, "'Like One of the Prophets of Old': Two Types of Popular Prophets at the Time of Jesus," *CBQ* 47 (1985): 435–63; Louis H. Feldman, "Prophets and Prophecy in Josephus," in *Prophets, Prophecy, and Prophetic Texts in Second Temple Judaism*, eds. M. H. Floyd and R. D. Haak (New York: T&T Clark, 2006), 210–39; Lester L. Grabbe, "Thus Spake the Prophet Josephus . . . : The Jewish Historian on Prophets and Prophecy," in *Prophets, Prophecy, and Prophetic Texts in Second Temple Judaism*, 240–47. Webb, *John the Baptizer and Prophet*; Taylor, *The Immerser*.

32. Possible links between John and Qumran are the desert/wilderness, Isa 40:3, asceticism, ritual immersion, priestly associations and sharing of property. Cf. J. Ian H. McDonald, "What Did You Go Out to See? John the Baptist, the Scrolls and Late Second Temple Judaism," in *The Dead Sea Scrolls in Their Historical Context*, ed. T. Lim (London: T&T Clark, 2004), 53–64; John A. T. Robinson, "The Baptism of John and the Qumran Community: Testing a Hypothesis," *HTR* 50.3 (1957): 175–92; Brownlee, "John the Baptist," 33–53; David Flusser, "The Baptism of John and the Dead Sea Sect," in *Essays on the Dead Sea Scrolls: In Memory of E. L. Sukenik*, eds. C. Rabin and Y. Yadin (Jerusalem: Hehal Ha-Sefer, 1961), 209–38; Otto Betz, "Was John an Essene?" in *Understanding the Dead Sea Scrolls: A Reader from the Biblical Archeology Review*, ed. H. Shanks (New York: Random House, 1992), 205–14; John C. Hutchinson, "Was John the Baptist an Essene from Qumran?" *BSac* 159 (2002): 187–200. For Josephus's view of John (*J.W.* 2.261; *Ant.* 20.169-70) see Scobie, *John the Baptist*, 17–21; Dapaah, *The Relationship between John the Baptist and Jesus of Nazareth*, 49; James D. G. Dunn, *Jesus Remembered: Christianity in the Making*, vol. 1 (Grand Rapids: Eerdmans, 2003), 658, esp. n.199; Webb, *John the Baptizer and Prophet*, 31–44, 307–48.

Matthew's Presentation of John the Baptist

John is introduced into Matthew's narrative with the title ὁ βαπτιστής, even though his baptizing activities are not described until v. 5.[33] This title is known by the narrator (and presumably his readers), Jesus, Herod, and the disciples.[34] While Matthew explains the meaning of "Immanuel," God with us (Matt 1:23), he does not do so for John's title.[35] His later activities in the Jordan River make the meaning clear. John's identity is not to be singularly understood as one who baptizes, but rather, Matthew's portrait of John emphasizes his prophetic status as he who was anticipated in the past, pronouncing heaven's verdict. Even if we should pass over the subsequent opinions of John catalogued in his gospel (Matt 11:9–14; 14:5; 21:26), there are sufficient signals in Matthew's initial introduction to draw the conclusion that he likewise considered John to be a prophet. John the Baptist comes to call Israel to an appropriate response of repentance in view of the coming of the kingdom (3:2). In his person, John is the Isaianic voice in the wilderness (3:3). Not only his proclamation, which is overladen with OT images, but also his Elijah-evoking attire (3:4)[36] and prophetic sign (3:6,11) points in the direction of a prophetic messenger sent at the behest of Yahweh.

Though Matthew gives no explicit criteria for what constitutes a prophet, his usage of προφήτης is stable and, taken collectively, readers are able to understand what Matthew means by such a usage and are able to follow the implications of such an understanding for John's ministry to Israel. We will proceed along three lines of related inquiry. First, we will consider the profile of the prophets: For Matthew, the identity, and therefore the definition, of a true prophet is properly discovered through the witness of the OT. Secondly, the prophets were those who predicted the future, often confronting God's wayward people with impending divine judgment. Thirdly, the prophets, broadly speaking, were rejected, persecuted, and killed by Israel. These points are important as they not only help to clarify John's role as a prophet, but they also provide the necessary groundwork for understanding the meaning of John's baptism in Matthew's Gospel. If John appears in Matthew's Gospel as a prophet, then his baptism takes on prophetic significance, as we will argue later.

The Profile of προφήτης in Matthew

No other NT writer uses προφήτης as often as Matthew.[37] Six of the thirty-seven instances occur in the first three chapters of Matthew's Gospel, four of which are

---

33. Gary Yamasaki, *John the Baptist in Life and Death: Audience-Oriented Criticism of Matthew's Narrative*, JSNTSup 167 (Sheffield: Sheffield Academic Press, 1998), 81; Carter, *Matthew and the Margins*, 92.

34. Dunn, *Jesus Remembered*, 356.

35. Yamasaki, *John the Baptist*, 81.

36. *Pace* Becker, "ist aber eher allgemeine Prophetentracht": Becker, *Jesus*, 51.

37. Matthew = thirty-seven times; Mark = eight; Luke = twenty-nine; John = fourteen; Acts = thirty. The number of occurrences in the remainder of the NT amounts to single digits in each book.

formula quotations. We will take our start with an overview of the data and then show their relevance for a proper understanding of Matthew's presentation of John the Baptist.

Matthew cites from the following prophets, sometimes by name and at other times omitting the name while clearly referencing the OT text:

Prophets	Occurrence(s)	Matthew
Isaiah	6	1:23; 3:3; 4:14–16; 8:17; 12:17; 3:14–15
Micah	1	2:6
Hosea	1	2:15
Jeremiah	2	2:18; 27:9
Malachi	1	11:10[38]
Psalm/Asaph[39]	1	13:35
Zechariah[40]	1	21:4
Daniel	1	24:15

Outside of the enigmatic reference to the fulfillment citations in 2:23 and 26:56, the first collective reference to the prophets is found in 5:12 where they are the objects of persecution. A few verses later, Matthew returns to the issue of fulfillment, this time to demonstrate that the view of Jesus himself is that of a mission to fulfill all the Law and the prophets (5:17). Christians are likewise to observe the rule of doing to others as they would like it done to them. This, Jesus says, is the substance of the Law and prophets (7:12). Jesus speaks of the one receiving a prophet also receiving a prophet's reward (10:41). In 11:9 he calls John a prophet and more—he is the one who will carry out the role of Mal 3:1. Therefore all the Law and the prophets prophesy until John (11:13). In 12:39 Jesus refers to Jonah as a prophetic sign—in this case a sign not only of what will become of Jesus, but also of Israel's judgment. The evil of the brood of vipers in v. 34, the explicit reference to judgment in vv. 36–37, and standing on the other side of the reference to Jonah are the men of Nineveh rising up in the judgment, and condemning the generation of Jesus (v. 41) suggests that for Matthew, the prophet Jonah was a warning not just to Nineveh, but also to Israel. The disciples of Jesus ask him why he speaks in parables (13:10). Jesus, in turn, cites Isaiah as prophetic evidence of Israel's inability to correctly see and hear the salvation Jesus brings. Of his time, characterized as a time of seeing and hearing, Jesus could say that many prophets longed to see and hear what his disciples visually and aurally experienced (13:17). Being rejected in his hometown, Jesus concludes that a prophet is not without honor, except in his hometown (13:57). Matthew then shifts back to John's death, citing the people's opinion of him as the reason for the delay of execution. Herod did not immediately put John to death because he feared the crowds who believed

---

38. Though not mentioned by name, Jesus proof texts John's identity as a prophet (11:9) by citing Mal 3:1.

39. Psalm 78:2; while only a heading, the superscription assigns the Psalm to Asaph.

40. Matthew might be seen here as giving a composite citation of Zech 9:9 with Isa 62:11, raising the number of references to Isaiah to seven.

John to be a prophet (14:5). After asking his disciples about the opinion of the people concerning the Son of Man, his disciples provide the following catalogue: John the Baptist, Elijah, Jeremiah, or one of the prophets (16:14). Upon his entry into Jerusalem, the opinion of the crowd becomes more precise: "This is the prophet Jesus" (21:11). Again, the crowd's opinion of John is that of a prophet (21:26), thereby causing the chief priests and elders to withhold their opinion of John's baptism. The chief priests and the Pharisees, like Herod, wish to arrest Jesus (κρατήσας; also in 14:3), but like Herod, they too feared the crowds who took Jesus to be a prophet (21:46; 14:5). One final time, the Law and the prophets are discussed. Jesus declares them both to be summarized by love (22:40). The scribes and the Pharisees are charged with the blood of the prophets in the next chapter (23:29–34, 37; for a total of five occurrences of προφήτης). Finally, when Jesus is arrested, the manner of his arrest is said to fulfill αἱ γραφαὶ τῶν προφητῶν (26:56).

Matthew's repeated use of προφήτης has a decidedly OT character and quality to it. When prophets are mentioned by name, it is always a name that is connected to an OT book or character (with the possible exception of Asaph—Matt 1:7–8). Never does Matthew provide names of prophets outside of the OT, except John the Baptist himself (Matt 11:9) and Jesus (e.g., Matt 13:57).

In the second place, when speaking of the prophets collectively, Matthew sometimes pairs them with νόμος (5:17; 7:12; 11:13; 22:40). Such an idiom was a familiar designation for the scriptures of Israel.[41]

Third, the unique Matthean expression προφῆται καὶ δίκαιοι is most readily understood as a reference to the OT prophets (13:16–17).[42] Jesus describes the prophets and the righteous as those who wanted to see and hear the things that his disciples were experiencing. Matthew places this saying immediately after the citation from Isaiah.[43] Isaiah prophesied that Israel would not see and hear correctly. This inability on the part of the majority of Israel is contrasted with the disciples' ability to see and hear. This expression (i.e., προφῆται καὶ δίκαιοι), placed after the Isaianic context, most naturally refers to the OT to which Isaiah belonged. There are no other contextual clues following Jesus's saying that would suggest otherwise. Additionally, there is an echo of Matt 5:12 in 13:17, which brings us to our fourth observation.[44]

In the Sermon on the Mount, Jesus pronounces a blessing upon those who are persecuted (Matt 5:12). Such mistreatment was also carried out against the prophets. Though προφήτης could be a more general designation for God's "spokespersons,"[45] Israel's rejection of God's prophets and subsequent rejection of

---

41. For examples of the expression in the Second Temple, Rabinical, Josephus, and NT literature, see Davies and Allison, *Matthew*, 1.484.

42. Note the identical parallel in 10:41, ὁ δεχόμενος προφήτην εἰς ὄνομα προφήτου μισθὸν προφήτου λήμψεται, καὶ ὁ δεχόμενος δίκαιον εἰς ὄνομα δικαίου μισθὸν δικαίου λήμψεται.

43. Already labeled a prophet in 1:22.

44. The shared words being μακάριοι (5:11/13:16), προφήτης (5:12/13:17).

45. Hagner, *Matthew*, 96.

Jesus is "clearly marked in the OT,"[46] and is a "well-established tradition."[47] While there is only a handful of passages that give accounts of the persecuted prophets (1 Kgs 18:4, 13; 19:10, 14; 2 Chr 24:20–21; 36:15-21; Jer 2:30; 26:20–24), there is a paradigmatic text for the violent fate of the prophets.[48] Nehemiah 9:26 reads, "Nevertheless, they were disobedient and rebelled against you and cast your law behind their back and killed your prophets, who had warned them in order to turn them back to you, and they committed great blasphemies."[49] The related themes of law and prophets, rejection and persecution, are taken up in the Sermon on the Mount (5:10–12, 17–18; 7:12). Rejection of the law ("casting behind the back") leads to persecution like that of the prophets, a treatment that the disciples and especially Jesus and John could expect to receive.

This persecution of the prophets is further developed in ch. 10 and expanded in ch. 23 where "prophets" and "persecution" reoccur (23:30–34) "so that on you may come all the righteous blood shed on earth, from the blood of righteous Abel to the blood of Zechariah the son of Barachiah, whom you murdered between the sanctuary and the altar" (23:35). While it is not possible to enter into the detailed and lengthy discussions of Zechariah's identity here,[50] on a surface level reading of the text the mention of prophets and Zechariah the son of Barachiah (Zech 1:1 = Matt 23:35) indicates that the prophets of the OT are in view.[51] For Matthew, the persecution of the prophets is an OT problem that was repeated during the time of Jesus.

John and Jesus

The remaining individuals who bear the title προφήτης in Matthew's Gospel are John the Baptist (11:9, 13; 14:5; 21:26) and Jesus (13:57; 16:14; 21:11, 46). Thus far, we have demonstrated that Matthew has done three things. First, he has named the individual prophets of the OT. Second, he has shown that the prophets prophesy, and third, he has described the fate of the prophets. As individuals who were foretold by the OT prophets (3:3; 1:22–23), both John and Jesus are called prophets

46. Nolland, *Matthew*, 209–10.

47. Davies and Allison, *Matthew*, 1.465. Cf. n. 59.

48. "Neh 9 ist der Locus classicus für die Vorstellung vom »gewaltsamen Geschick aller Propheten«". Anna Maria Schwemer, "Prophet, Zeuge und Märtyrer: Zur Entstehung des Märtyrerbegriffs im frühesten Christentum," *ZTK* 96.3 (1999): 325. Aune, *Prophecy*, 157–59.

49. Speaking of Israel's wandering years after the exodus and their interactions with foreign kings, Israel sang, "He rebuked kings on their account, saying, 'Touch not my anointed ones, do my prophets no harm'" (1 Chr 16:22). Ironically, Israel would engage in the very thing that God commanded foreign kings not to do.

50. Cf. Edmon L. Gallagher, "The Blood from Abel to Zechariah in the History of Interpretation," *NTS* 60.1 (2014): 121–38.

51. Note the concluding lament that brings the woes to an end, Ἰερουσαλὴμ Ἰερουσαλήμ, ἡ ἀποκτείνουσα τοὺς προφήτας καὶ λιθοβολοῦσα τοὺς ἀπεσταλμένους πρὸς αὐτήν (23:37).

(21:11, 26), engage in prophetic utterances and activities (3:7, 11–12; 12:40–45; 23:36; 24:3–25:46) and both will suffer the fate of a prophet.[52] To this, we add one final point that will be described below: both John and Jesus offered and/or preformed prophetic signs (3:6; 11; 12:38–39; 16:14; 21:12–13).[53]

Establishing the Expectation of a προφήτης

In chs. 1–2 Matthew has laid out the tension between Israel and Yahweh and thereby creates an expectation that Yahweh's response will be to confront his wayward people. He has drawn from the OT prophets: Isaiah, Micah, Hosea, and Jeremiah. All four references have been selected in order to show the fulfillment of God's plan for Israel. Matthew, citing the exile and its end (1:17), might reasonably be expected to place John in a position of heralding words of comfort (Isa 40:1). However, the intervening narrative between the genealogical reference to the end of the deportation (1:17) and the coming of John the Baptist (3:1) portrays a nation unprepared for the divine visitation that is shortly to befall it. In each of Matthew's citations in chs. 1 and 2, judgment is in the foreground. For Isaiah's Emmanuel, it is the Assyrian invasion that is being promised. Matthew's placement of the leaders' citation of Mic 5:2, while a positive promise, is used in the service of betrayal (i.e., Herod now knows where to find the rival king). This betrayal and rejection of Jesus is the reason for his exodus out of Israel, an event that Matthew sees as fulfilling Hos 11:1. The context of Hosea 11:1 is also that of Israel's ongoing rebellion and, by Matthew placing the citation into the account of Joseph taking his family *out* of Israel, Matthew negatively depicts Israel as spiritual Egypt from which God removes his son (Hos 11:1; Matt 2:15). The subsequent slaughter of the infant sons in Bethlehem likewise bears typological similarities to the devastation of the deportation that Jeremiah had told Israel to expect (Matt 2:16–18).

By incorporating these OT citations and typological associations, Matthew is not only highlighting the correspondence between the time of Jesus and the events of Israel's exodus from Egypt, but also prefiguring the typological story that he will

---

52. With regard to the death of John, Wink comments that, "Matthew's version of the death of John is comparable to the woe pronounced over the Pharisees for building the tombs of the prophets (23:29–36) and the parable of the vinedresser (21:33–43). This suffering of the prophets described in these passages is actually demonstrated by the death of John; his execution is proof of the axiom that the prophet must suffer": Wink, *John the Baptist*, 27.

53. While there are numerous healings and miracles performed by Jesus in the Gospel of Matthew that could potentially be treated under the category of prophetic sign, Cooper connects Jesus's statement about Israel's house (οἶκος, with 12:4, τὸν οἶκον τοῦ θεοῦ) being left desolate with Jesus's activity upon entering the temple/οἶκος, "As with the overturning of tables in 21.12–13 at the beginning of the section, Jesus physically leaving the Temple in 24.1 is also therefore a kind of prophetic sign act." Cooper, *Incorporated Servanthood*, 182–83.

tell in greater detail in his gospel. The antitype, to which the OT story pointed, is previewed in chs. 1 and 2 and then interwoven into the content of the remainder of his gospel.[54] It is no surprise that the ministry of John precedes that of Jesus (3:3; 11:10), neither is it unexpected that after the rejection of God's salvation (Matt 1:21; 2:5–6), a prophet arrives to confront Israel (Matt 3:1).[55]

Matthew's narrative is informed by Israel's prophets as well as the themes of Israel's larger OT narrative. As he tells the story of Jesus, he is retelling the unsuccessful story of Israel. Childs summarizes the Deuteronomic history this way,

> Israel's sad history of disobedience to God's law had been foreseen by the prophets, whom God sent in a constant stream, warning Israel to turn from its evil ways (II Kings 17.7ff.; cf. Jer. 16.10ff.; 25.1ff.). Accordingly, the history of Israel was patterned into a series of prophecies and fulfillments "until Yahweh removed Israel out of his sight, as he had spoken by his servants the prophets." (II Kings 17.23)[56]

Israel's disobedient relationship to God and to his prophets is built upon the Deuteronomistic interpretation of Israel's history.[57] In the Pentateuch, God raised up Moses to go to Israel, but Israel refused to believe God's word (Deut 1:32) and rebelled against God's prophet (Num 14:1–4; Deut 1:26–40). After the exodus from Egypt, the nation experienced exile, which ended in the death of the first generation (Deut 1:35). This pattern of Israel's unbelief, rejection of God's command(s) along with their indifference and persecution of the prophets is "alluded to" in both the former and latter prophets.[58] The appearance of a prophet often meant a decision was forced upon Israel. The arrival of God's messengers meant that Israel was once again standing at an all-too-familiar crossroad (Jer 44:4). According to Taylor, "Prophets have the specific function of calling Israel to repentance. Since Israel was continually disobedient, and this caused God to punish the nation through various calamities, God sent prophets to exhort Israel to repent and return to the Law."[59]

As the former and latter prophets resemble the activity of Moses, John the Baptist's activities and calls to repentance are consistent with the prophets that preceded him.[60] He is a prophet, but not one sent to offer Israel a baptism that will

---

54. See especially Allison, *The New Moses*, 137–270.

55. *Pace* Becker, "Nirgends begründet der Täufer, warum Gott zürnt": Becker, *Jesus*, 41.

56. Brevard Childs, *Biblical Theology: Old and New Testaments* (Minneapolis: Fortress, 1993), 170. For a similar overview see Odil Steck, *Israel und das gewaltsame Geschick der Propheten*, WMANT 23 (Neukirchen-Vluyn: Neukirchener Verlag, 1967), 184–86.

57. Turner, *Israel's Last Prophet*, 8.

58. Ibid.

59. Taylor, *The Immerser*, 226.

60. Intriguingly, John the Baptist takes the roles of both the former and the latter prophets. He resembles the greatest former prophet, namely Elijah (his dress, location, and

cleanse sin, or sanctify a nation in contrast to the temple and the corrupt sacrificial system. He comes with the authority of Yahweh, pronouncing the prophetic verdict, summoning Israel to repent and giving a prophetic sign. In the OT, the rejection of God was followed by severe consequences. But Yahweh's visitations in judgment were preceded by the appearance of prophets. Matthew has done something similar with John and one could say that with the deeper identity of John as Isaiah's voice (Matt 3:3) and Malachi's Elijah (Matt 11:10, 14), Matthew has increased the intensity of the eschatological crisis. Thus, "John is primarily a prophet of the coming end."[61] By the time Matthew finishes his presentation of John the Baptist, he has left his readers no other alternative but to understand that he was a prophet, and more (i.e., Mal 3:1).

In those days, the days of eschatological fulfillment, the prophet arrived, preaching in the wilderness. We now turn to the place of John's preaching and the content of his preaching.

The Wilderness[62]

John's appearance in the wilderness is recorded in the Synoptics, the Gospel of John and Josephus. John's locale is not only geographically suitable for drawing large crowds (Matt 3:5), but also theologically important as ἔρημος connects with his next OT citation (Matt 3:3/Isa 40:3). In the ἔρημος the voice cries out. This is probably one reason why Matthew introduces John the Baptist as a preacher first.

The wilderness was important to Israel's past, a past that Matthew carefully traces out in the first four chapters of his gospel. By OT citations, echoes, and allusions, he highlights that the OT events, people, and places are being recapitulated. We will first look at the role that the wilderness played in the life of Israel. After considering the importance of the wilderness motif, we will then turn to Matthew and the theological purposes the wilderness motif serves in his narrative.

The LXX used ἔρημος to translate a variety of Hebrew words: מדבר (Gen 14:6; Exod 16:1; Num 13:26/LXX= 13:27; Josh 16:1; 1 Sam 25:1; 1 Kgs 19:4; Ps 29:8/ LXX= 28:8; 106:14/LXX= 105:14; Isa 40:3; 41:18–19; Jer 2:31; Ezek 23:42; Hos 9:10), ישׁמ (Ps 68:7/LXX= 67:8; 107:4/LXX= 106:4), נגב (Gen 12:9; 13:1,3;), חרב (Ezra 9:9; Neh 2:17). A great majority of the uses of מדבר (and also נגב) have to do with a physical location, while the remaining words broadly convey notions such as desolation or ruin. The vast majority of LXX translations render מדבר as ἔρημος.

---

designation "Elijah who is to come"), and yet he does not perform any miraculous works, but instead performs a sign-act similar to the latter prophets: Isaiah, Jeremiah, and Ezekiel.

61. Kloppenborg, *The Formation of Q*, 105.

62. For a book-length treatment of the wilderness theme covering the OT more broadly and to a lesser degree the NT, see Robert B. Leal, *Wilderness in the Bible: Toward a Theology of Wilderness*, SBL 72 (New York: Peter Lang, 2004).

As Funk observed half a century ago, "ἔρημος and midbär are virtually tied to each other."[63]

In the OT, the wilderness is both literal and metaphorical. The wilderness was thought of as a place of escape (Jer 9:2) and refuge for Israel (Exod 5:1; Deut 2:7), David (1 Sam 23:15ff.; 24:1ff.) and the prophet Elijah (1 Kgs 17;1-7). It could also be used as an evocative symbol with layers of meaning.[64] The later wilderness symbolism was built upon the Deuteronomistic history. The pattern of Israel's founding event of the exodus, the faithfulness of God, the unbelief and judgment of the nation, followed by the wilderness wanderings and provisions for a new start in the Promised Land are the foundational-themes that the prophets lay hold of when building their theologies of deliverance from exile. As Mauser put it, "The constitutive elements of Israel's faith and life are rooted in the wilderness tradition."[65]

As a symbol, the wilderness could convey either positive or negative information about the relationship between God and his people. In the wilderness God revealed himself to Moses (Exod 3; 33:19; 34:6-7). After rescuing his people from slavery and drowning Pharaoh in the sea, Yahweh brought Israel into the wilderness. "The wilderness," writes Mauser, "is the place that threatens the very existence of Yahweh's chosen people, but it is also the stage which brightly illumines God's power and readiness to dispel the threat."[66] In the wilderness and under God's care, Israel had nothing and lacked nothing.[67] "He found him in a desert land, and in the howling waste of the wilderness; he encircled him, he cared for him, he kept him as the apple of his eye" (Deut 32:10). The wilderness that conveys reminders of God's favor and mercy is likewise the place of Israel's disobedience and unbelief. And so the divine lament, "The house of Israel rebelled against me in the wilderness" (Ezek 20:13).

God delivered Israel from slavery in Egypt, but not long thereafter, Israel, exasperated with God's will for the nation, spoke of returning to bondage in Egypt (Num 14:4). Standing on the outskirts of the land, they refused to go in (Num 14; Deut 1:19-25). Even the Lord's provisions of manna and water in the wilderness were the occasions for Israel's complaints against God (Num 11:6). Israel swore the oath, "All that the Lord has spoken we will do" (Exod19:8; 24:3), but while Moses was atop the mountain, Israel was below worshiping an image (Exod 32). The wilderness was a place of God's faithfulness and Israel's failure.

---

63. Robert W. Funk, "The Wilderness," *JBL* 78 (1959): 206.

64. Brian C. Jones, "Wilderness," NIDB, 5.849.

65. Ulrich Mauser, *Christ in the Wilderness: The Wilderness Theme in the Second Gospel and Its Basis in the Biblical Tradition* (London: SCM, 1963), 29.

66. Mauser, *Christ in the Wilderness*, 21.

67. Walter Brueggemann, *The Land: Place as Gift, Promise, and Challenge in Biblical Faith* (Minneapolis: Fortress, 2002), 27 cited in Bruce K. Waltke and Charles Yu, *An Old Testament Theology: An Exegetical, Canonical, and Thematic Approach* (Grand Rapids: Zondervan, 2007), 539.

Because the wilderness was not always the literal place "from which and to which Israel was headed," the prophets could juxtapose God's fidelity and Israel's infidelity with this symbol.[68] The wilderness "was a powerful tool for the prophetic poet, whether the goal of the oracular pronouncement was woe or weal."[69] The reminder of the wilderness was not infrequently embedded in the prophetic warnings: unless Israel repents and returns to Yahweh, Yahweh will turn them and their land into a wilderness (Isa 1:7; 6:11; 27:10; 54:3; 64:10; Jer 4:7, 26; 9:10–11; 22:6; 33:10/LXX 40:10; 34:22/LXX 41:22; Ezek 6:6; 12:19–20; 19:10–14; Hos 2:3; 13: 5–6, 15–16; Joel 2:3; Zech 7:14). The God who once brought Israel through the wilderness (Jer 2:6; Amos 2:10) would once again settle accounts with his people *in the wilderness*: "And I will bring you into the wilderness (τὴν ἔρημον) of the peoples, and there I will enter into judgment with you face to face" (Ezek 20:35).[70] Exile and wilderness can be viewed as roughly synonymous in the prophetic condemnation of Israel.

Yet even as the wilderness theme helped to forge a link between the failures of the prophets' contemporaries and the nation that left Egypt under Moses, so also the faithfulness of God would be demonstrated once more in the wilderness. God promised that though the land and people would fall under judgment and become a wilderness, new life paradoxically begins ἐν τῇ ἐρήμῳ. As Moses led captive Israel out of Egypt, God would return for his people and lead them out of their wilderness exile once more (Isa 40:3).

Isaiah especially sees a new start for Israel in the wilderness. When the divine king comes there will be streams in the dry land (Isa 32:1–2). The once-forsaken palace and deserted city will be transformed when the Spirit is poured out and the wilderness becomes a fruitful field (Isa 32:15; 35:1,8–10; 40:3–5; 41:18-19; 42:11; 43:19–20; 51:3; 55:12–13; 63:10–14). The return of Yahweh and his glory comes into Israel's exiled existence and transforms it. The one who made his heritage a ruin (Isa 25:3) will take away the reproach of his people (Isa 25:8; 29:22; 62:1-4) and the ransomed will return from their wilderness exile (Isa 35:10). Similar themes of return and a secured restoration can be found in Jeremiah (Jer 33:10-12/LXX40:10-12), Ezekiel (Ezek 34:25–28; 36:8–11; 38:8, 11–12), and Hosea (Hos 14:4–7).

In sum, the prophets utilized this tradition of Israel's founding event to convict the nation of its apostasy and rejection of Yahweh (even as their forefathers had done after leaving Egypt). It was also a convenient symbol that graphically portrayed what Israel would become if the people persisted in rebellion against God. The populated land would be depopulated, the cities ruined, and Israel would be reduced to a wilderness, desolate, and uninhabitable. Likewise, the preparation of the way and return of Yahweh in the wilderness signaled their restoration.

---

68. C. L. Eggleston, "Wilderness, Desert," *DOTP*, 4:845.

69. Ibid., 843.

70. O. Böcher, "Wilderness," *NIDNTTE*, 3.1006.

Wilderness in Matthew

Matthew's reference to the wilderness as the place of John's activities, along with his citation of Isa 40:3 to describe John, is consistent with these OT themes. It is also consistent with the eschatological points of interest that lead up to the arrival of John ἐν τῇ ἐρήμῳ. The wilderness is a place of foreboding and judgment, but it is likewise a place for return and renewal. John the Baptist is sent to the place with those two symbolic associations to announce the coming of those dual realities.

His function ἐν τῇ ἐρήμῳ was to call Israel out of their cities. But Matthew, unlike the other gospel writers, adds more geographical information. John came preaching ἐν τῇ ἐρήμῳ τῆς Ἰουδαίας. Matthew's "of Judea" serves the narratival purpose of providing a link back to Matt 2:1, 5, 22.[71] Judea was a place of danger, but "John's preaching in the wilderness of Judea offers a different sort of danger.... John proclaims the imminent reign or empire of God (βασιλεία, 3:2) in Judea. The cognate terms sharply juxtapose two reigns present in Judea. Conflict seems inevitable."[72]

Called by the prophetic voice, "Jerusalem and all Judea and all the region about the Jordan" (3:5) make their way into the wilderness to consider the words and sign of the last OT prophet (11:10–13). In the future, another sign would be given to Israel: τὸ βδέλυγμα τῆς ἐρημώσεως τὸ ῥηθὲν διὰ Δανιὴλ τοῦ προφήτου (24:15). On that day it will no longer be an option to leave. When that sign of "desolation" arrives (24:15 ἐρημώσεως; 3:5 "ἐρήμῳ"), τότε οἱ ἐν τῇ Ἰουδαίᾳ φευγέτωσαν εἰς τὰ ὄρη (24:16).

Wilderness in the Rest of Matthew As we have said, the wilderness is both a fitting place and theme for the exposition of Israel's failures (Ps 95:9–11) and hopes (Isa 31:2; 41:18–20; 51:3; Hos 2:14). Matthew's use of various OT typological lenses for the purposes of describing the events of Jesus's birth and infancy prepares readers for the theological significance of John's location. It is not difficult to see how the wilderness would play an important role in the ongoing story of Israel, now recapitulated through the activities of John (3:1–12) and in the life of Jesus (4:1–11). For one who is steeped in the OT tradition of the Law and the prophets, Israel's exodus and wilderness journey to Canaan (as well as the prophetic witness to a new exodus) would be revisited and retold. John's preaching in the wilderness conforms to the OT expectations of a new start for Israel as well as a warning. Matthew describes John as the anticipated wilderness voice, but it is a voice announcing the arrival of God's kingdom and king and therefore the need to repent (3:2, 11–12; 11:7, 10).

Following his baptism, Jesus is sent into the wilderness (4:1). Jesus undergoes an exodus out of Israel/spiritual Egypt: he crosses the waters of the Jordan in baptism and is led into the wilderness alone. None go with him because his test exclusively focuses upon his fidelity to God (3:17) as the true son of Abraham, David and

---

71. As does παρεγένοντο, found also in Matthew 2:1.

72. Carter, *Matthew and the Margins*, 92–93.

Israel (1:1–17). Matthew's readers, familiar with the story of Israel's first exodus, might be tempted to wonder where the people of Israel are in this time of testing of God's son. While they do enter the wilderness being warned by the preaching and baptism of John, there is still the lingering question as to whether or not they will experience God's care and provision as the first Israelites did upon their departure.

Matthew may have accented his gospel with this OT exodus theme of the feeding of God's people in the wilderness in ch. 14.[73] The feeding is preceded by John's beheading. This news causes Jesus to withdraw εἰς ἔρημον τόπον (14:13). Associations between the feeding story and the first exodus are more thematic than verbal in correspondence. The wilderness has consistently been called ὁ ἔρημος.[74] Matthew, following Mark, retains τόπος. A deserted place is not necessarily "the wilderness," but the feeding of Israel in the wilderness during the time of Moses "might" be alluded to. Jesus is in a wilderness place, feeding a large group of people, and the focus narrows from bread and fish (14:16) to bread (14:19).[75]

The OT paradigmatic wilderness feeding is the story of the exodus. God provided manna, the bread of heaven, for his people during their sojourn in the wilderness. That Matthew and the gospels provide a second bread feeding might also be a further reminder that God provided bread for Israel over an "extended period."[76] Matthew also mentions men, women, and children in the feeding narratives (14:21; 15:38), which might also reflect the provisions for Israel in the wilderness. If so, he is showing again that Jesus supersedes his OT counterpart in that Jesus, like God, provides enough bread for his people's needs. By such a connective referentiality, Matthew elevates the power of Jesus even over the greatest of OT prophets. "This miracle recalls God's miraculous, abundant provision of manna, 'bread,' ἄρτος in the LXX, in the wilderness (cf. Exod 16:13–35; Num 11:7–9, 31–32). The eschatological connotation of the manna miracle is evident in 2 Apoc. Bar. 29:8 (cf. Rev 2:17)."[77] Matthew portrays Jesus as the prophet greater than Moses (Deut 18:15–19).

The final two wilderness references are in chs. 23 and 24. In traditional prophetic idiom, Jesus announces the judgment upon Israel. In a short and terse summation, Israel's house will be left to them as ἔρημος (23:38). It is prophetic adjudication: θῶ σε εἰς ἔρημον (Jer 22:6), θήσομαί σε εἰς ἔρημον (Ezek 5:14), and the pairing of

---

73. Allison, *The New Moses*, 238–42.

74. Nolland, *Matthew*, 589.

75. The feeding of the five thousand is also a preview of the Lord's Supper. During the institution of the sacrament, ὁ Ἰησοῦς ἄρτον καὶ εὐλογήσας ἔκλασεν καὶ δοὺς τοῖς μαθηταῖς εἶπεν· λάβετε (26:26). Before feeding the crowds, εὐλόγησεν καὶ κλάσας ἔδωκεν τοῖς μαθηταῖς τοὺς ἄρτους (14:19). Read retrospectively, the verbal parallels are striking. Further, the Lord's Supper takes place during Passover (26:17–19), a commemoration of Israel's deliverance and start of their journey to Canaan through the wilderness.

76. Cf. France, *Matthew*, 559.

77. Donald A. Hagner, *Matthew 14-28*, WBC 33B (Nashville: Thomas Nelson, 1995), 418–19.

οἶκος and ἔρημος was a combination drawn from the OT (Isa 64:10–11; Jer 12:7; 22:5; Ezek 8:6; 11:22–25; 12:7; Hag 1:9).[78]

Finally, in the Olivet Discourse, Jesus warns his disciples that in the future the wilderness will only be the place of messianic pretenders (Matt 24:23–25). The return of Christ will not be in a remote place that would require travel for verification. He will appear as the lightening that flashes in the sky for all to see (Matt 24:26).

Summary

The wilderness theme in Matthew conforms to the OT wilderness symbolism of the prophets as a place connoting judgment, mercy, and the eschatological coming of God. In the wilderness John warns that the Lord's coming will be one of swift recompense. Fleeing to the wilderness will not shield the impenitent (3:7). The days of escape will end and Israel's house will become ἔρημος (Isa 23:38; Jer 4:23–26; 9:9–10; Ezek 14:10–14). But Matthew also shows his readers that Israel's past faithlessness in the wilderness has been answered by the obedience of Jesus to his father's will (3:15; 4:1–11). Both his willingness to go out to the wilderness and undergo baptism as well as his victory over the temptations of the devil are indicators that Jesus will be able to "save his people from their sins" (1:21). Those who follow him discover that he is more than able to provide what is needed for their bodies too (14:20). But for those (like the Pharisees and Sadduccees) who remain opposed to the kingdom of God and his son, there is no uncertainty as to what will befall them. The land of "milk and honey" will once more become ἔρημος.

Conclusion

When John arrives on the scene, he is a national figure sent to address the nation. A mere transition of time from the infant Jesus to the adult John (and Jesus) is unlikely, prima facie, to be Matthew's only communicative intention. His judicious use of prophetic citations in chs. 2–3, followed by the arrival of a prophet ἐν δὲ ταῖς ἡμέραις ἐκείναις and ἐν τῇ ἐρήμῳ, is hardly a colorless aside of elapsed time. On the contrary, it is an introduction that quickly begins to develop a growing sense of urgency and uncertainty for Israel.

Will national Israel's future be positive or negative? Will "those days" include the day of reckoning for sins committed, or the day of restoration after sins' payment? The one who is the Isaianic voice crying out in the wilderness (3:3), with the mantle of a prophet (3:4), speaks of Israel's future and gives a prophetic sign which leaves no doubt as to the urgency of the message and therefore the urgency of the hour. As readers come to find out, John, as the voice in the wilderness, is the last of the OT prophets (11:13), the Elijah to come (11:14). "Those days" shed

---

78. Davies and Allison, *Matthew*, 1.321.

light on this last OT prophet and his words and actions clarify the time in which national Israel finds itself.

If ἡμέραις ἐκείναις were not the start of the eschatological finale predicted by the prophets, then John would not have arrived, for he serves precisely this purpose in Matthew's Gospel. In Malachi it was promised that *the day* of God's visitation would come (Mal 4:1), but before the final day arrives, before that "great and awesome day of the Lord comes" (Mal 4:5), the prophet Elijah will make his appearance (Mal 4:5). Because John is the "Elijah to come" (Matt 11:14) God's kingdom would soon arrive.

With Matthew's penchant for typology, eschatology and fulfillment, there is no better place for the onset of the promised OT event and person than in the wilderness. But is the wilderness the symbolic location of Israel's new exodus? Will streams flow in the wilderness causing the blossoming and budding of vegetation, bringing new life to the world and especially to Israel? Or is the wilderness a symbolic reinforcement of Israel's approaching judgment and exile? On the one hand, Matthew cites Isa 40:3, a return from exile text. On the other hand, his message is less than the good tidings that go before a glorious future. Israel's sins were being called to account. The nation must leave Jerusalem and Judea and enter into the wilderness where the way of life is made known. Paradoxically, the repentant in the wilderness will be pardoned, but Jerusalem and Judea will be made a wilderness, void of human inhabitation.

Taken collectively and within this OT frame of reference, the rejection of Jesus in ch.2 and the three themes of time, person, and location in ch. 3 establish a reason for the final ultimatum delivered by prophetic word and sign. Individually considered, there are few eschatological implications to draw out of these themes. But when viewed collectively within the typological motifs Matthew has woven together, those days, a prophet, and the wilderness invite readers to anticipate that Israel is at the threshold of God's mercy and restoration, or wrath and judgment.

Chapter 9

THE PREACHING OF JUDGMENT

Introduction

In the previous chapter we considered Matthew's identification of John as a prophet. With his arrival, the days of eschatological expectancy ("those days") have been ushered forward. Moreover, John's location ("the wilderness") was the expected place of God's intervention, either for or against Israel (3:1). Building on Matthew's introductory verse, we will now consider John's prophetic summons to Israel. Matthew's account of the words and activity of John bear similarities to the OT prophets, which Matthew so regularly quotes and to which he alludes. We will proceed by examining the major themes and imagery drawn from John's preaching along with their correlation(s) to the OT prophets. Once we have analyzed the preaching of John, we will explore the meaning of his baptism in the chapter that follows. Our proposal is that Matthew's account of John's preaching and baptism is best understood against the backdrop of the preaching and sign-acts of the OT prophets.

This method of inquiry is justifiable for at least two reasons. First, in Matthew "prophet(s)" are (almost) exclusively tied to the OT. Second, Matthew contains repeated statements and affirmations about John's prophetic status. It would follow that Matthew expects readers to understand John's prophetic word, and baptismal sign, in light of the prophets who preceded him. Such a reading, we will suggest, solves the puzzling questions surrounding the nature and meaning of John's baptism. The interpretation offered here also provides greater clarity to the relationship between John's baptism and the baptism in the Holy Spirit and fire (Matt 3:11).

John's ministry, as it has come to us through the sources (Q, Mark, John, Josephus), was more multifaceted than what is being presented here. Nevertheless, what we are suggesting is that the quest for the historical John has, to a great degree, influenced the way in which John's preaching and especially his baptism are interpreted in Matthew. Matthew's exposition of John the Baptist has little to do with purification rituals, water rites of initiation, prefiguring of a gracious bestowal of the Spirit, or Christian baptism. His preoccupation is with the story of Israel and its fulfillment in Jesus. Matthew goes to great lengths in chs. 1–2 to show (e.g., the formula quotations, 1:22; 2:15; 2:17) that Israel's past is being recapitulated again, not only in the coming of Jesus as the true son of David who is the promised victor over his enemies and deliverer of his people, but also in the coming of the prophet John, who is sent to announce the imminent arrival of the king. Like the prophets Isaiah, Jeremiah, and Ezekiel, John does so by word and by sign.

The Prophetic Word

The opening words of John will be repeated in their entirety as Jesus begins his ministry, [καὶ] λέγων· μετανοεῖτε· ἤγγικεν γὰρ ἡ βασιλεία τῶν οὐρανῶν (Matt 3:2). Though in the wilderness, John's command is not specifically for individuals, but is national in scope (Matt 3:5–6). His first word, μετανοεῖτε, is in the form of an imperative and recalls the message of the prophets.[1] In the LXX, μετάνοια occurs seven times and eighteen times in its verbal cognate.[2] In the latter, it sometimes describes God's repenting/relenting (1 Sam 15:29; Jer 4:28; 18:8,10; Amos 7:3,6; Joel 2:13–14; Jonah 3:9–10; 4:2; Zech 8:14), while the remainder have to do with human responses (Prov 20:19 [20:25]; 20:24, 47; [30:1, 32]; Isa 46:8, 13; Jer 8:6; 38:19 [31:19]). The range of meaning can entail a change of mind, feelings of remorse and return to Yahweh (Wis 11:23; 12:10, 19; Sir 17:24; 44:16; Jub. 1:13; Pr. Man 7, 13; Sib. 1:128; Apocr. Ezek. 3:2).[3]

The Language of the Old Testament Prophets

For the OT prophets, repentance was a category of fundamental importance that contained a variety of prescribed words, acts, and feelings. In the case of Isaiah, Yahweh chided Israel for celebrating rather than repenting with weeping, mourning, and sackcloth (Isa 22:12–14). Joel identifies the desired response to the day of the Lord as a return to Yahweh with the whole heart, with fasting weeping and mourning (Joel 2:12–14). In the end, whether God gave Israel plenty or

---

1. Francis W. Beare, *The Gospel According to Matthew: Translation, Introduction and Commentary* (San Francisco: Harper & Row, 1981), 88; Bruner, *The Christbook: Matthew 1-12*, 86; Douglas R. Hare, *Matthew*, IBC (Louisville: Westminster John Knox, 1993), 18; D. A. Carson, *Matthew*, EBC 1 (Grand Rapids: Zondervan, 1995), 99; Keener, *A Commentary*, 120; Hagner, *Matthew 1-13*, 47. Michael Wilkins, *Matthew*, NIVAC (Grand Rapids: Zondervan, 2003), 131; France, *The Gospel According to Matthew*, 101.

2. Proverbs 14:15; Wis 11:13; 12:10, 19; Sir 44:16; Ode 8:8 (2x). Most frequently (fourteen of the eighteen occurrences) μετανοέω stands for נחם. "μετανοέω," *NIDNTTE*, Accordance Bible Software 11.1.6.

3. "μετανοέω, μετάνοια," *TDNT*, 991–92.

withheld rain, destroyed crops, sent pestilence (after the manner of Egypt), overthrowing some of their cities (in similar fashion to Sodom and Gomorrah), Amos's fivefold refrain is cast in the language of repentance: "yet you did not return to me" (Amos 4:6–13; cf. Jer 15:6). Despite the dispatch of prophets sent at God's command (Jer 25:4; 42:15 [35:15]; 51:3–4 [44:4–5]; Zech 1:6; 7:7,12), Israel remained largely unrepentant. They would not turn from their wickedness (Jer 5:3; 8:611:10; 18:7–8; 25:4–5; 33:2–3 [26:2–3]; 41:15–16 [34:15–16]; 42:15 [35:15]; 43:7 [36:7]; 51:3–4 [44:4–5]; 44:10–11; Ezek 13:22; 14:6, 8–11; 18:23–31; 33:9–11) and return to God (Isa 30:15; 31:1, 6; 45:19–22; 55:7; Jer 3:7–12; 4:1, 4; 8:4–5; 9:5; 12:17; 15:19; 24:7; 38:17–19; Hos 3:4–5; 5:4, 15; 6:1; 7:10; 11:5; 12:6; 14:2–4, 8; Joel 2:12–13; Amos 4:6–11; Hag 2:17; Zech 1:3–4; Mal 3:7).

According to Behm, "Of the basic structure of prophetic repentance as proclaimed from Hos. to Jer., it may be maintained that the chief concern is a turning to Yahweh with all one's being"[4] and as would be expected, a number of words can be used to describe such a call to repentance.

> Some have thought that whereas ἐπιστρέφω focuses on the concrete, physical motion implied by the OT use of שׁוב (e.g., going to the temple in Jerusalem, returning to the Holy Land), μετανοέω directs attention to the thought or the will. It would be a mistake, however, to think that this lexical aspect intellectualizes the concept. The term has in view the conversion of the whole person.[5]

Even though μετανοέω is the most common translation of נחם, and ἐπιστρέφω and ἀπιστρέφω of שׁוב, they collectively belong to the broader category of repent/repentance. With regard to their Hebrew counterparts, נחם and שׁוב, "though they have different meanings, both denote movement away from a position previously adopted."[6] A number of scholars have concurred that in addition to a change of mind

---

4. "μετανοέω, μετάνοια," *TDNT*, 4.985.

5. "μετανοέω," *NIDNTTE*, Accordance Bible Software 11.1.6. In Joel 2:14 there is a close association of meaning between ἐπιστρέφω and μετανοέω as both are used to describe a multifaceted response on the part of Yahweh, "τίς οἶδεν εἰ ἐπιστρέψει καὶ μετανοήσει . . ."

6. "μετανοέω, μετάνοια," *TDNT*, 4.989. The Greek manuscript evidence of the OT shows a shift in translating שׁוב:

> In the extant fragments of later Gk. transl. of the OT there are clear traces of a complete equation of μετανοέω and שׁוב. In 6 cases where שׁוב means "to convert" in the religious sense Σ transl. it by μετανοέω, Is. 31:6; 55:7; Jer 18:18; Ez. 33:12; Hos 11:5; Job 36:10. The linguistic material leads to the conclusion that for the Jewish Hellenistic world of the 2nd cent. A.D. μετανοέω was a common and even preferred equivalent of ἐπιστρέφομαι = שׁוב, "to turn," "to convert." "μετανοέω, μετάνοια," *TDNT*, 4.990.

and/or remorse, μετανοέω conveys the idea of turning from sin to God.[7] The evidence derived from the OT prophets supports such a meaning.

OT Prophetic Language—The Backdrop of John's Summons As John the Baptist called upon Israel to repent, the following preexilic and postexilic OT prescriptions would qualify as signs of repentance and would be a suitable background against which Matthew's account of the Baptist's proclamation could be properly understood.

Hosea details the severe judgment about to befall Israel. Because of their rebellion, Ephraim will be scorched by the רוח יהוה (Hos 13:15). Samaria's little ones will be dashed to pieces and the pregnant women will be ripped open (Hos 14:1). The divine plea follows: ἐπιστράφητε, Ἰσραήλ, πρὸς Κύριον τὸν θεόν σου (Hos 14:2). The specific content of their return consists in acknowledging their iniquity and offering to repay with the fruit (καρπός, cf. Matt 3:8) of lips (Hos 14:3). If Israel will trust in the Lord instead of the work of their hands, God will heal them and turn away his wrath (Hos 14:4). They will take root like the trees of Lebanon (Hos 14:6, LXX) and abound like grain (σῖτος, Hos 14:8 [14:7], cf. Matt 3:12).

In Jer 3:22 the Lord calls his faithless sons to return and be healed. Israel should respond with words of trust (Jer 3:22–23) and confession of their past and present shame and sin (Jer 3:24–25; cf. Matt 3:6). The removal of those things detestable to Yahweh is also required if there is to be a return (Jer 4:1–2).

Finally, the importance of the book of Joel for John's summons to repentance is not only to be found in the calls to repent/return (Joel 2:12, 13), but also in its heightened expectancy of the arrival of the day of the Lord (Joel 1:15) which John's preaching was likely modeled upon. Though John does not use the precise "day of the Lord" terminology, his summons and predictions of the arrival of the kingdom of heaven are the NT counterparts. "That the day of the Lord will be for Israel darkness and not light, judgment and not salvation, is a theme John took over from the OT."[8] But before the fire can consume (Joel 2:2) and Yahweh's army arrive (Joel 2:4–11), Israel is shown the way of escape, namely, by returning to God with the whole heart, with fasting and weeping and mourning as they seek his mercy (Joel 2:12–13). Those who will call upon the Lord in such a posture will be saved and escape God's wrath (Joel 2:32).

Matthew's choice of John's first word retrospectively reinforces the later connections made between John and the OT prophets (11:13–14). John speaks

---

7. Jürgen Becker, *Johannes der Täufer und Jesus von Nazareth*, BS 63 (Neukirchen-Vluyn: Neukirchener, 1972), 88; Hill, *Matthew*, 90; Beare, *The Gospel According to Matthew*, 88; Mounce, *Matthew*, 22; Keener, *A Commentary*, 120; Carson, *Matthew*, 99; Turner, *Matthew*, 106–07; Wilkins, *Matthew*, 131; Osborne, *Matthew*, 110; Reiser, *Jesus and Judgment*, 249–50.

8. Davies and Allison, *Matthew I-VII*, 306.

like a prophet, is dressed like a prophet, and is thought of as a prophet. By starting with the language of repentance, Matthew lays hold of what can only be an all-too-familiar theme for Israel. By taking up a word so characteristically descriptive of the OT prophetic message, the urgency and need in the shadow of the approaching future is laid bare. Israel must return to the Lord in a posture of repentance. By saying that repentance, as found in the gospels, is not "a change of mind," but rather a "turning" or "returning" to God, Keener creates an unnecessary bifurcation. A return to God, if it were to be acceptable to him, would necessarily require a "change of mind."[9]

According to Luz, "John is a prophet who is fundamentally different from his OT predecessors: he proclaims the nearness of the kingdom of heaven."[10] So also Behm: "But the summons is more categorical than it was on the lips of any prophet, for it stands under the urgency of the eschatological revelation of God."[11] One wonders how the eschatological warnings and summons of the OT prophets were somehow less categorical or urgent than John's (see especially Isa 2:10–21; 24:16–23; 26:20; Amos 5:18–20; Zeph 1:7–18). The prophets were sent ahead of Yahweh to warn Israel of his approach. That it was the great king himself who was coming to judge his wayward people is clear by the prophets' use of theophanic language in describing the divine ordeal (Joel 2:4–11; Mal 3:1–2; 4:1–3). John is not a different kind of prophet, he is, as Matthew would have his readers to understand, the last in a long line of prophets (Matt 11:13–14). But why does John the Baptist come with this announcement of Israel's need of repentance? Matthew gives two reasons that now must be explored.

Why Must Israel Repent? Why John bursts onto the narrative scene without any background information (such as is found in Luke), or any explanation as to the specific problems that have necessitated the new situation, have been puzzling to some. John does not explain why God is so angry with Israel.[12] Matthew's narrative does give at least two reasons why Israel must repent.

The Kingdom of Heaven The reason for Israel's summons to repentance is the arrival of the kingdom of heaven, μετανοεῖτε· ἤγγικεν γὰρ ἡ βασιλεία τῶν οὐρανῶν. The coordinating conjunction γάρ is explanatory, introducing the reason for the imperative.[13] The repetition of γάρ, repeated in v. 3 (οὗτος

---

9. Keener, *A Commentary*, 120.

10. Luz, *Matthew 1–7*, 135.

11. "μετανοέω, μετάνοια," *TDNT*, 4.1000.

12. Becker, *Jesus*, 41.

13. Daniel B. Wallace, *Greek Grammar beyond the Basics* (Grand Rapids: Zondervan, 1996), 673. Robertson calls this the illative (logically inferential) usage of the conjunction. A. T. Robertson, *A Grammar of the Greek New Testament in Light of Historical Research*, 3rd ed. (London: Hodder and Stoughton, 1919), 1191.

γάρ ἐστιν ὁ ῥηθεὶς διὰ Ἡσαΐου τοῦ προφήτου) might also be understood as introducing "various assertions of one and the same sentence confirmed one after the other."[14] Israel was being called to repent because the kingdom of heaven had drawn near, *and* because the Isaianic voice had now begun crying out in the wilderness.

The striking plural form of the genitive οὐρανῶν has long been a subject of scholarly interest. We will begin by taking a closer look at Pennington's analysis of this unique phrase since it is particularly important to the argument offered here. After the interpretive options have been discussed, we will consider the way in which ἡ βασιλεία τῶν οὐρανῶν functions in Matthew's Gospel and is to be understood in 3:2.

The most common explanation found in the literature is that τῶν οὐρανῶν is a Matthean circumlocution for the divine name. Matthew, it is thought, has substituted ἡ βασιλεία *τῶν οὐρανῶν* for the more common expression ἡ βασιλεία *τοῦ θεοῦ* (cf. Mark 1:15). While this might fit into a periphrastic practice of avoiding the divine name in various strands of Jewish literature, the problem with such a conclusion, at least as it relates to Matthew's Gospel, is that Matthew does use the more common ἡ βασιλεία τοῦ θεοῦ, four times (12:28; 19:24; 21:31, 43).[15] Positing a reluctance on the part of Matthew to use the divine name has yet to provide a compelling explanation for these four occasions where the divine name is found linked to the kingdom.

Matthew's unique expression has also been explored in relation to the alleged existence of multiple heavens in the OT (Deut 10:14; 1 Kgs 8:27; Neh 9:6; Ps 148:4;[16] 2 Chr 2:5 [MT]; 2 Chr 6:18; cf. 2 Cor 12:2) and other Jewish Apocalyptic writings.[17] In response to such possible influences, Pennington has offered the following critique:

> There is a marked difference between the use of heaven in the LXX (including the latest books) and the apocalyptic literature. In the LXX we have no heavenly journeys nor speculations about the levels of the heavens like we find in the later apocalyptic and rabbinic traditions. Any "levels" of heaven that may be discerned in the MT or LXX are quite vague and refer only to perceived differences of height in the created realm. This is a quite different sense of "levels of heaven" than the apocalyptic usage.[18]

---

14. "γάρ," *BDAG*, 189.

15. There is a text-critical question concerning Matt 6:33.

16. Psalm 148:4 contains the only plural (οἱ οὐρανοὶ τῶν οὐρανῶν) in the LXX.

17. Geerhard von Rad, "οὐρανός," *TDNT*, 5.503, cited in Jonathan Pennington, *Heaven and Earth in the Gospel of Matthew* (Grand Rapids: Baker, 2007), 102. Cf. 2 En. 11:1–6, 12:1–2, 13:1–2, 14:1–2, 15:1–3, 16:1–3, 17:1; 18:1–7; 19:1–3; 20:1–2, 21:3, 7–8; 22:1–10.

18. Pennington, *Heaven and Earth*, 102–03.

If Matthew was using his expression in such a fashion, it is surprising that there are no such hints of a "multilayered" heavenly realm in his gospel. Multiple heavens influencing Matthew's word choices can remain only a conjecture at best.

Perhaps the background influence upon Matthew's ἡ βασιλεία τῶν οὐρανῶν was not due to earlier apocalyptic traditions, but was the result of the lexical influence of the Hebrew grammar of the OT. Might the plural οὐρανοί be the result of the Hebrew duals (שמים, שמי השמים) influencing the LXX? Few would wish to deny that Matthew's Gospel bears marks of Semitic influence, but in this case one wonders why there are so few plurals in the LXX (41 plurals compared to 309 singular forms).[19] Matthew's reason may be found elsewhere.

The rhetorical function of "the heavens" in Matthew Building upon the observations of Betz[20] and Lohmeyer,[21] Pennington has advanced a comprehensive argument demonstrating that Matthew uses the plural form of the divine realm for literary, rhetorical, and polemic reasons.[22]

After surveying a number of Second Temple texts (Judith, 2 and 3 Maccabees, Psalms of Solomon, and Prayer of Manasseh), Pennington discovered no consistent pattern of singular and plural forms in these writings. "The only thing that can be said about these plurals is that they have one thing in common: they are all in words of praise and prayer addressed to God."[23] In Wisdom of Solomon and Testament of Abraham the findings are significantly different. Wisdom of Solomon shows no signs of multiple heavens, but does demonstrate a consistent pattern of the alternation of singular and plural forms of οὐρανός. There are six references in all and three of these are plural. In Wis 9:10, 16, and 18:15 the place of God's throne is described with the plural. In 13:2, 16:20, and 18:16 heaven is singular in form and refers to the sky.[24] Pennington observed a similar alternation between the singular (human realm) and plural (God's realm) in the Testament of Abraham[25] and wonders whether or not this is an example of a singular-plural distinction in the first century.[26] The implications for Matthew, and in particular the preaching of John the Baptist, extend far beyond a convenient way of specifying the world in distinction from heaven.

Matthew uses the plural forms of οὐρανός fifty-five times and the singular twenty-seven times. "In contrast with the singulars used in heaven and earth

19. Ibid., 102.

20. Hans D. Betz, *The Sermon on the Mount: A Commentary on the Sermon on the Mount, Including the Sermon on the Plain*, Hermenia (Minneapolis: Fortress, 1995).

21. Ernst Lohmeyer, *The Lord's Prayer*, trans. John Bowden (London: William Collins Sons & Co., 1965).

22. Pennington, *Heaven and Earth*, 339.

23. Ibid., 112.

24. Ibid., 113.

25. Ibid., 120–24.

26. Ibid., 123.

pairs and in reference to the visible world, the plural forms in Matthew refer to the invisible realm, usually explicitly God's realm or speaking of God indirectly through metonymy."[27] Out of those fifty-five instances thirty-two are found in Matthew's expression ἡ βασιλεία τῶν οὐρανῶν and unambiguously refer to God's kingdom or rule.[28]

Pennington further buttresses his argument by pointing out that the OT and other ancient Jewish writings have always understood heaven to be the place where God dwells, the place of his throne, such as in the opening chapters of the book of Job. Heaven is the place where the angels dwell and from where they are dispatched to do Yahweh's bidding. The same is the case for Matthew's theological understanding of heaven. "Heaven was the place of God's throne (Matt 5:34), the place of angels (18:10; 22:30; 24:36; 28:2) and the place from which God issued his help and judgment. ἡ βασιλεία τῶν οὐρανῶν always uses the plural form."[29] This spatial understanding on the part of Matthew was probably influenced by the book of Daniel.[30]

Is there a discernible purpose that extends beyond a distinction between the two realms? Pennington believes so. By using the plural ἡ βασιλεία τῶν οὐρανῶν, Matthew illustrates that this kingdom is not only distinct and separate from the kingdoms of the earth, but that it is in opposition to and stands over against them.[31] This antithetical purpose appears in Matt 8:11–12, "I tell you, many will come from east and west and recline at table with Abraham, Isaac, and Jacob in the kingdom of heaven (ἐν τῇ βασιλείᾳ τῶν οὐρανῶν), while the sons of the kingdom (οἱ δὲ υἱοὶ τῆς βασιλείας) will be thrown into the outer darkness. In that place there will be weeping and gnashing of teeth." In Matt 12:22–32 Satan's kingdom (12:26; βασιλεία αὐτοῦ) is assaulted by the kingdom that Jesus brings (12:28; ἡ βασιλεία τοῦ θεοῦ). In the Lord's Prayer (6:9–10) Christ's followers are commanded to pray for the coming of God's kingdom. After addressing God as Πάτερ ἡμῶν ὁ ἐν τοῖς οὐρανοῖς, what follows is the acknowledgment that the values of the kingdoms of this world are antithetical to the values of heaven: ἐλθέτω ἡ βασιλεία σου· γενηθήτω τὸ θέλημά σου, ὡς ἐν οὐρανῷ καὶ ἐπὶ γῆς. The secrets of the kingdom of heaven belong to the disciples, in contrast to those opposed to Jesus (13:11). The

27. Ibid., 140.

28. Ibid.

29. Ibid., 297.

30. Gundry, *Matthew*, 43. Pennington concurs,

> The Hebrew and Aramaic words for heaven appear quite frequently in Daniel (33x), especially in chapters 2–7 (28x) ... one of the recurrent uses of heaven is in the phrase "God of heaven" (2:18, 19, 37, 44) and the related God in heaven (2:28), Lord of heaven (4:23), and King of heaven (4:34) ... thirteen of the twenty-eight Aramaic references are joined in context with a reference to the earth, thus forming thematic pairs ...: Pennington, *Heaven and Earth*, 290.

31. Ibid., 313–14.

character and goals of the kingdom of heaven (as summarily comprehended in 5:3, 10, 19–20; 7:21; 18:1–4; 19:14, 23) are fundamentally different from the values and ideological outlook of the kingdoms of the world.

One of the final uses of ἡ βασιλεία τῶν οὐρανῶν is found in Matt 23:13 where Jesus excoriates the scribes and the Pharisees, pronouncing the prophetic "woe" upon them because "κλείετε τὴν βασιλείαν τῶν οὐρανῶν ἔμπροσθεν τῶν ἀνθρώπων· ὑμεῖς γὰρ οὐκ εἰσέρχεσθε οὐδὲ τοὺς εἰσερχομένους ἀφίετε εἰσελθεῖν." It is unmistakable that those who seek to shut the door of the kingdom of heaven in front of others are the enemies that the king will judge and cast away.

Like the emphasis of Dan 2–7, Matthew stresses that ἡ βασιλεία τῶν οὐρανῶν is not like the kingdoms of the earth. Shockingly, it does not belong to Israel either (Matt 8:11–12) because they are opposed to its values and ways. Pennington concludes, "The ultimate point of the important expression kingdom of heaven is that God's kingdom is very unlike earthly kingdoms, both in their Jewish and Roman manifestations, and will eschatologically replace them."[32]

With this understanding of Matthew's kingdom of heaven, it is little wonder that John the Baptist comes proclaiming the need for Israel's immediate repentance. God is coming to deal specifically with Israel's sin. His kingdom is set not only against the Roman Empire; John proclaims the kingdom of heaven is drawing near the nation of Israel. John's announcement is that of the prophets: God is drawing near for judgment and the judgment will be thorough, leaving neither root nor branch (Matt 3:10).

The Problem of Un-repentance Exasperated Outside of ch. 3 and the reduplication of John's message in 4:17, μετανοέω reoccurs two more times in Matthew's Gospel, both times to underscore the spiritual and moral failure of Israel.

In Matt 11:20–21 Jesus denounces the towns where his mighty acts were performed. The reason? They refused to repent. Like the prophets of the OT and John before him, Jesus's signs were rejected by the majority of the nation and the prophetic woe was the predictable consequence of such disbelief: "Woe to you, Chorazin! Woe to you, Bethsaida! For if the mighty works done in you had been done in Tyre and Sidon, they would have repented long ago in sackcloth and ashes" (Matt 11:21).

Tyre and Sidon were objects of prophetic woes (Isa 23; Ezek 20–23; 26–28; Jer 25:22; 47:4; Zech 9:2–4; Joel 3:4 [LXX 4:4]; Amos 1:9–10). The woe Jesus pronounces is worse still.[33] The day of judgment will be more bearable for Tyre and

---

32. Ibid., 342.

33. "Talk of the better position of Tyre and Sidon is not particularly to offer hope to Tyre and Sidon, but rather to identify the future situation of the inhabitants of Chorazin and Bethsaida as worse than that of cities identified in Scripture as ripe for judgment." Nolland, *Matthew*, 467.

Sidon than for the Jewish cities that refused to humble themselves in the presence of Jesus. The signs Jesus performed in those cities testified to the words that were spoken.[34] The disciples' message was nearly the same, the kingdom of heaven had approached (Matt 10:7). For those who resisted the urgency of the hour, "it will be more bearable on the day of judgment for the land of Sodom and Gomorrah than for that town" (Matt 10:15). The day of judgment provides a verbal link to the denunciation of Chorazin and Bethsaida in 11:20–21.

The second and final occurrence (outside the twin messages of John and Jesus) is Matt 12:41. "The men of Nineveh will rise up at the judgment with this generation and condemn it, for they repented at the preaching of Jonah, and behold, something greater than Jonah is here." The eschatological urgency is expanded. Whereas 11:20–21 contains a denunciation aimed against two cities in 12:41, the problem is the generation itself, μετὰ τῆς γενεᾶς ταύτης καὶ κατακρινοῦσιν αὐτήν. Nineveh repented at the preaching of Jonah, but the preaching of Jesus, Jonah's superior (ἰδοὺ πλεῖον Ἰωνᾶ ὧδε), produced no remorse or return to Yahweh or his son.[35]

Both Matt 11:20–21 and 12:41 have to do with signs and preaching to elicit repentance from Israel. The ties to John the Baptist, who also called for repentance in response to his enacted sign, completed what John had begun. The day of judgment, the arrival of the kingdom of heaven, meant a reckoning for Israel. What John as well as Jesus announced is nothing less than the universal judgment.[36]

We return to Becker's quandary that John nowhere explains why God is so angry. While the answer can be seen from John's invective directed at the Pharisees and Sadducees (Matt 3:8–12; they were not bearing the fruits of repentance), there is a Matthean reason provided.

The Reasons for John's First Words

Matthew has explained in chs. 1 and 2 why God is angry with Israel. At the announcement of Mary's pregnancy, Joseph thought to reject Jesus and put his mother away. But after the encounter with the angel, Joseph takes Mary as his wife and so embraces Jesus. In ch. 2 the question is put to the religious leaders via Herod: will they accept and submit to this newborn king's rule or reject him? Functionally speaking, they reject him not only by their words, but also by their inactivity to go and honor him as king. What is more, they tell Herod where Jesus can be found, which amounts to betraying him to those who would put him to death (Matt 2:4–5, 16–18). It is not only a rejection of Jesus by Herod and the

---

34. "In the logic of Matthew's narrative, these were the cities where Jesus had preached (11:1) after his disciples prepared the way (10:15, 23), carrying on his original mission of preaching the kingdom." Keener, *A Commentary*, 343.

35. Ulrich Luz, *Matthew 8-20*, Hermeneia, ed. Helmut Koester, trans. James E. Crouch (Minneapolis: Fortress, 2001), 218.

36. Davies and Allison, *Matthew VIII-XVIII*, 358.

religious leaders, the people's rejection of Jesus is already hinted at as they share in Herod's turmoil: ἀκούσας δὲ ὁ βασιλεὺς Ἡρῴδης ἐταράχθη καὶ πᾶσα Ἱεροσόλυμα μετ᾽ αὐτοῦ (Matt 2:3).[37]

As Matthew's narrative progresses, Israel is confronted by another announcement: the kingdom of heaven is at hand (3:2). Having implicitly rejected Jesus's kingship, the forerunner is sent into the wilderness of Judea with one final warning, "repent, for the kingdom of heaven is at hand."

Israel must repent because the king has been rejected, has left them as those who are spiritually speaking "Egypt" (Matt 2:15), and has returned only to live in obscurity in Nazareth. Then, at the time of his revealing, John was sent to announce that the time to repent was late, the kingdom was coming and the sign of the impact of this kingdom was dramatized in the baptismal waters.[38]

John's Rebuke (Matt 3:7–12)

The positive impact John had upon the Israelites is quickly discarded for his confrontation with the Pharisees and Sadducees. While five words encapsulate John's address to the multitudes, Matthew devotes 120 for the religious authorities.[39]

---

37. Gundry, *Matthew*, 28; Nolland, *Matthew*, 112. France in particular sees this as an ideological move on Matthew's part.

> Throughout his gospel Jerusalem will be portrayed as the place of opposition and rejection for the true Messiah . . . so that it is appropriate that, just as "all the city" will be "stirred up" by Jesus' arrival as the royal son of David in 21:10 (long after Herod is off the scene), so "all Jerusalem" is already perturbed at the prospect of a dynastic revolution. It will be there in Jerusalem that eventually "all the people" will accept responsibility for the death of their Messiah (27:24–25). France, *Matthew*, 70.

Carson, Morris, and Osborne think that the fear on the part of Jerusalem was over the reprisal of the paranoid king. Carson, *Matthew*, 286; Morris, *The Gospel According to Matthew*, 37; Osborne, *Matthew*, 88. Davies and Allison, Horsley, and Blomberg think that "all Jerusalem" primarily refers to the religious leaders who had a hand in the economic control of the city because their positions of authority were given to them by Herod. Davies and Allison, *Matthew*, 1.238–39; Richard A. Horsley, *The Liberation of Christmas: The Infancy Narratives in Social Context* (New York: Continuum, 1989), 49–52; Blomberg, *Matthew*, 63. Nolland thinks that the juxtaposition of "with him" in v. 3 and "gathering" in v. 4 hardly encourages such an identification. Nolland, *Matthew*, 112 n. 119. The next reference to Jerusalem takes place in Matt 3:5 where the city and all Judea come out to be baptized by John. Both accounts have to do with the announcement of kingship and the contrasting responses some thirty years later.

38. On which see ch. 10.

39. The original audience of John's scathing rebuke is debated in the literature. Nolland finds the defense of the religious leaders to be weak. "If the baptism is not being sought, then there is nothing to link John's question to." Nolland, *Matthew*, 142. Producing fruit unto repentance would then be nothing more than a renewed call to repent. Turner believes

Ἰδὼν δὲ πολλοὺς τῶν Φαρισαίων καὶ Σαδδουκαίων ἐρχομένους ἐπὶ τὸ βάπτισμα αὐτοῦ εἶπεν αὐτοῖς· γεννήματα ἐχιδνῶν, τίς ὑπέδειξεν ὑμῖν φυγεῖν ἀπὸ τῆς μελλούσης ὀργῆς (Matt 3:7).

The Pharisees and the Sadducees are a subgroup of the larger literary category of Jewish (religious) leaders. While they are distinguishable historically and narratively by different titles, they are, nevertheless, not singled out for their different functions and duties, but collectively serve the unifying purpose of opposing Jesus.[40]

In Matthew, the opponents of Jesus most often come in groups of two.[41] The Pharisees, being the most prominent antagonists, are listed first. To suppose that many of the Pharisees and Sadducees believed John's preaching and made no objection to his baptism misses Matthew's point.[42] When Jesus asks the chief priests and the elders of the people about the origin of John's baptism their unbelief of its heavenly origin is underscored (Matt 21:25). Luz finds it surprising that they, and not the crowds, are singled out first.[43] However, the chief priests and the scribes of the people capitulated to the demand of Herod and took their side against the newborn king (Matt 2:4). Matthew has singled out the spiritual leaders of the palace and of the people.

> As the two main ideological groups in the Sanhedrin, both the Sadducees (the "politically" dominant group from whom the priestly and temple hierarchy were drawn) and the Pharisees (a self-conscious "party" grouping committed to rigorous observance of the law) represented key elements in the Jerusalem establishment, the mention of them together probably suggests a sort of

that it is rhetorical; it exposes their unbelief that the wrath was about to come. They refuse to flee and so by asking such a question, John is in effect denying any connection between himself and the religious leader's pilgrimage to the Jordan. Turner, *Matthew*, 113. Webb contends that John's address is better-suited because (1) they are opposed to John's baptism; (2) John's preaching is unduly harsh; he cites Luke 3:10–14 where the audience's questions are answered with no hostility. Note as well that John "with many other words preached the good news" (Luke 3:18); and (3) If the answer to the question, "Who warned you to flee?" is for the masses coming to be baptized, the answer is "John did" which makes for a perplexing reading of the narrative. Webb, *John the Baptizer and Prophet*, 175–78. It is difficult to know if we are dealing with stylistic choice when Matthew describes the crowds going to John *to be baptized* and religious leaders *coming to his baptism.*

40. Cf. Kingsbury, *Matthew: Structure, Christology, Kingdom*, 115–28; Sjef van Tilborg, *The Jewish Leaders in Matthew's Gospel* (Leiden: Brill, 1979), 1–7; Anderson, *Narrative Web*, 97–125 and the supplemented list from van Tilborg (ibid., 97–98).

41. Luz, *Matthew*, 1.137.

42. Ridderbos, *Matthew*, 51; Nolland, *Matthew*, 142; Hagner cautiously allows some may have been sincere: Hagner, *Matthew*, 1.49.

43. Luz, *Matthew*, 1.137.

"cross-party delegation" who had come out to examine this disturbing new religious phenomenon down by the Jordan.[44]

Matthew has but one perspective on the religious leaders running throughout his gospel. The general enthusiasm of the crowds is offset by the Pharisees and Sadducees, and the crowd's positive estimation of Jesus will be turned by their spiritual leaders (Matt 27:20) joining together in mockery at the foot of the cross (Matt 27:39–41). It is not out of character for Matthew to narrow his focus to the religious leaders. Their interests, be they in John or Jesus, are never described in a positive manner. They come to Jesus in pretended neutrality (Matt 12:14), wishing to have Jesus perform a sign (Matt 12:38); they question Jesus (Matt 15:1–9), and the Pharisees and the Sadducees test him by seeking another sign from him (Matt 16:1–4). Because of Jesus's popularity they question his authority (Matt 21:23–27) and are indignant when they perceive that his parable was spoken against them (Matt 21:45).[45] These groups plot to discredit Jesus with their questions about paying taxes (Matt 22:15–16), the resurrection (Matt 22:23–33), and the greatest commandment (Matt 22:34–40; "to test him"). The questions of entrapment end just before the woes are pronounced, sealing their fate (Matt 23).

In Matthew's Gospel there is never mention of anything like a promise of salvation for the religious leaders of Israel.[46] No beatitude exists for them.[47] Why? Because they are three things: serpents, barren trees, and chaff destined for the fire (3:7, 10, 12).

Religious Leaders, Vipers, and Satan The epitaph "generation of serpents" (Matt 3:7) heads the list, making clear that they are more than simply unproductive fruit trees or chaff of no agricultural value. They are γεννήματα ἐχιδνῶν, the offspring of poisonous snakes.[48]

A similar idea, although worded differently, is found in Isa 14. In an oracle against Philistia, the nation is warned not to rejoice over the broken rod (probably Assyria[49]). The imagery then moves from the serpent's root (v. 29; σπέρματος

44. France, *Matthew*, 110.

45. Note the overlapping of the religious leaders: Matt 21:23 = the Chief Priests' and *Elders'* question, the conclusion of which given in Matt 21:45 = the Chief Priests' and *Pharisees'* desire to arrest him.

46. Contrast with John 3, 12:42. Note also, how Matthew deletes Mark's comment that Joseph of Arimathea was εὐσχήμων βουλευτής (Mark 15:43; Matt 27:57).

47. "Schon gar nicht kommit ihm ein 'Heil euch Gerechten, den eure Rettung naht!' über die Lippen." Becker, *Jesus*, 43.

48. Goppelt, *Theologie*, 85.

49. John N. Oswalt, *The Book of Isaiah: Chapters 1–39*, NICOT (Grand Rapids: Eerdmans, 1986), 331–32; Wildberger, *Isaiah 1-12*, 95–97; John Goldingay, *Isaiah*, NIBC (Peabody: Hendrickson, 2001), 104. Older interpreters saw the broken staff as a reference to Ahaz (v. 28).

ὄφεως) to its offspring, the flying serpent (v. 29; ὄφεις πετόμενοι). Isaiah 59 appears closer as a parallel. Zion's sins have separated them from the Lord (vv. 1–2), their hands are covered in blood (v. 3), and they lie and practice deception (v. 4). They are like hatched adders and vipers (v. 5; ἀσπίδων), committing iniquity (v. 6), evil (v. 7), shedding of blood (v. 7), injustice (v. 9), multiplying transgression, sin, and iniquity (v. 12), having turned from following God (v. 13). The serpent is a metaphor for the people of Israel and their destructive deeds. Similar negative connotations are conveyed by ὄφις (Num 21:6–9; Deut 8:15; Pss 57:4; 139:3; Prov 23:32; Amos 5:19; Sir 21.2; but see Gen 49:17 for a quasi-positive use).

As it relates to the religious leaders in Matthew's Gospel, the point of the comparison is simply reinforced: like the serpent, these opponents of both John and Jesus harm and kill (Matt 12:34; 23:33). Though ἔχιδνα is plural, there might be warrant for searching out a deeper understanding of the religious leaders beyond the abstract category of "evil" to Satan himself.

In the case of the temptation (4:1–11), Jesus's encounter with Satan anticipates Jesus's encounters with the religious leaders (12:34; 13:38–39). As the Tempter, the fountainhead of all evil (4:3; 6:13), Satan puts Jesus to the test (4:1–10). As those who are also evil (3:7), the religious leaders will repeatedly put Jesus to the test. In debate with Satan, Jesus has the last word, so that Satan leaves the scene (4:10–11). In debate with the leaders, Jesus will again have the last word. They too, will leave the scene (22:46–23:1).[50]

The next place where the religious leaders are assailed with the epithet is Matt 12:34 where both brood of vipers and trees bearing good/bad fruit are again brought together. The context is Jesus's power to cast out a demon from a man who was blind and mute. The Pharisees charge him with casting out demons by Beelzebub, the prince of demons. That Satan is so implied is made plain: "καὶ εἰ ὁ σατανᾶς τὸν σατανᾶν ἐκβάλλει, ἐφ᾽ ἑαυτὸν ἐμερίσθη· πῶς οὖν σταθήσεται ἡ βασιλεία αὐτοῦ" (12:26). Jesus makes clear that those who are not with him (Pharisees) are against him. Logically, they belong to Satan, being members of "τὴν οἰκίαν αὐτοῦ" (Matt 12:29).

Jesus assures them that they will not be forgiven in this age or in the age to come (v. 32). They are then described as a γεννήματα ἐχιδνῶν (v. 34) who will have to give an account for their words on the day of judgment (vv. 36–37). Immediately following Jesus's denunciation, the Pharisees ask for a sign and are answered that they belong to the evil and adulterous generation (vv. 38–39). Such a generation is, itself, possessed (v. 45)—by way of the analogy of the man liberated from his demonic oppressor.

Like the testing of Jesus (Matt 4:1–11), his final prophetic woe upon the brood of vipers follows their testing of him (Matt 21:23–27; 22:15–18, 23–33, 34–40).[51] In Matthew only Satan (4:1,3) and the Jewish leaders "test" Jesus (πειράζω, 16:1;

---

50. Kingsbury, *Matthew as Story*, 117.
51. Anderson, *Narrative Web*, 103.

19:3; 22:18, 35).[52] Satan's first temptation was for Jesus to prove his sonship by performing a sign (stone into bread, 4:3). The Pharisees and Sadducees begin the series of temptations with the request that Jesus perform a sign (16:1). "Matthew creates a specific link with the coming to Jesus of the tempter in 4:3, thus suggesting an alignment."[53]

In Matt 23 we have the third and final place where γεννήματα ἐχιδνῶν is used. Their designation, as serpents, is described as hell itself (23:33), the future abode of Satan (25:41). Being unable to escape the eternal fires is the corollary to Matthew's "unquenchable fire" (3:12). The reason for such a sentence is because they, like their fathers, persecuted those sent to them (23:34). That Jesus's fate and those before and after him are laid at the feet of the religious leaders is indicated by the additions of flogging and crucifying.[54] Jesus's lament in v. 37 likely includes the culpability of Jerusalem as well.[55]

Fruit of Repentance John does not explain what he means when he calls upon the religious leaders to produce "fruits of repentance" (Matt 3:8), but the remaining two occurrences found in the warning sayings of Jesus offer a Matthean perspective. False prophets will be known by their fruit (Matt 7:15–19), and once more, the religious leaders of Israel are chided for their unbelief (Matt 12:33–37). In all three passages the opposite of "fruits of repentance" is the rejection of the message/messenger.[56] As it was with Israel of old, with the prophets Yahweh sent, so also did John and Jesus find the same lack of receptivity.

Appeal to Abraham John follows his fierce depiction and demand for repentance by censuring any appeals to Abraham as father: καὶ μὴ δόξητε λέγειν ἐν ἑαυτοῖς· πατέρα ἔχομεν τὸν Ἀβραάμ. λέγω γὰρ ὑμῖν ὅτι δύναται ὁ θεὸς ἐκ τῶν λίθων τούτων ἐγεῖραι τέκνα τῷ Ἀβραάμ (Matt 3:9). This is probably in keeping with their identity as offspring of serpents. In the genealogy, Jesus is the son of Abraham. After John denies the religious leaders the right of appeal, the next mention of Abraham serves to reinforce the link to the patriarch through Jesus. In response to the gentile centurion's faith, Jesus declares that the sons of the kingdom (8:12; note the adversative οἱ δὲ υἱοὶ τῆς βασιλείας) will be thrown out, while many come in from the east and west to recline at the eschatological banquet table with Abraham. The centurion's faith that Jesus could heal his servant is sandwiched between Jesus's power to heal

---

52. Kingsbury, *Matthew as Story*, 117; Anderson, *Narrative Web*, 116.

53. Nolland, *Matthew*, 647.

54. Ibid., 945; Carson, *Matthew*, 316.

55. France, *Matthew*, 878.

56. *Pace* Reiser who thinks that John's call was for a return to Torah. Reiser, *Jesus and Judgment*, 253. Reiser does see a fundamental difference between Jesus's usages and that of John's. "Jesus' idea of repentance was turning to him and his message: it is this message, then, that supplies the content of the repentance he demands" (ibid., 254).

(8:1–4, 14–17), the very point that the religious authorities refuse to believe (Matt 9:3–4, 34; 12:24). Abraham's last appearance in Matthew is used to correct the Sadducees' disbelief in the resurrection. They know neither the scriptures nor the power of God (Matt 22:29).

Trees and Chaff John's remaining metaphors for the religious leaders are those of trees and chaff. The Pharisees and Sadducees being cut off from the blessings belonging to Abraham are vividly portrayed by the tree and axe imagery: ἤδη δὲ ἡ ἀξίνη πρὸς τὴν ῥίζαν τῶν δένδρων κεῖται· πᾶν οὖν δένδρον μὴ ποιοῦν καρπὸν καλὸν ἐκκόπτεται καὶ εἰς πῦρ βάλλεται (Matt 3:10). The winnowing of v. 12 and the chopping of v. 10 are parallel actions carried out by the Coming One. His winnowing fork/shovel is ἐν τῇ χειρὶ αὐτοῦ (3:12), which indicates that the final action is about to be carried out, even as the axe is ἤδη laid at the root of the tree. That the axe is brought out for the root rather than the branches indicates its removal in entirety, the exposed root heightening the eschatological urgency of the prophetic hour: "Das Endgericht ist so nahe wie die Spanne zwischen dem Ansetzen der Axt auf der freigelegten Wurzel und dem fällenden Schlag. Johannes vertritt, wie im Grunde alle Prophetie, die naherwartung."[57]

Was John thinking of the entire nation of Israel, so commonly described in arboreal imagery (cf. Isa 60:21; 61:3; Jub. 1:16; 16:26; 1 En. 93:4, 10; Ps 14:3–5)? That John is referring to the nation and can speak of only the trees not bearing fruit as fit for the fire, and the threshing floor being cleansed by the removal and burning of the chaff, implies a discriminating work that is carried out within the nation of Israel. The end of the unfruitful trees may be represented under the symbol of the lone fig tree (representing the temple/Jerusalem) that is cursed (Matt 21:19). In this case, there is no question as to the eschatological scenario that awaited them.

The intensification of πῦρ in v. 10 with the addition of ἄσβεστος in v. 12 point toward the final judgment.[58] One might expect the wind to carry away the chaff (Job 21:18; Ps 1:4; 35:5; Isa 17:13; 29:5; 41:15–16; Dan 2:35; Hos 13:3; Zeph 2:2),[59] but the simile of fire destroying the chaff/wicked is a prevalent Matthean theme (Matt 5:22; 7:19; 13:40; 17:15; 18:8–9; 25:41).

The parable of the weeds (Matt 13:24–30, 36–43) shares common vocabulary with ch. 3: πῦρ, κατακαίω, ἀποθήκη, σῖτος. In both the parable and the winnowing it is a separation with two outcomes: the barn and the fire. Being burned with fire is the fate of the unrepentant (weeds), which the parable twice describes as taking place at the end of the age (13:39–40; ἐν τῇ συντελείᾳ τοῦ αἰῶνος). A further

---

57. Goppelt, *Theologie*, 85.

58. "Unauslöschliches Feuer (Jes. 34,10; 66, 24) paßt freilich nicht mehr in Bild; hier ist schon an das jüngste Gericht gedacht. Dieses Ineinandegreifen von Bild und gemeinter Sache ist typisch für die Apokalyptik, die an der bald kommenden Endzeit mit ihren kosmichen Katastrophen interessiert ist." Eduard Schweizer, *Das Evangelium nach Matthäus* (Göttingen: Vandenhoeck & Ruprecht, 1973), 27.

59. Davies and Allison, *Matthew* 1.319.

distinction is made by the personal pronoun τὴν ἅλωνα αὐτοῦ and τὸν σῖτον αὐτοῦ contrasted with the adversative τὸ δὲ ἄχυρον (3:12).

The winnowing came to be understood as the eschatological day of universal judgment[60] where the wicked are consumed like "straw in the fire" (Joel 3:13; 1 En. 48:9)[61] at the eschatological harvest, the day of the Lord.[62] It is doubtful that Israel would not have been able to infer John's meaning from the stock images pulled from the OT. Some texts point to God or Israel threshing their enemies (Isa 41:14–17; Mic 4:12–13; Hab 3:12; Jer 51:33), but in this case John is not announcing the winnowing of Israel's enemies, but rather the winnowing of Israel (Matt 3:7). But at whose hands?

According to Ernst, it is God who is best understood as the agent of judgment.[63] The winnowing work and the felling of the trees in the OT and Second Temple literature (Ecclus 6:4; 23:25; Wis 4:3–5; 4 Ezra 4:30) are applied to God. In the OT the day of the Lord is the arrival of Yahweh (Mal 3:2; Hab 2:3) and there are no indications that Israel ought to expect otherwise. But the emergence of a heavenly being in a time of judgment (such as narrated in Dan 7 and Isa 11) laid the foundation for later messianic expectations that would crop up in the literature of the Second Temple era and the NT.

John is announcing the coming of a messianic figure, but as Goppelt points out, he does not access the typical OT designations that one would expect, such as *the* Messiah, Son of David, or Son of Man.[64] Whether or not John was thinking of the coming of God, or of a messianic figure, Matthew brings Jesus forward as John's "Coming One." As the king who brings the heavenly kingdom, Jesus comes as the eschatological judge and rightful ruler of Israel. Matthew goes on to describe Jesus in language similar to John's "Coming One." Far more often the reference is to Jesus coming in judgment (Matt 16:27; 24:27, 30, 39, 42, 44, 46; 25:10, 31 = Jesus; 21:40 = God). It would be but a small step for Matthew to take, in attributing such a function to Jesus, especially in light of the messianic expectations of judgment in the literature preceding him.[65]

---

60. Reiser, *Jesus and Judgment*, 179–80; Kraeling, *John the Baptist*, 41.

61. Keener, *A Commentary*, 129.

62. "Das heißt im Klartext: Israels Geschichte ist zu Ende. Israel steht vor dem letzten Gericht." Becker, *Jesus*, 44; Reiser, *Jesus and Judgment*, 172.

63. Josef Ernst, *Johannes der Täufer: Interpretation, Geschichte, Wirkungsgeschichte* (Berlin: Walter de Gruyter, 1989), 49–51.

64. "Er redet weder vom Messias noch vom Davidssohn noch com Menschensohn": Goppelt, *Theologie*, 90.

65. 1 Enoch 69:27-29; 2QMelch. 2; 2 Bar. 72:4; 4 Ezra 12:31-34; Pss. Sol. 17:21-23 cited in Davies and Allison, *Matthew*, 1.319.

Conclusion

Matthew has done several things to build his case against Israel. He describes John the Baptist in terms of Elijah (Matt 3:4; 11:10, 14; 17:10–13). In his role as Elijah, John is sent to prepare Israel for the coming of the day of the Lord. His speech is infused with judgment motifs that detail the prospects awaiting the nation. The baptism in the Holy Spirit and fire, far from being a positive, gracious alternative to the otherwise destructive language John uses, is in fact the pinnacle of his preaching.

As in the tradition of Malachi, he comes (Mal 3:1–2) against a brood of vipers (temple officials = Mal 2:1–3; 3:3).[66] This burning day will consume its objects, setting them on fire and leaving behind neither root nor branch (Mal 3:19 LXX). This one will strike those who do not submit to his rule, and his wrath is already kindled. He, like the root of Jesse, will be Spirit-endowed (Isa 11:2), striking the earth with the rod of his mouth and slaying the ungodly with the breath of his lips (Isa 11:4: καὶ ἐν πνεύματι διὰ χειλέων ἀνελεῖ ἀσεβῆ), while also gathering his remnant to himself (11:10–16). As we will see, Matthew understands the implications of John's announcement of the approaching king and kingdom as judgment upon Israel[67] (Matt 24), although the timing was not what John expected. It is a judgment against the serpents and unproductive trees, which were but chaff. Only the repentant could be spared his wrath, while the unfruitful trees and chaff could only experience the Spirit's fire. Only those who embark upon a new exodus, not to Israel for a fresh start but out of Israel and to Jesus, could be delivered from the messianic judgment.

Using the familiar categories of serpents, chaff, and unproductive trees to condemn Israel, John speaks words of destruction. The coming wrath has as its purpose to cast them into the fire. Their removal elucidates the meaning of the baptism in the Holy Spirit and fire and vice versa. In Matthew, John's target was the religious leaders, but his summons to repent was national. His warning applies to those who would follow their leaders. Yet to do so would be their undoing. Only those who turn to God in repentance and, as Matthew will go on to state, only those who submit to Jesus will escape the judgment he brings. As John's words indicated, so his baptism displayed: the coming of the kingdom in judgment. Not only his words, but also his action, bore a resemblance to the OT prophets. John came to Israel performing a prophetic sign-act of God's ultimatum and it is to that sign we now must turn. Like the water submerging the baptized, God's wrath would come and the one who would bring it, John promised, would pour it out upon the nation in the Holy Spirit and fire.

---

66. Jeffry A. Trumbower, "The Role of Malachi in the Career of John the Baptist," in *The Gospels and the Scriptures of Israel*, JSNTS 104, eds. Craig A. Evans and W. Richard Stegner (London: Sheffield Academic Press, 1994), 28–41.

67. Cf. the similar evaluation of Luz, *Matthew*, 1.137. Cf. Str-B 4.1075–76.

Chapter 10

BAPTISM AS THE SIGN-ACT OF JUDGMENT

Introduction

Having examined the themes of John's preaching, we now turn to his baptism and explore the meaning Matthew narratively ascribes to it. The scholarly literature on the meaning of the baptism of John is multifarious and therefore requires a brief but representative survey of the major interpretations and potential backgrounds for John's rite. After listing the several interpretations and possible backgrounds of John's baptism, we will proceed to look at John's baptism through a prophetic sign-act lens. The ways in which others have understood the meaning of his sign-act will also be treated. We will then turn to a definition and evaluation of the prophetic sign-acts and apply our findings to the baptism of John. When we do, we will see that various scholarly treatments have in some cases anticipated parts of the position advocated here, namely that from the perspective of Matthew's Gospel, John's sign-act was not a symbol of cleansing but of judgment. This perspective is able to harmonize the preaching and baptizing of John (especially the relationship of his baptism to the future baptism in the Holy Spirit and fire) and uniquely fits Matthew's context, narrative, and theological interests, while conforming to the practices and situations of the OT prophets, to which John belonged.

Survey of Interpretations

Everett Ferguson provides the following list as a sample of interpretations derived from the primary sources: the Gospels and Josephus. To this list we have added the names of scholars as representatives of the categories. John's baptism

(1) expressed conversionary repentance, a turning to a new way of life.[1] (2) It mediated divine forgiveness.[2] (3) It purified from uncleanness, ritual, and

---

1. Beasley-Murray, *Baptism*, 33–35.
2. Kraeling, *John the Baptist*, 121–22; Webb, *John the Baptizer and Prophet*.

moral.[3] (4) It foreshadowed the ministry of an expected figure (from the Christian perspective this made John the forerunner of Jesus Christ), so it had an eschatological dimension.[4] (5) It was an initiation into the "true Israel"—not, however, a closed community like Qumran but the renewed people of God.[5] (6) It was a protest against the temple establishment by offering an alternative means of forgiveness of sins.[6]

To this we may add one final proposal, some scholars have discussed John's baptism as a judgment ordeal, to which the baptized penitents were released from the liability to which the baptism pointed.[7]

As Ferguson suggests, some of the ideas about John's baptism are not mutually exclusive. Points one and three could be combined. One who turns to Yahweh and is baptized as an expression of trust in God could be considered religiously "clean" or morally purified by turning from sin and embracing John's baptism. The fifth category would also seem to be a natural addition to points one and three. The "repentants" who turn to God and take upon themselves the symbol of cleansing and purity would, by baptism, become an insider and thus belong to God's people. John's baptism could also be an act of protest against a corrupt temple hierarchy and so include point six. So also, a suitable pairing could be made of point four and the addition of a judgment ordeal at the hand of the expected figure. This last combination lies close to the argument that will be presented shortly, but first we must say a word about the background(s) of John's baptism.

---

3. J. Stockton Axtell, *The Mystery of Baptism* (London: Bible Churchmen's Missionary Society, n.d.), 91–95; Scobie, *John the Baptist*, 110–16.

4. Reiser, *Jesus and Judgment*, 186; Davies and Allison, *Matthew I-VII*, 299; Kraeling's view also fits under this category. Kraeling, *John the Baptist*, 113–22.

5. Oscar Cullmann, *Die Tauflehre des Neuen Testaments* (Zurich: Zwingli-Verlag, 1948), 5; Geoffrey W. H. Lampe, *The Seal of the Spirit: A Study in the Doctrine of Baptism and Confirmation in the New Testament and the Fathers* (London: SPCK, 1967), 22. Lampe also thinks it is "probable that John believed his baptism to effect forgiveness of sins by both water and inward repentance" (ibid., 22).

6. Everett Ferguson, *Baptism in the Early Church: History, Theology, and Liturgy in the First Five Centuries* (Grand Rapids: Eerdmans, 2009), 93. Ferguson's list is drawn from Robert L. Webb, "Jesus' Baptism: Its Historicity and Implications," *BBR* 10.2 (2000), 261–309.

7. Carl-Martin Edsman, *Le baptême de feu* (Uppsala: Lundsquistska Bok-handeln, 1940); Kraeling, *John the Baptist*, 117–18; Meredith G. Kline, *By Oath Consigned* (Grand Rapids: Eerdmans, 1968), 55–62; Richard R. de Ridder, *Discipling the Nations* (Grand Rapids: Baker, 1971), 128–37; John V. Fesko, *Word, Water, and Spirit: A Reformed Perspective on Baptism* (Grand Rapids: Reformation Heritage Books, 2010), 228–58.

Potential antecedents for John's baptism include (1) OT lustrations,[8] (2) Qumran washings,[9] (3) Jewish initiatory rite,[10] and (4) OT prophetic sign-acts.

After providing a sizable and detailed analysis of the origins of John's baptism, Beasley-Murray appears to concur with those who wish to assign more broadly the OT as the proper background from which John's activities emerged.[11] Ready at hand are the statements in the prophets that describe a symbolic fusion of cleansing with water and the purifying activities of God in the last days (cf. Isa 1:16; 44:3; Jer 4:14; Ezek 36:25; Zech 13:1). According to Beasley-Murray, OT ritual illustrations and the prophetic words and actions of Israel's prophets best explain the source from which John's activity arose.[12] Turner goes even further, suggesting connections to biblical ritual cleansings, Jewish proselyte baptism, and the cleansing rituals of the Qumran community."[13]

The difficulties of trying to pinpoint a background for John's baptism are well known, and for every proposal one finds the existence of numerous counterpoints. The nature of John's baptism remains controverted in the scholarly literature.[14]

In summary fashion, Davies and Allison conclude that the baptism of John "was directed towards the nation as a whole (contrast Qumran), administered once and for all (contrast OT ablutions), and was for Jews only (contrast proselyte baptism). Most important of all, it was eschatological and probably sealed the repentant, marking them as those who would pass through the coming judgment

---

8. Lev 14:7, 52; Num 8:7; 19:17; Ps 51:6–9; Isa 1:16–17; 4:4; 44:3; Jer 4:11–14; Ezek 36:25–27; Zech 13:1.

9. 1 QS 3:6–9; 4:20–22; 1GH 7:6–7; 17:26; 1QS 3:4–12; 5:13–14.

10. Though later than John's baptism, see the discussion of baptism as a conversionary rite in *b. Yebam.* 46a. Harold H. Rowley, *From Moses to Qumran: Studies in the Old Testament* (New York: Association Press, 1963), 211–25; Joachim Jeremias, *Infant Baptism in the First Four Centuries* (Philadelphia: Westminster Press, 1960), 24–29. Jeremias believes that the T. Levi 14:6 may represent the oldest evidence for proselyte baptism. The difficulty is that 14:6 does not use βαπτίζω when speaking of purifying gentiles with unlawful purifications. Charlesworth's point is worth noting in this regard, "The discovery of Aramaic fragments of a Testament of Levi does not prove the pre-Christian origin of all of the Testament of Levi, let alone the thoroughly redacted Testaments of the Twelve Patriarchs": James H. Charlesworth, *The Old Testament Pseudepigrapha and the New Testament: Prolegomena for the Study of Christian Origins* (Cambridge: Cambridge University Press, 1985), 38.

11. Beasley-Murray, *Baptism*, 1–44.

12. Ibid., 44.

13. David L. Turner, *Matthew*, BECNT (Grand Rapids: Baker Academic, 2008), 110.

14. Meier, *A Marginal Jew*, 49–52; Taylor, *The Immerser*, 49–100; Webb, *John the Baptizer and Prophet*, 122–30; Witherington, "John the Baptist," 386; Beasley-Murray, *Baptism*, 11–31; Hagner, *Matthew*, 1.46; Nolland, *Matthew*, 141.

to enter the Messianic age."[15] These authors have raised what we deem to be a crucial point concerning the origin and meaning of John's baptism. *John's baptism was eschatological.*[16] We will now argue that as a prophet, John's baptism was an eschatological sign-act; this act was as portentous as his preaching, and was in keeping with his OT prophet-predecessors.

In taking this line of approach, it is believed that the solution to the quandary posed by Witherington can be satisfactorily answered: "John the Baptist called his audience to repentance. One major theme of John's preaching was that Yahweh's eschatological wrath would soon fall on Israel. What is not clear is the relationship between John's preaching of repentance and his baptismal practice."[17] When careful consideration is given to the OT prophets, John's words and action are uniformly coherent. John comes as a prophet of ultimatum, denouncing Israel and its leaders and giving a sign of the coming wrath of God.

We will proceed by looking at the range of meaning of βαπτίζω and then answer three questions. As a prophetic sign-act, (1) what was the nature of John's baptism, (2) how does it connect to the signs given by prophets of the OT, and (3) how does one relate John's baptism to his preaching? The answers given by those who understand John's baptizing activity to be in the form of a sign-act have been remarkably similar and need to be evaluated first.

Semantic Range of βαπτίζω

βάπτω and βαπτίζω convey the meanings of "to dip, plunge, wash, purify, or immerse."[18] The transliteration of the term came to denote a Christian ritual initiation with spiritual or metaphorical meanings associated with it.[19] Prior to this, the word could be used to indicate a disastrous action carried out with water. In Polybius it is used to describe the sinking of ships (*The Histories* 1.51.6–7;

---

15. Davies and Allison, *Matthew*, 1.299. While the great majority of the baptized were Jewish, Luke's account may suggest that gentiles also partook of John's baptism (cf. Luke 3:14).

16. Even those who look to Josephus to glean information of John have largely concluded that Josephus has downplayed the eschatological impulse that Q, and the gospels reveal to be at work in John's wilderness ministry. Meier calls this observation "commonplace" and cites Dibehus, Klausner, Scobie, Ernst, Backhaus, and E. P. Sanders. John P. Meier, "John the Baptist in Josephus: Philology and Exegesis," *JBL* 111.2 (1992): 225–37.

17. Witherington, "John the Baptist," 387.

18. A. Oepke, "βάπτω," et al., *TDNT*, 1.529–46; "βάπτω," *NIDNTTE*, Accordance Bible Software 11.1.6.

19. I. Howard Marshall, "The Meaning of the Verb 'Baptize,'" in *Dimensions of Baptism: Biblical and Theological Studies*, JSNTSup 234, eds. Stanley E. Porter and Anthony R. Cross (London: Sheffield Academic Press, 2002), 8–9.

5.47.2) and drowning (e.g., *Diod. Sic.* 16.80; Jos. *B.J.* 4.525).[20] The nonliteral usage of βαπτίζω during the first century CE was not always spiritual, "Josephus uses it of Jerusalem being brought to disaster during the Roman siege by the entry of brigands (*War* 4.137); in this case the metaphor is not of something being dipped into water but rather of a stream of water overwhelming an object."[21] Elsewhere, it is used in the metaphorical sense for Jesus's suffering and death (Mark 10:38; Luke 12:28).[22]

The gospel writers chose βαπτίζω as a description of John's actions in the Jordan River (Mark 1:4; Luke 3:7; John 1:28), even though his baptism was of a different kind and therefore not to be equated with Christian baptism (e.g., Matt 28:19). What, then, are we to make of this verb? It might simply be used to describe the plunging of a person into the water, in this case, immersion. Obviously, the gospels did not think of John as drowning the penitents in the waters. So we can set aside the nonfigurative meaning of "to drown." This leaves nonphysical and metaphorical uses of "overwhelm" or "devastate." In the case of Matthew, we wish to suggest that the meaning of "overwhelm" is a better explanation for the *meaning* of John's baptism and it is a meaning that was sometimes conveyed by βαπτίζω. John's baptism with water symbolized the devastating messianic baptism in Spirit and fire that would be poured out upon the nation of Israel. John's baptism as a sign-act conveyed the reality of judgment: "In terms of the results there is not a lot of difference in the end between being immersed in water or being overwhelmed by a torrent or being caught in a cloudburst (like Noah's flood): one is soaked to the skin and if the event is on a grand scale the results can equally be fatal."[23]

Reflections on the Nature of John's Sign-Act, Past to Present

The perspective that John's baptism was a sign-act like those offered by the OT prophets dates back to at least the turn of the twentieth century. Johannes Lindblom is thought to be the first to propose that the OT antecedent to Christian baptism lies in the sign-acts of Israel's OT prophets.[24] Seven years later, Wheeler Robinson discussed the nature of the sign-acts of Israel's prophets.[25] He argued

---

20. "βάπτω," *NIDNTTE*, Accordance Bible Software 11.1.6. Gerhard, "ΒΑΡΤΙΣΜΑ ΒΑΠΓΙΣΘΗΝΑΙ," *NovT* 2 (1958): 100.

21. Marshall, "The Meaning," 17. "He overwhelmed the city": ἐβάπτισεν τὴν πόλιν (*Bell.* 4.137), "βαπτίζω," *BDAG*, 132.

22. Richard B. Gaffin, "Justification in Luke-Acts," in *Right with God: Justification in the Bible and the World*, ed. D. A. Carson (Grand Rapids: Baker, 1992), 110–11.

23. Marshall, "The Meaning," 18.

24. Johannes Lindblom, *Jesu Missions-och Dopbefallning, Mt. 28, 18-20 Tillika en Studie over det kristna Dopeti Ursprung* (Uppsala, 1919), 196–201. Cited in Beasley-Murray, *Baptism*, 43.

25. H. Wheeler Robinson, "Prophetic Symbolism," in *Old Testament Essays*, ed. D. C. Simpson (London: Charles Griffin and Company, 1927), 1–17.

that the future of Israel was affected by the prophetic act.[26] In an unpublished essay, "Hebrew Psychology; being notes of work subsequent to date of Kennicott Essay,"[27] Robinson stated that "a practical application of these results might be made in regard to the conception of primitive Christian baptism, probably an effective symbolism of this kind. This might show that even in Paul the Hellenistic element is not so great as has been argued."[28] Robinson spoke of "the act as a 'word' of an intenser kind, which initiated and liberated objective forces."[29] And again, "The prophet's act enters into the purpose, and so acquires the power of Yahweh. The prophet might equally well have said, 'Thus doth Yahweh' of his own symbolic act, as he does say, of his own spoken word, 'Thus saith Yahweh.'"[30] Applying his observations to Rom 6:35, Robinson surmises: "On the one hand the water-baptism symbolically reproduces the death, burial and resurrection of Jesus, on the other the death to sin and the resurrection to life of the believer made one with Him by faith."[31] In this, he sees not only a positive sign-act, but also a sign-act that participates in the positive result: "The apostle does not teach that the act will infallibly produce the results he assumes, but it seems not less clear that he regards the act as instrumental to the results, since his appeal is to the act of baptism."[32]

William Flemington In 1948 Flemington took up Robinson's suggestion that prophetic symbolism might prove a helpful category in illuminating the meaning of Christian baptism and applied Robinson's findings to John's baptism.[33] Proceeding with the premise that the baptism of John was an extension of the symbolic prophetic action, Flemington avowed that "just as Isaiah or Jeremiah expressed their prophetic insight into the moral realities present in a particular historical situation, by performing a symbolic act, so John gathered up his conviction about divine judgment, and the need for "turning" to God, in this 'baptism of repentance unto remission of sins."[34] If John's sign is expressed "just as" Isaiah or Jeremiah expressed their own, what does it mean? It was the escape from the day of the

---

26. "The prophetic act is itself a part of the will of Yahweh, to whose complete fulfillment it points; it brings that will nearer to its completion, not only by declaring it, but in some small degree as affecting it": Robinson, "Prophetic Symbolism," 15. H. Wheeler Robinson, "Hebrew Sacrifice and Prophetic Symbolism," *JTS* 43 (1942): 129–39.

27. Angus Library, Regent's Park College, Oxford, p. 117.

28. Max E. Polley, "The Place of Henry Wheeler Robinson among Old Testament Scholars," *Baptist Quarterly* 24.6 (1972): 277.

29. Robinson, "Hebrew Sacrifice," 132.

30. Ibid.

31. Ibid., 138.

32. Ibid.

33. Flemington, *The New Testament Doctrine*, 20–23.

34. Ibid., 22.

Lord. In this way his sign was effective of the divine will—the baptized could know that "their repentance was accepted and sins would be forgiven."[35] Presumably this means that baptism is a sign of God's forgiveness. Whereas Robinson looked at baptism as a sign-act of the work of Christ who brought people to new life, Flemington's position is that John's baptism was offered to assure repentant people of God's mercy and, as he put it, "that their membership of the future messianic community was secure."[36] In short, Flemington's position is more or less a conflation of one and the same principle: baptism is in some way instrumental in the securing of the repentant person's position before God.

Alec Gilmore Following Flemington and Robinson, Alec Gilmore attempted to advance the discussion further still.[37] While not establishing any criteria for determining what constitutes a prophetic sign-act,[38] Gilmore posits that if John was to be linked to the prophets, he goes beyond them by calling for moral renewal, announcing the coming of the Messiah, and urging Israel to express their repentance in baptism.[39] This is in keeping with his assessment that John's baptism was eschatological in orientation.[40] For Gilmore, the most important aspect of John's message was his call to moral renewal: "The people who accept this aspect of John's teaching must cut adrift from the old by repentance, and take up the new, and such an acceptance must find its expression in a changed life. All this was adequately symbolized in baptism."[41]

It is assumed (and understandably so given the statements from the previous authors) that John's baptismal sign proffered inner cleansing and a new start.[42] John's sign was solely to signify repentance and cleansing. Presumably, then, those who rejected his sign could expect the negative aspects of his preaching to be applicable. The problem with such an understanding is that while it is true the prophets spoke of cleansing and purification of the hearts of God's people (Jer 31:33; Ezek 36:25; Joel 2:28–29), nowhere in the OT do we find a prophetic sign-act conveying such a meaning. Without some evidence from the OT, the arguments look suspiciously like arguments for the meaning of Christian baptism.

Gilmore concludes on a note about the effectiveness of John's sign. If the sign given communicates cleansing and repentance, what would happen if the people changed their minds and turned their backs on their baptisms? Gilmore believed

---

35. Ibid.

36. Ibid.

37. Alec Gilmore, *Christian Baptism: A Fresh Attempt to Understand the Rite in Terms of Scripture, History, and Theology* (Chicago: The Judson Press, 1959), 54–83.

38. Gilmore makes brief reference to Elisha as approximating the sign-acts of the major prophets, but does not discuss any of the latter in his essay. Gilmore, "Jewish Antecedents," 76.

39. Ibid., 79.

40. Ibid., 73–74.

41. Ibid., 80.

42. Ibid.

that John's baptism would then be made of "no effect."[43] This conclusion, though logically following the premises, is the exact opposite of the situation. Going back upon their baptisms and refusing to walk in repentance would not make John's baptismal sign-act null and void; on the contrary, it would in that case seal to them the judgment that was announced in both John's preaching and his prophetic sign. This raises one last issue that concerns the relationship of John's water baptism to the future Spirit and fire baptism of the "one to come" (Matt 3:11).

If one grants the aforementioned premises, then the baptism in the Holy Spirit and fire would almost certainly need to be interpreted as a positive, gracious outpouring. But as we have sought to demonstrate, the dative construction of Spirit and fire, along with the casting of the trees into the fire (Matt 3:10) on one side of the logion (Matt 3:11) and the chaff thrown into the fire on the other side (Matt 3:12), does not support such a view of the future Spirit and fire baptism. Quite the contrary: though John surely did warn his listeners that they must repent, he did not offer Israel a sign of *repentance*; the sign was that of God's kingdom in conflict *with* and coming *against* the nation of Israel.

Recent Studies With the groundwork laid, the few scholars who have advocated for a sign-act interpretation of John's baptism have added relatively nothing new to the discussion. Lampe,[44] Dunn,[45] Brooks,[46] Meier,[47] Hooker,[48] and Bergin[49] have taken the position that John's baptism was a prophetic sign of cleansing and renewal.[50] The texts most often cited to further substantiate such an interpretation are Isa 1:16–20; Jer 4:14; Ezek 36:25–28; 47:1–12, and Zech 13:1. These OT texts speak of the cleansing work of God, some of which are given in eschatological

---

43. Ibid., 82.

44. Lampe, *The Seal of the Spirit*, 19–31.

45. Dunn, *Baptism in the Holy Spirit*, 17.

46. Oscar S. Brooks, *The Drama of Decision: Baptism in the New Testament* (Peabody: Hendrickson, 1987), 30–32.

47. Meier, *A Marginal Jew*, 2.40, 54–55. While Meier does refer to John as a prophet and speaks about his baptism as a symbolic sign, he also calls John's baptism a ritual symbol (ibid., 54).

48. Hooker, *The Signs of a Prophet*, 9–13, esp. 12. Idem., "John's Baptism: A Prophetic Sign," in *The Holy Spirit and Christian Origins: Essays in Honor of James D. G. Dunn*, eds. Graham Stanton, Bruce W. Longenecker, and Stephen C. Barton (Grand Rapids: Eerdmans, 2004), 22–40.

49. Liam Bergin, *O Propheticum Lavacrum: Baptism as Symbolic Act of Eschatological Salvation*, Analecta Gregoriana 277 (Rome: Gregorian University, 1999), 111–42.

50. This is probably the understanding of Friedrich who comments, "One may ask whether the baptism of John is not to be understood as a prophetic action." Gerhard Friedrich, "προφήτης," TDNT, 6.837. Friedrich then goes on to cite Lampe and Flemmington, ibid., n. 353.

contexts.[51] Furthermore, they are texts that come from the OT prophets. But the point at issue is not whether or not there are OT passages that speak of the washing and cleansing of God's people through his Spirit. The substance of the matter is whether or not this cleaning emphasis was ever signified by way of prophetic sign. The problem remains that none of the aforesaid texts are situated within the context of prophetic signs. It is, of course, *possible* that John's sign does indicate such a new meaning, but such a decision should only be reached after the meanings of the OT sign-acts have been ruled out as disanalogous.

Meredith Kline Among the more recent interpreters, Meredith Kline stands out as one who has taken a view of John's baptism that is theologically important, but often overlooked.[52] Although not using the language of sign-acts, Kline attempted to analyze the ministry of John the Baptist in terms of the mission of the OT prophets to Israel as covenant lawyers sent to prosecute Israel for their violations of the treaty between Yahweh and his people.[53] As a prophet, John's message was a divine ultimatum of eschatological judgment for disobedience.[54] Kline rejected the Levitical lustrations and the prophetic promises of the pouring out and cleansing work of the Spirit (e.g., Ezek. 36:25) as the primary antecedents to John's baptism. Instead of interpreting John's water rite as an acted-out extension of those prophesies, Kline viewed John's baptism as analogous to the OT water ordeals, the outcomes of which were both negative and positive: "But the possibility must be probed whether this water rite did not dramatize more plainly and pointedly the dominant theme in John's proclamation . . . namely, the impending judicial ordeal which would discriminate and separate between the chaff and the wheat, rendering a verdict of acceptance but also of rejection."[55]

Kline compares John's baptismal rite to the Flood account in Genesis, the "archetype of water ordeals."[56] In the NT, the retrospective comments of Peter (2 Pet 3:5–7) indicate that the future day of judgment will be akin to the flooding of the world in Noah's day. God's past destruction of the wicked by water and his

---

51. The religious washings of Second Temple Judaism do not account for John's baptism, but the prophesied eschatological purification of the Spirit, found in the OT, does. According to Goppelt, the meaning of John's baptism is to be found in these OT announcements as well as in John's prophetic intuition. Goppelt, *Theologie*, 89.

52. More recently, Ridder and Fesko have followed Kline's observations. Ridder, *Discipling the Nations*, 128–37; Fesko, *Word, Water, and Spirit*, 228–58.

53. Kline, *By Oath Consigned*, 52.

54. Ibid., 54.

55. Ibid.

56. Ibid., 55.

future judgment of the ungodly by fire are linked.[57] The second water ordeal is the crossings of the Red Sea and the Jordan River:

> These, too, were acts of redemptive judgment wherein God vindicated the cause of those who called upon his name and condemned their adversaries. The exodus ordeal, with Israel coming forth safe and the Egyptians overwhelmed in the depths, strikingly exemplified the dual potential of the ordeal process. In the Jordan ordeal, the dispossession of the condemned by the acquitted was prominent. At that historical juncture the rightful ownership of Canaan was precisely the legal issue at stake and God declared in favor of Israel by delivering them from Jordan's overflowing torrents. Thereby Israel's contemplated conquest of the land was vindicated as a holy war, a judgment of God.[58]

Both the flood and the exodus through the Red Sea are, for Kline, water ordeals that communicated God's judicial verdict on behalf of his people and against his enemies. Read in this way, the water is not only the sign of the ordeal, but also the actual instrument through which God's people passed and their enemies were destroyed (in the case of the Egyptians). If Kline is correct, particularly in his reading of John's baptism against the exodus, then John's choice of the Jordan's waters would be something of an irony for Israel. The river where God gave a sign of his favor toward Israel and judgment against the nations (ending in their dispossession of the land) is the place where John calls Israel to confess their forfeiture of the land in the prospect of the divine wrath that was shortly to come against them. In summary,

> John the Baptist was sent as a messenger of the Old Covenant to its final generation. His concern was not to prepare the world at large for the coming of Christ but to summon Israel unto the Lord to whom they had sworn allegiance at Sinai, ere his wrath broke upon them and the Mosaic kingdom was terminated in the flames of messianic judgment. The demand which John brought to Israel was focused in his call to baptism. This baptism was not an ordinance to be observed by Israel in their generations but a special sign for that terminal generation epitomizing the particular crisis in covenant history represented by the mission of John as messenger of the Lord's ultimatum.[59]

In much more abbreviated fashion, Kline speaks of John's baptism from the angle of repentance and faith and concludes that from this perspective, "John's ultimatum could be seen as a gracious invitation . . . as a seal of the remission of sins."[60] In the

---

57. Ibid. Kline also briefly mentions the second law of Hammurabi's Code as a symbolic water ordeal (ibid., 55). This, he believes, finds a fitting parallel with the comparison of John's baptism in water and the Coming One's baptism in the Holy Spirit and fire (ibid., 57).

58. Ibid., 56.

59. Ibid., 61.

60. Ibid.

end, though, the emphasis is upon the judgment: "To this overflowing wrath the waters of John's baptism had pointed, as well as to the remission of sins received by the remnant according to the election of grace."[61]

Evaluation of Kline As it relates to Matthew, it is debatable that the flood is the antecedent to John's baptism.[62] Israel's exodus, on the other hand, is more analogous. As we observed, Matthew has woven exodus themes throughout the opening of his narrative (Matt 2:15). In the immediate context, the mention of John as the Isaianic voice in the wilderness (Matt 3:3) and the nation of Israel entering the waters of the Jordan and confessing sin (Matt 3:5-6) suggests another exodus: "As it was at the time of the nation's first crossing into the Promised Land under Joshua, or at the time of apostasy and crisis when Elijah stood alone, *so now all Israel was summoned to the Jordan to be reminded of this sacred past and the fearful judgment that was soon to come.*"[63]

Kline has come closer to the meaning of John's baptism by interpreting it as a judgment ordeal. John's baptism was a "sign" of crisis.[64] Yet the force of the argument is perhaps weakened by an attempt to also derive a gracious meaning from the sign itself. This decision is in keeping with Kline's emphasis on the dual sanctions of the covenant which lies at the heart of John's words and action.[65] Though only tentative and passing, it is difficult to see how John's baptism can be both the sign of crisis and a "seal" of "a verdict of remission of sin."[66] With those criticisms noted, Kline has helpfully moved the discussion of John's baptism forward and in the right general direction.

Now that we have surveyed the ways in which John's baptism has been understood as the sign of a prophet, it is time to reconsider the purpose of the sign-acts of the OT prophets.[67] We do so in order to determine not only if John's

---

61. Ibid., 62.

62. Peter connects the flood to baptism (ὃ καὶ ὑμᾶς ἀντίτυπον νῦν σῴζει βάπτισμα; 1 Pet 3:20), but it is clearly Christian baptism that serves as the analogue (δι᾽ ἀναστάσεως Ἰησοῦ Χριστοῦ; 1 Pet 3:21). While Matthew's first words take readers back to Genesis, there are no clear references to the Genesis flood until Matt 24:37. If Matt 3 is, as we will argue, further elucidated in ch. 24, then a link could be indirectly made.

63. Craig A. Evans, "The Baptism of John in a Typological Context," in *Dimensions of Baptism: Biblical and Theological Studies*, 52. Emphasis mine.

64. Kline, *By Oath Consigned*, 61.

65. Cf. Ibid., 39-49.

66. Ibid., 57.

67. As we proceed, we will set aside the question of whether or not the OT prophets actually performed their sign-acts. We will have to pass over the question of whether or not John's baptism was sacramentally efficacious, as well as the more general and voluminous discussions on the potential relationship of prophetic sign-acts to magic.

sign-act bears any resemblance to theirs, but also to understand better and to clarify the meaning of the actions both they and John performed.

Identifying and Defining Sign-Acts

In this section we will outline the OT meanings of sign-acts and the OT texts that contain them. This will help us to gauge the meaning of John's baptism in Matthew's Gospel.

Fohrer treated the component parts of the prophets' sign-acts under the term *symbolischen Handlungen* ("symbolic actions").[68] In his outline of the symbolischen Handlungen, Fohrer acknowledged that his outline was neither exhaustive nor completely representative of every element in the "symbolic acts." The reason he gave was that the symbolic actions' characteristics take various forms.[69] He then proceeded to give the main characteristics: (1) God's command to the prophet to perform the symbolic act, (2) a report of the carrying out of the symbolic action, and (3) an interpretation of the symbolic action.[70]

W. D. Stacey has provided his own expansive definitional category by which the various details of the sign-acts can be classified. Stacey stated what should be fairly obvious: a sign-act points beyond itself to another referent.[71] Typically, the actions of the prophet stand over and against some important reality or state of affairs.[72] In other words, the prophetic sign was never a private sign to be given to a specific individual that communicated something about his or her destiny. The signs the prophets performed were national signs that conveyed important and often devastating changes, particularly in the case of Israel's national life in relation to God as well as the nations. The prophet is himself a symbol; he performed his actions at the command of God, the actions taking place in a "once-for-all fashion" (i.e., not repeated actions). The particular signs were chosen for particular situations. Lastly, the sign-acts were typically accompanied by an oracle of explanation.[73]

At this point it might be asked how John's baptism could be a sign-act since the signs that prophets performed allegedly were not repeated, but John's certainly

---

68. Georg Fohrer, "Die Gattung der Berichte über symbolische Handlungen der Propheten," *ZAW* 64.2 (1952): 101–20. This particular language has been criticized as being too vague. According to Zimmerli, "It does not make it clear enough that the prophet wants these acts to represent something more than the symbolic." Walther Zimmerli, *The Fiery Throne: The Prophets and Old Testament Theology* (Minneapolis: Fortress, 2003), 110.

69. Fohrer, "Die Gattung," 103.

70. Ibid.

71. W. David Stacey, *Prophetic Drama in the Old Testament* (London: Epworth Press, 1990), 64.

72. Stacey, *Prophetic Drama*, 65.

73. Ibid., 61–62.

was. In his analysis of the signs of Jeremiah and Ezekiel,[74] Friebel has adequately demonstrated that some of the sign-acts were indeed repetitive. Jeremiah's celibacy (Jer 16:2) and his absence from attending feasts and funerals (Jer 16:5–8) were ongoing signs leading up to the fall of Jerusalem.[75] Such an analysis has a bearing upon the sign-act performed by John the Baptist. Repetition is not a disqualification for his act to be comparable to the sign-acts of the OT prophets.

But what exactly does such an act communicate? According to Zimmerli, the prophet's visible action is a sign of what Yahweh has declared he will do.[76] The action is more than a symbol and more than just acted-out words; it brings the event into effect. The action carried out by the prophet guarantees that the event proclaimed will take place.[77] Though we would agree that the sign is not empty, it does not appear to have the power to effect any change, but is instead part of the divine process of the reordering of events when the sign is future-oriented.

Sign-acts, or what Hutton calls "illocutionary" and "perlocutionary" actions, generate a new condition (illocutionary function), but part of that new condition is a response required of the audience (perlocutionary function).[78] The purpose of the performed acts is to motivate the onlookers to change their behavior.[79] Such a motivation most often was to be prompted by the threatening nature of the signs performed by the prophets. Many of the threatening sign-acts contained no indications that the judgment could be averted.[80] Onlookers could *infer* from the sign that only a change in behavior could potentially alter the visual pronouncement of doom, but it is worth noting that Jeremiah and Ezekiel do not give any assurances of escape as they conducted their signs (Ezek 4:6, 12–13; 5:2b–4; Jer 13:4–10; 43:8–13).[81] Friebel concludes: "The coordination of the nonverbal and verbal therefore had a building effect: the nonverbal attracted the audience's attention, conveyed

---

74. Friebel limited his study to these two prophets since most of the sign-acts are found in their books.

75. Kelvin G. Friebel, *Jeremiah's and Ezekiel's Sign-Act*, JSOTSup 283 (Sheffield: Sheffield Academic Press, 1999), 456. Friebel also references the yoke worn by Jeremiah (Jer 27:2), Ezekiel's years of speechlessness (Ezek 3:26), his siege and other actions recorded in chs. 4–5, his sign of trembling while eating (Ezek 12:17–20) and refraining from the customary week of mourning (Ezek 24:15–24), all demonstrate that the sign-acts performed by Jeremiah and Ezekiel at times were ongoing. Friebel, *Jeremiah's*, 456–57. We could add Isaiah's sign-act of walking about naked for three years (Isa 20:1–4) as additional evidence that such signs were not "once-for-all acts."

76. Walther Zimmerli, *Ezekiel 1: A Commentary on the Book of the Prophet Ezekiel, Chapters 1–24*, trans. R. E. Clements (Philadelphia: Fortress, 1969), 28.

77. Zimmerli, *Ezekiel 1*, 156.

78. Rodney R. Hutton, "Magic or Street-Theater? The Power of the Prophetic Word," *ZAW* 107 (1995): 256–57. Cf. Stacey, *Prophetic Drama*, 265.

79. Paul A. Kruger, "אות," NIDOT, 1.332. Cf. Friebel, *Jeremiah's*, 30.

80. Friebel, *Jeremiah's*, 449, 451.

81. Ibid., 448.

the message in an ambiguous manner, caused the audience to think about the action as they attempted to ascertain its meaning, then through the verbal channel, full comprehension was given."[82]

John's sign-act functioned in a similar way. As the crowds of people went out to the wilderness to see the strange spectacle, they were confronted with a sign performed in the Jordan waters. Yet quite unlike the Jewish lustrations of the OT or those of the Qumran community, John plunged the people under the waters, hence earning himself the name "the Baptizer." The event called for some explanation. He performed the sign upon the nation in anticipation of the oncoming kingdom of heaven. This was not a means of putting out the imminent fire; it was a symbol of the fiery Spirit that would soon descend and submerge the nation with devastating effect. Water, after all, was not solely a symbol of a gracious reviving work of God. The flood account in the book of Genesis easily demonstrates that water could be used for the purposes of judgment. Job 38:16–17; Ps 74:13; 89:10, and Jonah 2 also have to do with the destructive and frightful aspects of water. Like the prophets of old, John gives not only the prophetic sign but also the meaning through "the verbal channel" (Matt 3:11). The reason Israel must repent is the imminent arrival of the heavenly kingdom. The function of that kingdom is dramatized through the sign and explained through the verbal channel: the felling of trees, the burning of the chaff and, positioned between the two, the Holy Spirit and fire.

Interpreting John's sign-act as a symbol of judgment also corresponds to the limited number of positive sign-acts performed by the OT prophets in comparison to the overwhelming majority of judgment signs. A detailed analysis is not possible here, but the following summary by Friebel clearly shows that the preponderance of signs offered to Israel were that of curse and threat. [83]

1. Isaiah 20:1–4: Isaiah goes naked for three years to represent the people of Cush and Egypt being led away naked as captives by the Assyrians.
2. Jeremiah 13:1–11: Jeremiah buys, wears, and buries, by the River Perat, a waist sash to illustrate the people's initial closeness to God and their subsequent deterioration.
3. Jeremiah 16:1–9: Jeremiah does not marry or attend funerals or feasts, representing the people's future decimation such that they would be devoid of family members and occasions of ritual mourning and festivity.
4. Jeremiah 19:1–13: Jeremiah shatters an earthenware jar, demonstrating that God will shatter Jerusalem.
5. Jeremiah 27: Jeremiah wears a yoke to advise Judah to continue its submission to Babylon. In response, Hananiah (cf. Jer 28:10–11) breaks the yoke to symbolize the divine breaking of the Babylonians' rule.

---

82. Ibid., 454.

83. This summary is fairly representative of list(s) found in the literature.

6. Jeremiah 32: Jeremiah purchases a parcel of land to signify that, in the future, fields would once again be bought and sold by the Judahites.

7. Jeremiah 35: Jeremiah offers wine to the Rechabites, who refuse to drink it out of commitment to their ancestral oath. Their faithfulness is then verbally contrasted with the Judahites' failure to keep their covenant with God.

8. Jeremiah 43:8–13: In Tahpanhes, Egypt, Jeremiah buries a stone to indicate that the king of Babylon would invade Egypt and construct a throne on that very location.

9. Jeremiah 51:59–64: Jeremiah sends with Seraiah a scroll to Babylon, which is thrown into the Euphrates to signify the demise of Babylon.

10. Ezekiel 3:24–27; 24:25–27; 33:21–22: Ezekiel remains speechless from the time of his calling as a prophet until he receives the news that Jerusalem has fallen.

11. Ezekiel 4–5: Ezekiel performs multiple actions revolving around a brick with "Jerusalem" inscribed on it. He lays siege to the city, sets an iron griddle next to it, and sets his face against the griddle; he lies on his left side for 390 days and then on his right side for 40 days to symbolize the bearing of the people's iniquities; he consumes both rationed portions of food and water to represent the scarcity of food during the siege; he bakes his bread on dung to symbolize the unclean food of the exile; he shaves off his hair, divides it into three portions and then, to show the threefold fate of the inhabitants of Jerusalem, burns one-third upon the model siege, chops up another third with his sword, and scatters the last third to the wind and chases after it with the sword.

12. Ezekiel 6:11–12: Ezekiel claps his hands and cries "Ah!" to display God's indignation over the people's wicked practices.

13. Ezekiel 12:1–16: Ezekiel prepares a bag, digs a hole in the wall of his house, places the bag upon his shoulder, exits through the hole with his eyes covered, and departs from the city to represent the people of Jerusalem going off into exile.

14. Ezekiel 12:17–20: Ezekiel eats and drinks with trembling to show the Jerusalemites' emotional distress during the Babylonian invasion.

15. Ezekiel 21:6–7: Ezekiel groans to demonstrate the people's response to the news of God's impending judgment.

16. Ezekiel 21:8–17: Ezekiel cries out and strikes his thigh to depict the people's gestures of grief. Later, he claps his hands to show the divine indignation toward the people.

17. Ezekiel 21:18–23: Ezekiel sets up a signpost to show the ways the king of Babylon might take in his march against the west.

18. Ezekiel 24:15–24: Ezekiel refrains from weeping or performing the normal mourning rituals at his wife's death to illustrate how the people should respond to the news of the fall of Jerusalem.

19. Ezekiel 37:15–28: Ezekiel joins two pieces of wood to signify the reunification of Israel and Judah.

20. Hosea 1:2–9: Hosea takes a wife of harlotry, symbolizing God's relationship to his people.
21. Hosea 3: Hosea buys back his wife to symbolize God's taking back and restoring his wayward people.
22. Zechariah 6:9–15: Zechariah makes a crown and places it on the high priest Joshua to show God's crowning of the person who will rebuild the temple.[84]

This list of the sign-acts of the prophets gives some important information for understanding the sign-acts of the Bible. Counting the individual actions found in Ezek 4–5, the number of sign-acts increases to twenty-seven. Of the twenty-seven, twenty have to do with the judgment of God upon his people and their exile.[85] Groaning, trembling, violence, sword, desolation, and exile are the messages conveyed through the meaning-laden signs. The prophets were signifying through those acts that God would punish Israel on account of their sinful rebellion. Israel had become "not my people," because he was not their God (Hos 1:9).

Three additional signs indicate that God's wrath and judgment would befall the nations of Egypt, Cush, and Babylon. The remaining sign-acts were more positive in scope and hope-inspiring. Jer 32, Ezek 37:15–28, and Hos 3 foretell the end of the exile and the return of the people, while Zechariah's sign-act refers to the one who would rebuild the ruined temple, helped by those who return from the exile (Zech 6:15).

Twenty of the twenty-four sign-acts performed for Israel were graphic actions given for the purposes of displaying God's disfavor and Israel's doom. The additional *verbal* images of things like "sword" and "fire" served the purpose of reinforcing the acts' message and meaning. The remaining four sign-acts all have to do with God's determination to return Israel to their land. In other words, all four positive sign-acts are declarations of what will take place *after the fall of Israel*. The sign-acts of the latter prophets signify either judgment and ruin (twenty times), or return after exile (four times).

Baptism: John's Sign-Act

The Gospel of Matthew repeatedly claims a prophetic status for John (11:9; 14:5; 21:25–26). As the last prophet of the Old Covenant, John performed a final sign

---

84. Kelvin G. Friebel, "Sign Acts," *DOTP*, 708–09.

85. While Jeremiah's loin cloth and the wine offered to the Rechabites might better be understood as Israel's unfaithfulness before the Lord, surely the unfaithfulness of Israel is a necessary point for the other sign-acts to be correctly understood. Furthermore, the meanings given are Israel "shall be like this [ruined] loincloth, which is good for nothing" (Jer 13:10). The issue concerning the Rechabites is that they obeyed their father and Israel, but Israel had not obeyed God. The sign signified disobedience which Jeremiah was commanded to explain (Jer 35:12–16) and in language much like the other sign-acts, the explanation contained the promise that disaster would fall upon Israel (Jer 35:17).

for national Israel. John's baptismal sign, like the OT prophets, was a sign of judgment.[86] John was not offering Israel a sign of what they could expect *in place of* or *after* the judgment. The Matthean context does not bear the weight of such an interpretation. There is no mention of a return to the land in Matthew's account. In Matthew's Gospel, John is a preacher of judgment and his sign bore the same meaning.

By baptizing the nation, John gives Israel a sign of impending doom. He reinforces the sign by calling for repentance, as did the prophets before him. Israel must turn from their sins and seek God's mercy, or the kingdom of heaven would submerge them under the divine wrath. The trees not yielding the fruits characteristic of repentance would be chopped down and thrown into the fire. The fiery Holy Spirit that would be poured out upon Israel was the reality to which John's sign pointed. The symbolism is not only to be found in his baptizing, but also in his preaching: cutting down and burning of trees = Israel's judgment; wheat and chaff thrown into the fire = Israel's judgment; water baptism and Spirit and fire baptism = Israel's judgment.

There was one additional element to John's verbal message that the listeners could count on. And this, in good story making fashion, Matthew saves for last. Like the wheat, the truly repentant would be gathered up and spared. This theme is not foreign to the OT. When God's people "meditated upon their defeat and deliverance by God, the idea of being spared from the waters is present (Pss 18:16; 42:7; 69:1ff.)."[87]

John is called a prophet, speaks like a prophet, and carries out a prophetic action. Unless there are good contextual clues suggesting that this rite should be viewed in preparatory terms (such as for Christian baptism), readers ought to go back to the OT that Matthew is so fond of utilizing, to consider the prophets' roles as preachers and sign-givers. When this is done, the connection between John and the prophets is illuminating. His baptism is a sign like theirs. The circumstances are similar—Israel has erred and is called to return to Yahweh. The warnings are similar and must not be ignored. The promised results are similar—Israel will be judged and laid waste, the wicked will not be spared. And the signs are similar—they conveyed the overthrow of Israel.

The outlook was that Israel would experience the deluge in the Spirit and fire even as their ancestors felt the stinging displeasure of God's recompense. This is

---

86. Though Kraeling does not discuss John's baptism as a sign-act, he does understand his baptism as a symbolic enactment, not of the judgment of national Israel, but as the final judgment, "The waters of baptism represents and symbolizes the fiery torrent of judgment, and that the individual by voluntarily immersing himself in the water enacts in advance before God his willing submission to the divine judgment, which the river of fire will perform." Kraeling, *John the Baptist*, 117. Like M. G. Kline, Witherington also leaves open the possibility that John drew on the ancient trial by water ordeal. Witherington, "John the Baptist," 386.

87. Brooks, *The Drama of Decision*, 32.

how Matthew is able to connect John's baptism with the judgment baptism in Spirit and fire. The baptism of John was his prophetic sign-act signifying, that like in the days of old, so also in the time of this last prophet, God's wrath would soon fall.

The Relationship between the Two Baptisms In Matt 3:11 John declares, Ἐγὼ μὲν ὑμᾶς βαπτίζω ἐν ὕδατι εἰς μετάνοιαν . . . αὐτὸς ὑμᾶς βαπτίσει ἐν πνεύματι ἁγίῳ καὶ πυρί. As a prophetic sign-act it is not given to symbolize repentance, *which no OT sign-act ever signified.* The opposite, as Becker noted, is equally negated: "Für die Gemeindegründung des Lehrers und die Taufe des Johannes gibt es bei den Propheten des Alten Testaments keine brauchbare Analogie, denn die Gleichnishandlungen der Propheten wirken nicht selbst heilsspendend."[88] John's baptism is not an efficacious sacramental sign either. The sign is given for another reason which better fits Matthew's theological perspective. It is a visual sign of an impending reality.

The εἰς + accusative fits the grammatical category of the intended "purpose" or "result" of the baptism. John likely baptizes in order to incite the people to repent (purpose). These categories overlap to a degree, making a decision difficult, if not unnecessary. Given the nature of John's sign-act, the purpose or result meanings not only make his statement intelligible, they conform to Matthew's theological point that forgiveness of sins is through Jesus alone.

This reading of εἰς μετάνοιαν is further strengthened by Matthew's displacement of Mark's "for the forgiveness of sins" (Mark 1:4) and relocation to Jesus's words in the institution of the Eucharist (Matt 26:28). In the upper room with his disciples, Jesus says, "τοῦτο γάρ ἐστιν τὸ αἷμά μου τῆς διαθήκης τὸ περὶ πολλῶν ἐκχυννόμενον εἰς ἄφεσιν ἁμαρτιῶν." Readers of Matthew already know that the cup of wine does not communicate forgiveness of sins. Matthew has already made that clear (Matt 1:21). The purpose or result uses of the εἰς + accusative fit naturally here. The cup symbolized Christ's blood poured out for the forgiveness of sins, or with the result that sins will be pardoned.

John's sign was for the purpose of eliciting confession of sin. Jesus's sign (no less a sign of judgment) pointed to the reality of his shed blood for the purpose (or result) that sins would be forgiven. In this way, Matthew can assure his readers that their repentance of sin was answered in Christ's cross of suffering.

Conclusion

As the last of the OT prophets, John's message and sign, though initially producing an enthusiastic response from the crowds, ended up failing to achieve its purpose. Such was the case with the prophets before him. For the most part, the crowds'

---

88. "The parabolic acts of the prophets do not, on their own, provide salvation." Becker, *Johannes der Täufer*, 62.

repentance was not lasting. The confession of sin (3:6) is narratively "drowned out" with the cry to crucify him (27:22).

To interpret the prophet's baptism as a sign-act provides a unified explanation of his message and sign. His sign-act was the message. To return to Witherington's question, John's baptism displays the meaning of his words and they are dramatized in the sign. In Matthew's narrative, baptism was ironically a sign for a nation on the brink of divine destruction. Its meaning did not communicate the way of escape, but rather something which John's audience needed to escape from. Such a reading is in harmony with the rejected king motif (e.g., Matt 2) and the nature and demands of the kingdom of the "heavens".

Regardless of whether or not every single individual had undergone John's baptism, the sign-act had been issued and carried out on the national level. Ignorance could not be feigned, but the repentant could find protection.

In Matt 3:12 John speaks of the wheat *not* passing through the messianic fires of v. 11.[89] The wheat is gathered into the barn. What is less than surprising, but nevertheless significant for Matthew's theological agenda, is that the barn is not Israel. John's ministry was to prepare people to leave Israel, to be gathered up out of Israel, or to be destroyed in the fiery messianic deluge of Israel. This gathering (συνάξει τὸν σῖτον αὐτοῦ εἰς τὴν ἀποθήκην) is picked up in the parables (cf. Matt 13:30, 47; 22:10) and then explained and expanded in Matt 24. John's sign was an eschatological sign of the end of the age. This is also the meaning Jesus gives to the end of the age in Matt 24:31. At the end of the age Jesus will send his angels καὶ ἐπισυνάξουσιν τοὺς ἐκλεκτοὺς αὐτοῦ.

John's sign pointed to the eschatological finale. John baptized for the purposes of repentance because the one coming after him would baptize with the Holy Spirit and fire. In OT terms, John was describing what had already been foretold in such places as Isa 11 and Dan 7. John's description was in both word and deed. For Israel to experience the end of the exile and restoration of peace to the world they would have to submit to God's verdict. They would have to confess their sins and take part in the national and dramatic declaration that the judgment to which John's baptismal sign pointed could only be averted by turning to God in repentance and being gathered out of the nation that John, and later Jesus, saw as ripe for judgment. Read in this way, it is little wonder that the gathering of the wheat into the barn and the angels gathering the elect out of the four corners of the earth would mean in the interim, an apostolic dispatch to gather up disciples of all nations, βαπτίζον τες αὐτοὺς εἰς τὸ ὄνομα τοῦ πατρὸς καὶ τοῦ υἱοῦ καὶ τοῦ ἁγίου πνεύματος (Matt 28:19).

How this evaluation of John's prophetic sign coheres with Matthew's editorial insertion that John was to be viewed in terms of the Isaianic voice of the new exodus will now be explored in terms of John's baptism of Jesus in the Jordon River. Specifically, what is the significance of the baptism of Jesus at the hand of John?

89. *Pace* Kraeling, *John the Baptist*, 117–18; Dunn, "Spirit-and-Fire Baptism," 86; Davies and Allison, *Matthew*, 1.316.

Chapter 11

THE MEANING OF THE JUDGMENT
IN THE BAPTISM OF JESUS

Introduction

The eschatological urgency underscored by John's sign-act will now be explored in its relationship to the baptism Jesus receives. Does our interpretation of John's preaching and sign-act (as oracular and visual messages of the impending eschatological judgment in the Holy Spirit and fire) cohere with Jesus's undergoing of the rite? The reason(s) Jesus came to be baptized are left unsaid apart from the provocative response that such an act is carried out πληρῶσαι πᾶσαν δικαιοσύνην (Matt 3:15). Predictably, the theological explanations of the saying are numerous.[1] To this the perplexing question is often added: Why did Jesus feel it necessary to be baptized by John?[2] While we cannot but doubt that different redactional and narratival readings of Matthew will turn up different answers to those questions, we will seek to demonstrate that our understanding of John's sign-act is consistent with Jesus's task of redemption of his people by judgment in his person. When framed within the Matthean interpretation of John's OT prophetic status and baptismal sign-act, we will discover that the baptism of Jesus is a further development of the initial promise that Jesus will save his people from their sins (Matt 1:21). His baptism was an acting-out of the royal son's messianic mission as the faithful embodiment of Israel. He came to fulfill the Father's will by undergoing the wrath of God to deliver his people from the judgment because of sin. Put succinctly, Jesus's messianic judgment makes the way for the deliverance of the new and repentant Israel and secures for them the promised new exodus. This is, conceivably, the main point of his baptism.

---

1. For an overview of interpretations see Davies and Allison, *Matthew I-VII*, 325–27.

2. Nolland cites nine different explanations and asserts that they all share one thing in common—they are "little more than projections from understandings of the historical Jesus held on other grounds." Nolland, *Matthew*, 152.

The Arrival of Jesus

Matthew distinguishes the religious leaders ἐρχομένους ἐπὶ τὸ βάπτισμα αὐτοῦ (Matt 3:7) with the coming of Jesus πρὸς τὸν Ἰωάννην τοῦ βαπτισθῆναι ὑπ᾽ αὐτοῦ (Matt 3:13).[3] John's stinging rebuke stands in pointed contrast to the divine acceptance of Jesus after his baptism. Matthew has presented the arrival of John the Baptist in the wilderness and Jesus at the Jordan with similar vocabulary and word order, which helps readers to conclude that both Jesus and John are operating according to the divine will: John by baptizing, Jesus by being baptized.[4]

Matthew's infinitive of purpose, πρὸς τὸν Ἰωάννην τοῦ βαπτισθῆναι ὑπ᾽ αὐτοῦ, suggests not that Jesus was eventually persuaded of the rightness of John's message, but that Jesus undertook the journey ἀπὸ τῆς Γαλιλαίας ἐπὶ τὸν Ἰορδάνην because he was already compelled to undergo the baptismal rite. To the narrative brevity, Matthew adds a short dialogue between John and Jesus to provide an explanation of the meaning of John's baptism of Jesus.

The Question of John

ὁ δὲ Ἰωάννης διεκώλυεν αὐτὸν λέγων· ἐγὼ χρείαν ἔχω ὑπὸ σοῦ βαπτισθῆναι, καὶ σὺ ἔρχῃ πρός με (Matt 3:14). The imperfect tense form of the *hapax legomenon* "διεκώλυεν" probably indicates a repeated yet unsuccessful attempt to circumvent Jesus' decision (cf. Jdt 4:7 [LXX 4:6]; 12:7 [LXX 12:6]).[5] Many commentators draw the reason for John's protest from the preceding pericope.[6] John announced that the one coming after him would baptize in the Holy Spirit and fire and understood Jesus to be the one he proclaimed.[7]

---

3. While ἐπί can convey the sense of opposition ("against"), their arrival is probably for the purposes of critical observation. Robert H. Gundry, *Matthew* (Grand Rapids: Eerdmans, 1982), 42. Carter thinks that they came to oppose John and persuade his audience not to be baptized by him. Carter, *Matthew and the Margins*, 97.

4. Temporal note + παραγίνεται + proper name (+ verb) + place name + verb. So Davies and Allison, *Matthew*, 1.321.

5. A conative use of the imperfect. Robertson, *A Grammar of the Greek New Testament*, 885. Wallace, *Greek Grammar*, 550.

6. Meier, *Matthew*, 26; Gundry, *Matthew*, 83; Davies and Allison, *Matthew*, 1.323–24; Hagner, *Matthew 1-13*, 55; Keener, *A Commentary*, 131–32; Garland, *Reading Matthew*; Nolland, *Matthew*, 153. France leaves John's objection on the basis of messianic baptism in the realm of possibility. France, *The Gospel According to Matthew*, 119.

7. A question commonly raised without answer in the literature is how John knew Jesus was the Coming One. Cf. David Hill, *The Gospel of Matthew* (London: Marshall, Morgan & Scott, 1972; repr., Grand Rapids: Eerdmans, 1986), 96. As the prophetic voice of Isa 40:3, this insight of John is consonant with his prophetic status. A prophet's knowledge of the future is predicated on receiving illumination from the divine.

Was John referring to his need to be baptized by Jesus with the Holy Spirit and fire, or does ἐγὼ χρείαν ἔχω ὑπὸ σοῦ βαπτισθῆναι refer to water baptism? There are three reasons that suggest John's statement refers to water baptism. The first is that Spirit and fire baptism are missing from the interchange (3:14–15). This is inferred and read back into John's protest. Second, a reference to the Spirit and fire baptism bypasses v. 13, Τότε παραγίνεται ὁ Ἰησοῦς ἀπὸ τῆς Γαλιλαίας ἐπὶ τὸν Ἰορδάνην πρὸς τὸν Ἰωάννην τοῦ βαπτισθῆναι ὑπ᾽ αὐτοῦ. The baptism of the Holy Spirit and fire is one pericope removed from John's reaction to Jesus's request, making water baptism the closest antecedent. The third reason hinges upon the nature of the baptism of the Holy Spirit and fire. We have shown that John's preaching of judgment underlies the sign. John declared that the baptism in the Holy Spirit and fire was an inundation of eschatological judgment to be escaped, and therefore, it would be incongruous to think that he would then ask to be baptized with the reality his baptism signified. But to conclude that Matthew understood the meaning of the baptism in the Holy Spirit and fire to be an announcement of something gracious runs into the difficulty of explaining John's later question to Jesus. If John conceived of the baptism in the Holy Spirit and fire as a gracious outpouring of blessing, renewal, and purification, then why after hearing of Jesus's mighty works does he ask Jesus if he is the One to Come (Matt 11:2–3)? If John was predicting a gracious work of the Spirit at the hand of the Coming One, Jesus's actions would be demonstrable proof of John's prediction. But it is precisely the lack of judgment (by Spirit and fire) that gives rise to the question. Mathew has collocated a number of Jesus's miraculous works in the lead up to John's request for clarification: the healing of the leper, centurion's servant and multitudes (8:1–4, 5–13, 14–17), casting out demons (vv. 8:28–34; 9:32–33), raising of a dead girl (9:18–26), opening the eyes of the blind (9:27–31), proclaiming the good news and healing "every affliction" (9:35–38). Matthew strategically places John's question after the healings, the spread of the reports and the commission of the disciples to preach and perform miracles, thereby replicating Jesus's activities (ch. 10). By including this later question by John, Matthew clarifies the meaning of the baptism in the Holy Spirit and fire. If John was not referring to eschatological judgment, then his question would make little sense.[8]

John was not predicting a work of blessing, but of a curse. The deeds of Christ did not fit the category John had used to describe the Coming One's work. The narrative transitional marker τότε and his later question can account for John's question. His rejoinder is simply that the water roles ought to be reversed.[9] As we

8. The difficulty is even felt by those who would interpret the baptism in the Holy Spirit as purificatory and fire as destructive. Commenting on 11:3, Nolland writes, "It is not clear how we are to relate John's confidence about Jesus' identity implicit in 3:14 with the present questioning, but a certain discomforting tension between John's expectations and what Jesus did is common property to Mt. 3:14, 9:14, and 11:3." Nolland, *Matthew*, 147, 450.

9. Witherington, *Matthew*, 81; Craig Evans, *Matthew*, NCBC (Cambridge: Cambridge University Press, 2012), 76; Morris, *The Gospel According to Matthew*, 64.

will see, this has less to do with an embarrassed demotion of John on the part of the Christian church, but is rather to provide an salvation-historical explanation for the reason Jesus must be baptized by John.

The Response of Jesus

For the moment (ἄφες ἄρτι), John must set aside his scruples and baptize Jesus: οὕτως γὰρ πρέπον ἐστὶν ἡμῖν πληρῶσαι πᾶσαν δικαιοσύνην (3:15). The anarthrous δικαιοσύνην is definite due to the pronominal adjective πᾶσαν.[10] Matthew has already used πληρόω to speak of the fulfillment of scripture (1:22; 2:15, 17, 23). Here, the adverbial use of the infinitive is for the purpose of fulfillment. What it fulfills is a multifaceted scriptural concept. The broad range of meaning of δικαιο σύνη can be summarized as the salvation-historical work of God, or human behavior conforming to God's revealed will/law. A combination of the two is also possible: by obeying God's will, Jesus will accomplish the salvation-historical purposes of God.

Przybylski believes that "the righteousness God demands" is Matthew's meaning and even *exclusive* usage.[11] Those who hunger and thirst for righteousness are blessed (5:6, 10); righteousness must exceed that of the scribes and the Pharisees (5:20) and must not be paraded before others (6:1). God's people must seek his righteousness (6:32).[12] Finally, John is also linked to righteousness (3:15; 21:32). While caution should be used in presupposing that Matthew and Paul are using the δικ—root in exactly the same way, it is equally questionable to dispense with OT usages, especially since Matthew makes such copious use of the OT throughout his gospel. On the one hand there is an ethical force to δικαιοσύνη that is difficult to deny in the Gospel of Matthew. On the other hand, πληρόω is most often the fulfillment of scripture in Matthew (13:48 and 23:32 are the only exceptions) and therefore salvation-historical in character.

Matthew's placement of the unique saying of Jesus into his narrative framework (exile, exodus/new exodus, wilderness testing) is not contrary to the ethical demands associated with δικαιοσύνη. As Jesus has already undergone his own exodus and exile (2:15), so he also faithfully obeys his father's will (3:15). Jesus has come to save his people from their sins (1:21) and it is the path of obedience that secures their salvation. The salvation-historical fulfillment is achieved by the son's obedience.

---

10. Wallace, *Greek Grammar*, 253.

11. Benno Przybylski, *Righteousness in Matthew and His World of Thought*, SNTSM 41 (Cambridge: Cambridge University Press, 1980), 78–99, esp. 115.

12. Nolland, 'In Such a Manner It Is Fitting for Us to Fulfill All Righteousness,' 65.

John and Jesus have a specific role to fulfill. France is correct in pointing out that πρέπον ἐστὶν ἡμῖν ("it is fitting for *us*") "indicates that Jesus is thinking of something specific to his own and John's role rather than of a general principle."[13] While John is the preparatory voice in the wilderness, Jesus is the embodiment of Israel, undergoing judgment for the purposes of the new exodus. The temptation narrative, with its citations from Deuteronomy, contrasts the faithful adherence of Jesus to God's Law with that of the past failure on the part of national Israel to do the same (4:1–11). But the statement in question includes John (ἡμῖν) and his baptism (21:25). John's inclusion is later explained by the position he holds in salvation history. All the prophets and the law prophesied until John (11:13). He is the Elijah to come (11:14). John came announcing the way of righteousness (21:32); Jesus came to walk in it. Fulfilling all righteousness is not only the requirement of the positive demands of God's Law, but also the punitive requisition for violations to the Law of God. Such an undertaking on behalf of his people is salvation-historical and, as we will now suggest in his baptism, the punitive side of fulfilling all righteousness is prominent.

Righteousness Fulfilled by Judgment

The context for the baptism of Jesus is prefaced by warning (Matt 3:2) and is judgment-laden (3:7–12). John's sign-act communicated the same. In symbolic fashion, Jesus undergoes his "trial by ordeal," passing through the judgment waters with the aim of fulfilling the righteousness required by God.[14]

The way of righteousness for Jesus is the obedience that takes him into suffering. His death/exile and resurrection/exodus are alluded to in the infancy narrative and symbolized by his baptism. With his baptism, Jesus begins his suffering.[15] Jesus's baptism pointed to his suffering. The eschatological Son of God/Son of Man comes to die.[16] His task is to lay down his life as a ransom for many.[17] He must rise from the dead as the one who has received the heavenly approbation after emerging from the waters of judgment.[18] What John later questions is the delay of judgment (11:1–3). The reason for the delay is the redemption of God's people: σώσει τὸν λαὸν αὐτοῦ ἀπὸ τῶν ἁμαρτιῶν αὐτῶν (Matt 1:21) and the way of their salvation is

---

13. France, *Matthew*, 120.

14. For analysis of the ancient trial by ordeal see Meredith G. Kline, "Oath and Ordeal Signs," *WTJ* 27.2 (1965): 115–39.

15. Gerhard Maier, *Matthäus-Evangelium*, BKZNT 1 (Stuttgart: Hänssler, 1983), 59.

16. Matt 12:40 (note the connection to the final judgment in vv. 41–42); 16:4, 21; 17:9–13, 22; 20:17–19, 28; 21:37–43; 26:26–29.

17. Substitution and representation are Matthean themes (20:28; 26:28).

18. Matt 16:21; 17:9, 23; 20:19; 26:29.

the cross. In brief, Jesus recapitulates Israel's history and experiences (4:1–12; 26:17–25), including their judgment. As Meier has summarized:

> The baptism indicates that Jesus knew, presumably by hearing it firsthand, the basic eschatological message of John and agreed with it . . . (1) The end of Israel's history as Israel had experienced it up until now was fast approaching. (2) Israel as a people had gone astray, had in effect apostatized; and so all Israel was in danger of being consumed by the fire of God's wrathful judgment, soon to come. (3) The only way to pass from the present sinful state in which Abraham's children were caught to the state of those Israelites who would be saved on the last day was to undergo a basic change of mind and heart. This interior change had to be reflected in a basic change in the way one lived one's life, and it had to be sealed by submission to the special, once-and-for-all, ritual immersion administered by John . . . (4) Implicit in all this is Jesus' recognition of John as a prophet sent by God to all Israel in the short, critical time left before the judgment. In other words, Jesus acknowledged John to be *a* or *the* eschatological prophet.[19]

The only way to be saved was for Jesus to stand in the place of sinners.[20] Jesus does not come to John to *confess* sin, but to undertake the *payment* of sin, to bear the judgment and to secure eternal life (Matt 8:11–12; 22:1–14; 25:1–13; 26:28–29). Read in such a way, salvation comes through the judgment of Jesus. John came to announce the judgment of God against the nation of Israel, and the way of escape would be more than confessing sin and being initiated into the judgment waters. It could only be escaped by Jesus's work, figuratively displayed in baptism and carried out on the cross. The judgment of Jesus, as we will later see, also seals the fate of the unrepentant.

The Gift of the Spirit and Old Testament Background

The giving of the Spirit follows the baptism of Jesus. Once Jesus undergoes the judgment sign and emerges from the waters, the heavens are opened: βαπτισθεὶς δὲ ὁ Ἰησοῦς εὐθὺς ἀνέβη ἀπὸ τοῦ ὕδατος· καὶ ἰδοὺ ἠνεῴχθησαν [αὐτῷ] οἱ οὐρανοί, καὶ εἶδεν [τὸ] πνεῦμα [τοῦ] θεοῦ καταβαῖνον ὡσεὶ περιστερὰν [καὶ] ἐρχόμενον ἐπ᾽ αὐτόν (Matt 3:16).

The main differences in the synoptic accounts are that both Matthew and Luke have ἀνοίγω (Q?) where Mark reads σχιζομένους (Mark 1:10). In Matthew and Mark Jesus sees the heavens opening and descent of the Spirit (Matt 3:16; Mark 1:10), while Luke writes that the heavenly opening and descent occur while Jesus

---

19. Meier, *A Marginal Jew*, 109–10. Emphasis is Meier's.

20. Jeffrey A. Gibbs, "Israel Standing with Israel: The Baptism of Jesus in Matthew's Gospel (Matt 3:13–17)," *CBQ* 64 (2002): 522.

is praying (Lk 3:21). As will be explored, Matthew's modifications of Mark and differences from Luke are for the purposes of OT echo.

Matthew's text, while not a formal citation, is closest to Ezekiel in terms of conceptual similarity, diction, and word order. Both experiences occur near rivers and describe the opening of the heavens, theophanic manifestations, and a heavenly voice of explanation (Ezek 1:1, 4, 28; 2:1–3:12; Matt 3:16).[21] Matthew's choice of words and word order are almost certainly drawn from the apocalyptic introduction to Ezekiel's revelation:[22]

Matthew 3:16	Ezekiel 1:1
ἰδοὺ ἠνεῴχθησαν [αὐτῷ] οἱ οὐρανοί,	καὶ ἠνοίχθησαν οἱ οὐρανοί, καὶ εἶδον
καὶ εἶδεν [τὸ] πνεῦμα [τοῦ] θεοῦ . . .[23]	ὁράσεις θεοῦ.

This apocalyptic entry point not only alerts Matthew's readers to the visionary nature of the following temptation, but also suggests that Jesus's ministry will bear some resemblance to that of Ezekiel's.[24] Jesus not only begins his work in a way similar to Ezekiel, but his messianic task is reminiscent of Ezekiel. He too must go to Israel with messages of judgment, exile, and the salvation of God's people.

Ezekiel's first task is to pronounce judgment. In the words of Dumbrell,

> The prophetic word to Israel is one of undeviating judgment relating to the destruction of city and temple. Any messages of hope in chapters 1-24 beyond this destruction do not weaken the stark character of the prophetic threat directed against Jerusalem and her temple in its historical context. The very symbols of the community's faith were marked out by the message for destruction, a message completely unacceptable to the Israel of Ezekiel's day.[25]

Standing by the river, Ezekiel sees the heavens open (Ezek 1:1), after which comes the theophany (Ezek 1:4–28), followed by the divine voice (Ezek 2:1–7). Ezekiel is

---

21. The Spirit also plays an important role in the visionary experiences of each (Ezek 2:1; 3:12, 14; 11:1, 24; 43:5; Matt 3:16; 4:1). The coming of the Spirit upon Jesus in Matt 3:16 (ἐρχόμενον ἐπ᾽ αὐτόν) might also allude to the coming of the Spirit in Ezek 3:24 (καὶ ἦλθεν ἐπ᾽ ἐμὲ πνεῦμα).

22. David Mathewson, "The Apocalyptic Vision of Jesus according to the Gospel of Matthew: Reading Matthew 3:16–4:11 Intertextually," *TynBul* 62.1 (2011): 93–94; David B. Capes, "Intertextual Echoes in the Matthean Baptismal Narrative," *BBR* 9 (1999): 37–49, esp. 42. Ezekiel 1:1 is the only OT reference cited in NA28.

23. The earliest reading is difficult to decide. Did copyists add αὐτῷ for greater clarity or omit it as unnecessary? Bruce Metzger, *A Textual Commentary on the Greek New Testament* (Stuttgart: United Bible Society, 1975), 11.

24. In the place of a heavenly journey, some apocalypses contain "ecstatic journeys to earthly locales." Mathewson, "Apocalyptic Vision," 100.

25. Dumbrell, *Faith of Israel*, 130.

to go to a people who are rebellious (vv. 3, 5–7) and stubborn (v. 4). Similarly, Jesus is in (or near) the Jordan River, the heavens are opened, and the Spirit alights upon him. But the divine words that follow are decidedly different. In contrast to faithless Israel, Jesus is the faithful son.[26] Jesus will prove to be faithful, even though national Israel recapitulates the Israel of Ezekiel's day by rejecting the way of God's rule through his son. Israel was baptized and confession of sin was made (Matt 3:6). When Jesus is baptized, it is not a confession of sin that follows, but a heavenly declaration of sonship.

By undergoing the sign of judgment as the embodiment of Israel, Jesus receives the Spirit. This pattern of judgment followed by the giving of the Spirit is found in several places in the OT (Isa 32:15–20; 44:3–4; 59:20–21; Ezek 39:25–29; Joel 2:28–29). One could say that the exile is not over until the Spirit is poured out upon Israel. Jesus secures the Spirit for the repentant through his work as the faithful son that Israel had failed to be. As in the case of Ezekiel, Matthew's apocalyptic insertion shows what will be. Ezekiel is told that Israel would continue to be rebellious (Ezek 2:1–7; 3:7). Jerusalem would be besieged and judged (Ezek 4–32), but the Lord also promised that he would be the God of the remnant and David would be their prince (Ezek 34:23–24). Yahweh will gather them from their exile (Ezek 39:25–28) and pour out his Spirit upon the house of Israel (Ezek 39:29). In those days he would cleanse and restore a new Jerusalem with its eschatological temple (chs. 40–48) and the glory of the Lord would fill it (Ezek 43:5).[27]

Judgment, exile, salvation, and the pouring out of the Spirit are the themes of Ezekiel and they are the themes of Matt 3. With this allusion to Ezekiel, Matthew's biblical-theological narrative returns to an important theme in the genealogy, the deportation to Babylon: Ἰωσίας δὲ ἐγέννησεν τὸν Ἰεχονίαν καὶ τοὺς ἀδελφοὺς αὐτοῦ ἐπὶ τῆς μετοικεσίας Βαβυλῶνος (Matt 1:11). With the arrival of ὁ Χριστός (Matt 1:1, 16–18; 2:4), his undergoing of John's sign of judgment, the approval and anointing of the Spirit (Matt 3:16), the conclusion to Matthew's genealogical history of Israel have been reached: . . . καὶ ἀπὸ τῆς μετοικεσίας Βαβυλῶνος ἕως τοῦ Χριστοῦ γενεαὶ δεκατέσσαρες (Matt 1:17). The deportation that Ezekiel saw and experienced ends with Jesus.

The Descent of the Spirit

The opening of the heavens is not unique to Ezekiel (2 Sam 22:10; Pss 18:9; 102:26; 144:5; Isa 64:1; Ezk 1:1; Acts 7:56; 10:11; Rev 19:11).[28] As we have already observed in Matt 3:2, the plural οὐρανοι is part of Matthew's idiolectic usage of heaven and

---

26. Cf. G. H. P. Thompson, "Called-Proved-Obedient: A Study in the Baptism and Temptation Narratives of Matthew and Luke," *JTS* 11.1 (1960): 1–12.

27. Note the reference to the first vision that links the restoration and renewal with the vision of judgment (Ezek 43:3).

28. Rowland, *The Open Heaven*, 358–67.

is most likely used here as the realm of God.[29] The passive ἠνεῴχθησαν would then be an indication of the action of God (a "divine passive") in response to Jesus's submission to baptism and the implications that flow from it.[30] The conflict between the kingdom of heaven and earthly kingdoms (Matt 2:3, 16; 3:2) will not only be overcome through judgment brought by Jesus (Matt 3:7–12), but also the promised endowment of the Spirit for the purposes of renewal and restoration (Isa 11:1–5; cf. Matt 12:18–21).[31]

The Role of the Spirit

Though not described in terms of theophany, the Spirit rested upon judges (Judg 3:10), kings (1 Sam 11:6; 16:13), prophets (2 Chr 15:1), and upon the messiah, equipping him for his work (Isa 11:1; 42:1; 61:1; Pss. Sol. 17:37; 1 En. 49:3; T. Levi 18:6–14). The imparting of the Spirit was for the subduing of Israel's enemies and the blessing of Israel and the world. Matthew does not tell his readers why the Spirit was given.[32] Following the baptism, the first activity of the Spirit is to lead Jesus into the wilderness to be tempted by the devil (4:1). Matthew makes no mention of the Spirit's help while Jesus is being tempted, but the positive and prophesied work of the Spirit in liberation and restoration is implied through Jesus's ability to heal (12:15–21). We also note that the specific phrase, πνεῦμα [τοῦ] θεοῦ, appears only at the baptism of Jesus and the liberation of a demon-oppressed man (12:28). In response to the accusation that Jesus casts out demons by the prince of demons, Jesus declares that such an assertion is blasphemy against πνεύματος τοῦ ἁγίου which will not be forgiven (12:32). This is Matthew's last mention of the Spirit's role in the work of Jesus. In Matthew, the messianic task is one of healing and judgment (i.e., against the evil spirit of the blind-mute). The Spirit is involved in both.

The Description of the Spirit

The descent of the Spirit like a dove is a puzzling.[33] France and Keener think that Noah's dove might be the most suitable background, while others detect a possible

29. Cf. Ezek 1:1–4; 2 Bar 22:1–3a; T. Levi 2.6; Acts 10:11; Rev 10:1. See also, Fritzleo Lentzen-Deis, *Die Taufe nach den Synoptikern: Literarkritische und gattungsgeschichtliche Untersuchungen* (Frankfurt am Main: Joseph Knecht, 1970), 99–119.

30. Carter, *Matthew and the Margins*, 103; Hagner, *Matthew*, 1.57. Proceeding upon the basis of Markan priority, Matthew has changed Mark's splitting of the heavens, σχιζομένους τοὺς οὐρανοὺς (1:10) to "the heavens were opened," ἠνεῴχθησαν οἱ οὐρανοί. This adjustment would further the link to Ezekiel.

31. Pennington, *Heaven and Earth*, 342–43.

32. The OT expectations of messianic endowment for the purposes of carrying out the will of God would be suitable for Matthew's usage.

33. Davies and Allison list sixteen interpretations: Davies and Allison, *Matthew*, 1.331–32; cf. Luz, *Matthew 1–7*, 1434–45.

allusion to Gen 1 in the hovering of the Spirit over the waters.[34] The book of Genesis links the flood with the account of creation. Such points of contact include the world returning to a watery state (Gen 1:2; 7:19–20), differentiation of water and sky (Gen 1:6–8; 8:2), land appearing on the third day and the appearance of the mountaintops on the third dated event (Gen 1:9; 8:5) and the repeated command that birds, animals, and humans be fruitful and multiply (Gen 1:22, 28; 8:17–19; 9:1, 7).[35] To this one could add the connection of eating/drinking (Adam = fruit of the tree, Gen 3:6–7; Noah = fruit of the vine, 9:21), the covering of nakedness (Gen 3:21; 9:23), and pronouncement of curses (Gen 3:17; 9:25). In the NT, flood symbolism is incorporated into explanations of the end of the age with the return of Christ and recreation of the earth. Matthew, like other NT writers, views the flood as paradigmatic for the final judgment (Matt 24:36–44; cf. 1 Pet 3:20–21; 2 Pet 3:6–7).[36]

If we are to understand the hovering of the Spirit as a dove over the baptismal waters to be a signal of new creation, it would then follow (from our analysis of John's baptismal sign) that Jesus's undertaking of the curse and emerging through the symbolic waters of judgment brings the gift of the Spirit and new creation as a result of his work. These themes of water and the hovering of the Spirit might then be suggestive of the end of judgment and the exodus.[37] If the Spirit's descent like a dove is meant to encourage recollection of the first instance of the dove in the Bible (Gen 8), then the waters of baptism, so interpreted, could recall divine judgment. It is the dove's return with the olive leaf that assures Noah and his family of the water ordeal's abatement and their deliverance. Such connections, as we have traced them, are suggestive implications drawn from creation/new creation motifs that are themselves possible, but not certain.

The Heavenly Approbation

The divine voice coming through the opened heavens is the attestation to Jesus's identity, and indirectly to his mission. Proposals for OT backgrounds include Isa

---

34. Keener, *Matthew*, 132–33; France, *Matthew*, 122; Rowland, *Open Heaven*, 361–63; Davies and Allison, *Matthew*, 1.334; Hagner, *Matthew* 1.58; Carter, *Matthew and the Margins*, 103; Warren A. Gage, *The Gospel of Genesis: Studies in Protology and Eschatology* (Winona Lake: Carpenter Books, 1984), 129.

35. Joseph Blenkinsopp, *Creation, Un-creation, Re-creation: A Discursive Commentary on Genesis 1-11* (London: T&T Clark, 2011), 131–54; Waltke and Yu, *An Old Testament Theology*, 293–94; Gordon J. Wenham, *Genesis 1-15*, WBC 1 (Nashville: Thomas Nelson, 1987), 185; John H. Sailhamer, *The Pentateuch as Narrative* (Grand Rapids: Zondervan, 1992), 127.

36. Keener, *Matthew*, 133.

37. In the Jewish mind the Exodus was linked with the act of creation. Davies and Allison, *Matthew*, 1.153.

42:1, Ps 2:7, Gen 22:2, Jer 38:20 (LXX), Exod 4:22–23 and Deut 32.[38] The majority position understands a combination of Isa 40:2 and Ps 2:7 to be behind Matt 3:17.[39] Despite scholarly demurrals, Ps 2:7 and Isa 42:1 continue to be the most widely held and discussed viewpoints.[40] We will begin with what is probably a secondary allusion and therefore more tenuous, namely Ps 2:7.

Psalm 2:7

There are four primary objections that Ps 2:7 lies behind the heavenly approbation. In the first place, the predominant narrative themes are Christological and recapitulatory of Israel. Secondly, the theme of Davidic royalty is lacking in the preaching of John. Thirdly, the begetting of Jesus is located in ch. 1, not 3:17, and

---

38. For Gen 22:2 see Geza Vermes, *Scripture and Tradition in Judaism: Haggadic Studies* (Leiden: Brill, 1973), 221–23, Leroy A. Huizenga, *The New Isaac: Tradition and Intertextuality in the Gospel of Matthew*, SNT (Leiden: Brill, 2009); Gibbs, "Israel Standing with Israel," 522–26; Paul G. Bretscher, "Exodus 4:22-23 and the Voice from Heaven," *JBL* 87 (1968): 301–11; Brandon D. Crowe, *The Obedient Son: Deuteronomy and Christology in the Gospel of Matthew*, BZNW 188 (Berlin: Walter de Gruyter, 2012), 194–200.

39. Dunn, *Jesus Remembered*, 374.

40. Morna Hooker analyzes the three words used to describe Jesus (beloved, son, and well-pleased) and concludes that these words conceptually describe Israel, and therefore can only be dubiously ascribed to Isa 42: Morna D. Hooker, *Jesus and the Servant: The Influence of the Servant Concept of Deutero-Isaiah in the New Testament* (London: SPCK, 1959), 73. For arguments against an allusion to Ps 2:7 see Joachim Jeremias and Walther Zimmerli, *The Servant of God* (London: SCM, 1957), 80–81; Oscar Cullmann, *Christology of the New Testament* (London: SCM, 1963), 66; Reginald H. Fuller, *The Foundations of New Testament Christology* (London: Collins, 1969), 170; Gibbs, "Israel Standing with Israel," 511–26; Hooker, *Jesus and the Servant*, 67–73; Huizenga, *The New Isaac*, 156–66. Crowe, *Obedient Son*, 187–89. For those who attribute the echo to Ps 2 (with varying degrees of probability), see: William Barclay, *The Gospel of Matthew*, 2 vols. (Philadelphia: Westminster Press, 1958), 1.53; W. F. Albright and C. S. Mann, *Matthew*, AB (New York: Doubleday, 1971), 30–31; Hill, *Matthew*, 1972, 97–98; Kingsbury, *Matthew: Structure, Christology, Kingdom*, 48–50; Beare, *The Gospel According to Matthew*, 100–04; Davies and Allison, *Matthew*, 1.336–39; Robert H. Smith, *Matthew*, ACNT (Minneapolis: Augsburg, 1989), 59; Frederick D. Bruner, *Matthew: A Commentary*, 2 vols. (Waco: Word, 1990), 2.607; John P. Meier, *The Vision of Matthew: Christ, Church, and Morality in the First Gospel* (Eugene: Wipf & Stock, 1991), 58–59; Harrington, *Matthew*, 62; Blomberg, *Matthew*, 82; Hagner, *Matthew*, 1.58–59; Dunn, *Jesus Remembered*, 1.372–74; Carter, *Matthew and the Margins*, 104; Nolland, *Matthew*, 157; France, *Matthew*, 123–24; Turner, *Matthew*, 120; Kennedy, *Recapitulation*, 179–82; Osborne, *Matthew*, 125; Craig Evans, *Matthew*, NCBC (Cambridge: Cambridge University Press, 2012), 78.

finally, there are several discrepancies in the wording of the so-called allusion: "Psalm 2:7 speaks of the king only as 'my son,' not 'my beloved son' and uses the third person singular 'this is my son' instead of the second person 'you are my son.'"[41]

Gibbs acknowledges that a royal Davidic messianic motif runs through chs. 1–2, but doubts such is the case for ch. 3.[42] Furthermore, "in Matthew 3 and especially in the Baptist's proclamation concerning the Coming One, there is no discernible reference to the theme of the royal Davidic Messiah."[43] But the continuation of the royal son motif in chs. 1–2 is a logical explanation for John's announcement that "the kingdom of heaven is at hand." It is not likely that Matthew conceives of a kingdom coming, minus the king, or a different king than the one presented in Matt 1–2. Matthew has made such a Davidic kingship connection logically necessary (Matt 1:1, 6, 17; 2:6). He is introduced in chs 1–2, his approaching kingdom is announced by the coming of the herald (Matt 3:1–3), he is endowed with the Spirit (Isa 11; 42:1) and to him belongs "all the kingdoms of the world and their glory" (Matt 4:8).

Another reason for rejecting Ps 2:7 is that Matthew has already spoken of the "begetting" ἐκ πνεύματος ἁγίου (1:18–20). Finding an allusion to Ps 2:7 in 3:17 would generate two begettings of Jesus. Therefore, Matthew's readers "will in no way think of Jesus's baptism as the 'today' of Ps 2:7 when Jesus is begotten by God."[44] The difficulty with such a statement lies in the meaning attributed to Ps 2:7. As the NT documents indicate, Ps 2:7 was never used by the early church as a physical begetting or conception of Jesus (Acts 13:33; Heb 1:5; 5:5). Such a view attaches a meaning to "begetting" that neither Ps 2:7 nor the NT supports. In Ps 2:6 the king is already seated upon his throne. This is not a reference to his birth, but to his installation and enthronement which the NT writers understand to take place after his resurrection. John's baptism as an enacted sign of judgment (and Jesus's undergoing and emerging from the water) is a foreshadowing of his death and exaltation thereby making Ps 2:7 a suitable OT echo.

The difference in wording (the addition of "beloved" and the change from the second-person form of address "you are my son" to the third person "this is my son") is not very significant. Matthew combines OT texts (cf. 2:6) and modifies them to fit his narrative purposes (11:10).[45] As we will go on to show, Matthew's altering of the original wording makes better sense as an adjustment to conform the heavenly voice at Jesus's baptism to the voice at his transfiguration (17:5).

What possible contribution might the psalm have for the baptism of Jesus? Psalm 2, as we have observed, is the coronation of the king who would reign over all the nations. Those who oppose him will perish. Both John and the psalmist make similar points. The son as king will judge his enemies even as he will surely

---

41. Gibbs, "Israel Standing with Israel," 512–25.

42. Ibid., 513.

43. Ibid.

44. Ibid.

45. Note how Matthew changes the wording of Mal 3:1 from "he will prepare the way before me" to "he will prepare the way before you."

rule over all peoples. The preaching of John and the wording of the psalm relate this king, eschatologically, to the climax of God's kingdom and work. If Matthew intends an echo of this coronation psalm, then it follows immediately upon his symbolic act of suffering death. Such a composition conforms to the understanding of the early church which saw in the resurrection of the Son the attending coronation of the messianic king.

In the case of Matthew, Jesus is the rightful king who is declared the Son of God after his baptism and transfiguration. Matthew has laid down the themes of sonship and kingship in his genealogy and has described the infancy narrative as a conflict between kings. Through John, the announcement of the kingdom comes to Israel and, upon the baptism of Jesus, the Davidic king is proclaimed to be the Son. Sonship and suffering are anticipated in the OT (2 Sam 7:14; Pss 2:7; 89:26–27). With regard to the latter motif, a good case can be made via David who was pursued by Saul, his enemy, as well as by his son Absalom and the great majority of Israelites who backed his revolt. Psalms of kingship give expression to the distress and suffering of the Davidic king (Pss 20:9; 63:11). Yet in the end, David is exalted over all Israel and his enemies are either destroyed or subjugated to him.

After the baptism of Jesus the voice of approval is announced. He is the Son whom God will exalt. The son's work is indicated by his baptism and by the second OT echo from Isa 42:1.

Isaiah 42:1

The reasons most commonly cited for this Isaianic reference include the descent of the Spirit "upon him," τὸ πνεῦμά μου ἐπ᾽ αὐτόν (Isa 42:1; the targum reads "my holy spirit"), the translation εὐδόκησεν in Theodotion and Symmachus, and Matthew's formula quotation of Isa 42:1 applied to Jesus in 12:18. Though not without its difficulties, we will proceed to look at the potential meanings and illumination Isa 42:1 has for the understanding and approval of Jesus's work which is enacted in baptism. [46]

The difficulties of assessing the servant theme in Isa 40–55 are well known. Collective interpretations understand the servant to be either Israel, or a portion/remnant of Israel, while the individual interpretations cover a spectrum of historical figures.[47] Childs draws the interpretive difficulties together with the following broad overview:

---

46. For arguments against Isa 42:1 in Matt 3:17 see Gerhard Barth, "Matthew's Understanding of the Law," in *Tradition and Interpretation in Matthew*, eds. Günther Bornkamm, Gerhard Barth, and Heinz Joachim Held, trans. P. Scott (London: SCM, 1963), 126; Schweizer, *TDNT*, 8.368; Hooker, *Jesus and the Servant*, 72; Huizenga, *The New Isaac*, 163–66.

47. Individual interpretations include Zerubbabel, Jehoiachin, Moses, Uzziah, Ezekiel, Isaiah, a leper and Cyrus. Dillard and Longman, *Introduction*, 278.

On the one hand, the servant is viewed as collective Israel; on the other, he is an individual. Collective Israel is pictured as blind and deaf, unable to understand, a people robbed and plundered (42.18ff.), whereas the other servant is described as alert and sensitive to the word of God (50.4ff.). Collective Israel is guilty of her punishment; the other servant is innocent. Collective Israel suffers from the abuse of the nations, whereas the other servant is rejected by his own people. Finally, collective Israel is portrayed in typical, representative language, while the other servant appears as a historical figure who suffered and died at a particular time.[48]

Isaiah 42:1–9 has been described as the installation of the servant of the Lord.[49] The divine legitimation of the servant is reminiscent of the royal psalms (Pss 2; 72; 89; 110), addressed in the third person to the listeners, be they heavenly or earthly.[50] In Ps 2:7 and Isa 42:1 Yahweh describes the work of his son/servant. The LXX identifies the unnamed servant of 42:1 as Israel, Ἰακὼβ ὁ παῖς μου, ἀντιλήμψομαι αὐτοῦ· Ἰσραὴλ ὁ ἐκλεκτός μου, προσεδέξατο αὐτὸν ἡ ψυχή μου. This is probably in keeping with the previous reference to Isaiah's servant (41:8).

The profile of the Isa 42:1 servant is one of correspondence and contrast. The servant has been identified as "Israel," "Jacob" and the "offspring of Abraham" (41:8). On the other hand, the servant of 42:1 may also be conceived of as a singular individual contrasted with the servant of 41:8 that had become corrupt by their idolatry. The "servant" "Jacob" (41:8) is addressed and rebuked by the King of Jacob (41:21). But the servant of 42:1 is delighted in and is faithful to Yahweh. After speaking of the servant's task which includes the opening of the eyes of the blind (42:7), he is then described as blind (42:19). Idolatry has ensnared the servant (43:10), even though God has chosen Israel that they would know that only Yahweh is Lord and the idolatry of the nations is futile (44:9–22). The continuity and contrast of the servant(s) continues throughout Isa 40–55 and reaches an unexpected crescendo in ch. 53 with suffering and death.

From a literary perspective there appears to be two Israels: the faithless and the faithful. The Lord promises his servant that he will blot out transgressions (44:21–22). Even though Israel disregarded the Lord's commandments (48:18–19), Yahweh will redeem his servant Jacob and they will leave Babylon (48:20). The servant later responds that he has labored in vain (49:4).[51] But God declares that the servant will

---

48. Childs, *Introduction*, 1982, 334–35.

49. Klaus Baltzer, "Zur formgeschichtlichen Bestimmung der Texte vom Gottesknecht im Deuterojesaja Buch," in *Probleme biblischer Theologie*, eds. Gerhard Von Rad and Hans W. Wolff (München: Chr. Kaiser, 1971), 27–43.

50. "It Is Jacob–Israel": John Goldingay and David Payne, *A Critical and Exegetical Commentary on Isaiah 40-55*, 2 vols., ICC (London: T&T Clark, 2006), 212.

51. Quite unlike the servant of 42:4 who does not grow faint and is not discouraged.

not only bring Israel back (the new exodus), but will be a light to the nations (49:6; cf. 42:6), causing salvation to extend to the ends of the earth. In ch. 53 the Lord is pleased to take away the travail of the servant's soul and: to justify the righteous one who serves many, and he will bear their sins (δικαιῶσαι δίκαιον εὖ δουλεύοντα πολλοῖς, καὶ τὰς ἁμαρτίας αὐτῶν αὐτὸς ἀνοίσει, Isa 53:11). The Isaianic contours of the servant's function are that he/they function on behalf of sinful Israel, while at the same time benefiting the nations (42:1, 6–7). Judgment against Israel has passed, and the restoration and liberation from exile comes through him:

> And now the Lord says, he who formed me from the womb to be his servant, to bring Jacob back to him; and that Israel might be gathered to him—for I am honored in the eyes of the Lord, and my God has become my strength—he says: "It is too light a thing that you should be my servant to raise up the tribes of Jacob and to bring back the preserved of Israel; I will make you as a light for the nations, that my salvation may reach to the end of the earth." (Isa 49:5–6)

Read as a literary whole, as Matthew would most certainly have done, the faithful servant who is chosen and endowed with the Spirit to bring justice and light to the nations (note that Matthew cites this Isaianic theme after the temptation of Jesus, 4:15–16), who opens the eyes of the blind and delivers the prisoners, is the servant who gives his life: ἁμαρτίας αὐτῶν αὐτὸς ἀνοίσει (53:11). This faithful servant is a substitute for the faithless and is delivered over to death: ἀνθ᾽ ὧν παρεδόθη εἰς θάνατον ἡ ψυχὴ αὐτοῦ, being numbered among the lawless: καὶ ἐν τοῖς ἀνόμοις ἐλογίσθη, bearing their sins: καὶ αὐτὸς ἁμαρτίας πολλῶν ἀνήνεγκεν (53:12). His reward for his sacrificial work is guaranteed, κληρονομήσει πολλούς (53:12). Note also how Matthew takes up Isa 42:1–4 and applies it to the healings of Jesus (12:15–20) which are set against the backdrop of his opponents conspiring to kill him: ἐξελθόντες δὲ οἱ Φαρισαῖοι συμβούλιον ἔλαβον κατ᾽ αὐτοῦ ὅπως αὐτὸν ἀπολέσωσιν. Ὁ δὲ Ἰησοῦς γνοὺς ἀνεχώρησεν ἐκεῖθεν (Matt 12:14–15a).

Does Matthew have the entire work of the Isaianic servant in mind in the baptismal scene? The servant who is the hope of the nation and who suffers for the sins of his people fits within the interpretive framework Matthew has provided. The one who saves his people from their sins (Matt 1:21) is the one who endures the judgment on their behalf (Matt 3:16). In response, Yahweh declares him to be his Son and endows him with the Holy Spirit to accomplish God's plan. Jesus, as the obedient Israel who is contrasted with the disobedient Israel, is not unlike the obedient servant (be he an individual or collective from the perspective of Isaiah) who is also contrasted with the disobedient servant. In both cases, the work of the servant and son is for the benefit of others. In both Isaiah and Matthew, the servant-son must suffer on behalf of others. This is prefigured in the baptism of Jesus, but even more succinctly it is foretold in the account of the transfiguration which Matthew has verbally linked to the baptism. If the sufferings of the son are typified in his baptism, they are expressly stated in the transfiguration and connected by a common link, to which we now turn before drawing this chapter to a close.

The Elaboration of Jesus's Baptism in the Transfiguration

Matthew's typological interests return to Moses and Elijah in ch. 17, and in the case of Moses, such a typology has been noted above (ch. 7).[52] Both Moses and Jesus ascend a mountain after six days (Exod 24:16, 12, 15–18; Matt 17:1) accompanied by three named individuals (Exod 24:1; Matt 17:1), the faces of Moses and Jesus shine (Exod 34:29–35; Matt 17:2), a luminescent cloud overshadows the mountain (Exod 24:15–18; Matt 17:5) with a voice proceeding from it (Exod 24:16; Matt 17:5), and the response of the onlookers is fear (Exod 34: 29–30; Matt 17:6). Whereas Mark reads καὶ ὤφθη αὐτοῖς Ἠλίας σὺν Μωϋσεῖ (Mark 9:4), Matthew has changed the order to reflect the primacy of Moses: καὶ ἰδοὺ ὤφθη αὐτοῖς Μωϋσῆς καὶ Ἠλίας (17:3).[53] Other possible connections to Moses might be drawn from ἐπισκιάζω, which is used to describe the cloud overshadowing the tabernacle (LXX, Exod 40:35), and Peter's proposal to build booths/tents ("σκηνάς," Matt 17:4; Exod 29:4; 33:7–10).[54]

The transfiguration is followed by a heavenly voice and content that is nearly identical to that of the baptism of Jesus with the addition of "hear him." Neither Mark nor Luke have ἐν ᾧ εὐδόκησα (Mark 9:7; Luke 9:35). Matthew has reduplicated it in order to further the parallel to the voice at Jesus's baptism:[55]

Matthew 3:17	**Matthew 17:5**
καὶ ἰδοὺ φωνὴ ἐκ τῶν οὐρανῶν λέγουσα· οὗτός ἐστιν ὁ υἱός μου ὁ ἀγαπητός, ἐν ᾧ εὐδόκησα.	καὶ ἰδοὺ φωνὴ ἐκ τῆς νεφέλης λέγουσα· οὗτός ἐστιν ὁ υἱός μου ὁ ἀγαπητός, ἐν ᾧ εὐδόκησα· ἀκούετε αὐτοῦ.

The additional "hear him" adds another layer to the Mosaic typology. Jesus is the prophet like Moses: "him you shall hear" (Deut 18:15).[56] In the OT, Israel was to hear the commands of the Lord. But what are the disciples to hear? It could be the instructions that follow (17:9–12), what has preceded (16:21–28), or both. The nature of the instruction in both instances shares (at least) this common theme: Jesus must die. This also, we have argued, is a primary meaning for the baptismal account.

In a salvation-historical sense, "hear him/ἀκούετε αὐτοῦ" (17:5) probably alludes to Jesus as the prophet to come (Deut 18:15–19). Contextually, it signals to readers a point previously made: Jesus's words to his disciples about his identity and mission (16:21). The divine word attests to Peter's confession, σὺ εἶ ὁ χριστὸς

---

52. Cf. Allison, *The New Moses*, 243–48.

53. Davies and Allison, *Matthew VIII-XVIII*, 685.

54. Davies and Allison, *Matthew*, 2.699–700, 701; Carter, *Matthew and the Margins*, 348–49.

55. Gundry, *Matthew*, 344.

56. Meier, *Matthew*, 191.

ὁ υἱὸς τοῦ θεοῦ τοῦ ζῶντος (16:16). What the disciples had not grasped was that sonship entailed death. Peter's response to Jesus's question contains an ironic twist: while Jesus is the son of the *living* God (ὁ υἱὸς τοῦ θεοῦ τοῦ ζῶντος), the Son of God will most certainly die. Peter's *beatitude*, "blessed are you Peter," is followed by a *rebuke* when he objects to Jesus's mission of suffering, death and resurrection (16:21). The baptism and transfiguration of Jesus are both preceded by objections (3:14; 16:22)

The glorification of the Son of God and his arrival in "his kingdom" are not hindered by death. Rather, it is through suffering, death, and resurrection that the king of the kingdom must pass. Of this the divine voice testifies and the radiance of Jesus's kingdom glory is manifested to the disciples on the mountain. On their way down the mountain, Jesus speaks to his disciples of his resurrection from the dead (17:9). The glory that the disciples see on the mountain is the preview of his resurrection glory. For their part, the disciples are left pondering the place of Elijah in salvation history. The much-debated subject of whether or not Elijah was *anticipated* by the scribes need not deter us here.[57] Our interest is in Matthew's connection of John the Baptist to Elijah and his relationship to Jesus. Matthew has described John in ch. 3 with Elijah-like imagery (3:4) and as the Isaianic voice who prepares the way (3:3). Jesus's own perspective on John is the same (11:9, 14). More importantly the rejection of John has already been indicated and, in keeping with Matthew's Jesus-John parallelism, so has the rejection of Jesus (11:18–19). Both forerunner and Coming One will share in the same fate, but the transfiguration shows the disciples what lies on the other side of his death.

Once again, the echoes of Isa 42:1 and Ps 2:7 bear upon the meaning of the transfiguration even as they did upon the baptism. "Together," writes Bruner, "psalm and Isaiah say that the Father's Voice over Jesus means this: Jesus is God's Son (psalm) and God's (Isaiah) Servant, the One bequeathed the ends of the earth (Ps 2:8; cf. Matt 28:18) and who, endowed by the Spirit, will bring forth justice to the nations (Isa 42:1b; 49:6; cf. Matt 12:18b)."[58] But the servant who is installed as king must paradoxically suffer mistreatment and death:

> The transfiguration narrative has a remarkable twin of sorts in the account of Jesus' execution, 27.32–54. In the one, a private epiphany, an exalted Jesus, with garments glistening, stands on a high mountain and is flanked by two religious giants of the past. All is light. In the other, a public spectacle, a humiliated Jesus,

57. Cf. Morris M. Faierstein, "Why Do the Scribes Say That Elijah Must Come First?" *JBL* 100 (1981): 75–86; followed by Allison's response, Dale C. Allison Jr., "Elijah Must Come First," *JBL* 103 (1984): 256–58; and the rejoinder by Fitzmyer, Joseph A. Fitzmyer, "More about Elijah Coming First," *JBL* 104 (1985): 295–96; T. W. Manson, *The Sayings of Jesus: As Recorded in the Gospels According to St. Matthew and St. Luke* (Grand Rapids: Eerdmans, 1979), 69–70.

58. Bruner, *Matthew*, 607.

whose clothes have been torn from him and divided, is lifted upon a cross and flanked by two common, convicted criminals. All is darkness. We have here pictorial antithetical parallelism, a diptych in which the two plates have similar lines but different colours.[59]

Such is the first meaning of the transfiguration on the mountain. Its connotation, shared with the baptism—suffering precedes glory.

The second is the eschatological vindication of God, this time not with the giving of the Spirit for the work of the Messiah, but the conclusion of the self-sacrificing work by the transformation of the earthly reality into its heavenly counterpart. Carter explains, "The scene confirms Jesus as God's son who manifests God's reign in the present (Matt 4:17; cf. Ps 72). It anticipates his installation as the eschatological king on Zion after his resurrection and at his return."[60]

The implication for the people Jesus comes to save (1:21; 20:28) is that the new exodus transcends the earthly realms. Jesus's exodus from death and ensuing glorification is an anticipation of the glory into which the Servant-King brings his people. Of these heavenly realities, the long-since departed Moses and Elijah were testimonial witnesses. As "the Elijah to come," John prepared the way. For Matthew, Jesus, the leader of the new exodus, is once again the New Moses (cf. 2:15). And in keeping with Matthew's emphasis on Jesus's typological fulfillment, Moses and Elijah disappear from the scene, leaving Jesus to explain and carry out the work foreshadowed in the Law and the prophets.[61]

On either side of the mountain, the critical information concerning the rejection, death, and resurrection of Jesus is given. Upon the mountain, his glory and the divine attestation of the way of glory through suffering is reaffirmed. By assimilating the voice at Jesus's baptism to his transfiguration, Matthew leads his readers to accept both the witness of the OT and of Jesus that suffering and exaltation are constituent parts of messianic sonship (16:16, 19). This is the way that John the Baptist, as Elijah, has prepared (3:3; 17:11–12), and such is the meaning of Jesus's baptism at the hands of John. The glorified Servant-King on the mountain is the suffering Servant-King in the Jordan River whose death served God's salvation-historical plan, fulfilling what was spoken (in the OT). *Where the accents of his baptism and transfiguration differ is that his baptism is into death, while his transfiguration is an indicator of what follows death, which is to say, his resurrection and glorification.*

59. Davies and Allison, *Matthew*, 2.706.
60. Carter, *Matthew and the Margins*, 348.
61. Bruner, *Matthew*, 613.

Conclusion

We conclude by drawing out some implications from our findings. In the first place, Matthew brings out the exchange between Jesus and John to explain the purpose of his baptism. Far from being a disconnected insertion arising from the embarrassment of Jesus's baptism by John, Matthew sees in the account the symbolic fulfillment of God's plan. His explanation, "to fulfill all righteousness," answers two dilemmas: (1) The repeated inability of Israel to be perfectly faithful to fulfill all that God commands. John prepares the way for Jesus to enter upon his work as the perfectly obedient Son of God. (2) The expectation of judgment for breaking God's Law. As the faithful Son, Jesus submits himself to the wrath of God, symbolized in John's baptism. The announcement from heaven and the impartation of the Spirit signals that the messianic endeavor would be successful. Jesus, the beloved Son, will faithfully live, suffer, and die for his people. But he will also be vindicated by being raised from the dead.

Secondly, this means that from the perspective of Matthew, the baptism of Jesus has nothing to do with the question of whether or not proselyte baptism is the interpretive key to unlock the meaning of John's baptism. The baptism of John was not a discipleship-making event. For Matthew, John is the last prophet of the OT, his baptism is a sign-act of the judgment he proclaimed against Israel, and Jesus's commitment to obey and experience the judgment of God fulfilled the righteous requirements of the divine will. Jesus's baptism might be thought of as a pledge to secure the salvation-historical beatitude of heaven and the indwelling presence of the Spirit on behalf of his people. Death, resurrection, and eschatological exaltation are the themes of both the baptism and the transfiguration (each with its own accent), linked by the divine voice. Matthew makes clear that rejection and suffering are the way of the Lord. Matthew's assimilation of the divine voices encourages readers to read each account in light of the other.

In conclusion, the words from heaven (and the cloud) validate the work of Jesus and show him to be the exalted messianic king and servant. The eschatological vision at the Jordan and the mountain confirms his messianic task of suffering as well as his right as the victor to lead a new Israel by way of a new exodus, the departure of which begins in Jerusalem, spreads throughout the world and has as its destination the fullness of the kingdom of heaven. The final instructions of the risen Christ are for disciples to be made of all the nations. The baptism that is to be administered is carried out under the name and authority of the Father, Son, and Holy Spirit (28:19), which is an announcement of approval and reception of the one baptized. Such an approval has been achieved by the baptism-suffering of Jesus. Jesus, the Servant-King and leader of the new exodus, has the final word in the Gospel of Matthew: "I am with you always, even unto the end of the age" (28:20). The way of suffering pictured in the baptism of Jesus opens the way to the age to come, a kingdom and glorified existence to be experienced, around the righteous son with whom the Father is well-pleased.

Chapter 12

THE JUDGMENT(S) TO COME IN MATTHEW'S GOSPEL

Introduction

In the Gospel of Matthew, John the Baptist is portrayed as the last of the OT prophets (11:13). His assigned role, cloaked in the typological mantle of Elijah (3:4; 11:14), was to represent in his person the time of eschatological fulfillment (3:3; Isa 40:3). But the fulfillment envisioned by Matthew has been accented in such a way as to make John a harbinger of disaster. His words for Israel, though less abrasive than those to the Pharisees and Sadducees, are nevertheless calamitous. Israel must repent for the kingdom of heaven has drawn near (3:2). The impact of the kingdom is perhaps best understood by the work of the Coming One. The kingdom of heaven brings with it one who will pour out the fiery Holy Spirit on those who do not repent and flee from the coming wrath (3:7,11). To this preaching of eschatological crisis, the prophet added his sign-act of water baptism which symbolized the coming ordeal. In those days (3:1), reparation would be required of Israel for the nation's failure and culpability (2:15–18; 3:2,6) and, while the possibility of averting the disaster is less prominent it is presupposed by submitting to baptism and confessing sin (3:6). Moreover, the symbolism of trees being spared and wheat being gathered into the barn (3:10–12) held out some measure of hope, if ever so indirectly.

The reminder of the deportation (1:11–12), which was God's response to Israel's rejection of Yahweh's rule (Jer 15:1–6), is followed by the rejection of Jesus: by Herod, the religious leaders, and implicitly "all Jerusalem" (2:3), thus raising the specter of future recompense. Chapter 3 confirms such a reading, as Israel is once again confronted with a prophet announcing the wrath to come (3:7) for the express purpose of eliminating the fruitless trees and the chaff (3:10–12). The "first word" for Israel is the birth of the king (2:1–3); the "second" is the need for national repentance in view of Israel's imminent confrontation with the kingdom of heaven. Despite what appears to be a sizable and affirmative response on the part of the people, the envisioned eschatological visitation would not be forestalled (11:20–24). Judgment remains a central and recurring motif throughout this gospel.[1] The second aspect of Israel's judgment turns, typologically, to the faithful son. The one who comes *as judge* (3:11) paradoxically comes to *be judged*. The one who executes the judgment by the fiery Spirit is the one who is appointed to death upon a cross.

We will now consider how this warning of judgment is developed on the global, national, and individual levels (i.e., Jesus). Such an overview of this Matthean theme naturally requires that we probe beyond the lexical occurrences of κριτής/κρίσις and their cognates to include judgment-like sayings, imagery, and actions that convey the concept. The task is not simply to identify those places where the theme of judgment is carried on from Matt 3, but also to explain the narrative reasons for the judgment theme.[2] We will begin our survey of the theme of judgment in the remainder of Matthew's Gospel with the actions and words of Jesus that lead up to the pronouncement of the woes over the Galilean towns of Chorazin, Bethsaida, and Capernaum (11:20–24).

Jesus's Mighty Words and Deeds: The Reasons for Judgment

After revealing John's salvation-historical identity as Elijah (11:10, 14; Mal 3:1; 4:5), Jesus turns to offer his assessment of Israel's response to John's ministry as well as that of his own: "But to what shall I compare this generation? It is like children sitting in the marketplaces and calling to their playmates, 'We played the flute for you, and you did not dance; we sang a dirge, and you did not mourn'" (11:16–17).

Some have understood the children sitting in the marketplace as Israel.[3] "This generation" *is like* the children who call out to their playmates, rather than the children who refuse to play: ὁμοία ἐστὶν παιδίοις καθημένοις ἐν ταῖς ἀγοραῖς ἃ προσφωνοῦντα τοῖς ἑτέροις. The parallelism between the complaints of the

---

1. Book-length treatments of the judgment theme in Matthew can be found in Daniel Marguerat, *Le jugement dans l'Evangile de Matthieu* (Geneva: Labor et Fides, 1981); Blaine Charette, *The Theme of Recompense in Matthew's Gospel*, JSNTSup 79 (Sheffield: JSOT, 1992). For a general treatment of the theme of judgment in the Gospels see Reiser, *Jesus and Judgment*.

2. For works which view apocalyptic eschatology as arising from the *Sitz im Leben* facing the Matthean community, see Graham Stanton, "The Gospel of Matthew and Judaism," *BJRL* 66 (1984): 264–84; Sim, *Apocalyptic Eschatology*. For a challenge to the majority position see Stephen L. Cook, *Prophecy & Apocalypticism: The Postexilic Setting* (Minneapolis: Fortress, 1995). For the paraenetic function of the judgment theme in Matthew, see Günther Bornkamm, "End-Expectation and Church in Matthew," in *Tradition and Interpretation in Matthew*, 15–51.

3. Davies and Allison, *Matthew VIII-XVIII*, 261–62; Hagner, *Matthew 1-13*, 310.

children corresponds with the later statements that John has a demon and Jesus is a glutton and drunkard (vv. 18–19). Others have thought John and Jesus are the children.[4] A decision is difficult, as both readings have their own unique contextual strengths. The former flows naturally out of the introductory question: Τίνι δὲ ὁμοιώσω τὴν γενεὰν ταύτην (11:16), yet the latter better fits the theme of the rejection of Jesus and refusal to respond in repentance (vv. 20–24).

The simile illustrates Israel's failure to believe and embrace the warnings of John and the teachings and confirmatory miracles of Jesus. Matthew has structured this assessment of Israel after a twofold profile of Jesus's preaching and miracles which are marked by an inclusio:

4:23 Καὶ περιῆγεν ἐν ὅλῃ τῇ Γαλιλαίᾳ διδάσκων ἐν ταῖς συναγωγαῖς αὐτῶν καὶ κηρύσσων τὸ εὐαγγέλιον τῆς βασιλείας καὶ θεραπεύων πᾶσαν νόσον καὶ πᾶσαν μαλακίαν ἐν τῷ λαῷ.

Chapters 5–7 the teaching of Jesus

Chapters 8–9 the miraculous deeds of Jesus

9:35 Καὶ περιῆγεν ὁ Ἰησοῦς τὰς πόλεις πάσας καὶ τὰς κώμας διδάσκων ἐν ταῖς συναγωγαῖς αὐτῶν καὶ κηρύσσων τὸ εὐαγγέλιον τῆς βασιλείας καὶ θεραπεύων πᾶσαν νόσον καὶ πᾶσαν μαλακίαν.

The Sermon on the Mount ends with two pericopes which assert that the future blessedness or curse of human beings is determined by one's relationship and obedience to Jesus. Both underscore Jesus's authority as judge and the one by which entrance into the kingdom of heaven is granted.[5] Those who know Jesus will do what he says (7:24) and live, even as false disciples will be revealed as workers of lawlessness (7:23) who come to a disastrous end (7:27).

Three triads of miracles follow the Sermon on the Mount:

1. 8:1–4 healing of a leper;
2. 8:5–13 healing of a centurion's servant;
3. 8:14–15 healing of Peter's mother.

1. 8:23–27 calming of the storm;
2. 8:28–34 the exorcism of two demoniacs;
3. 9:1–8 healing of the paralytic.

---

4. Donald J. Verseput, *The Rejection of the Humble Messianic King: A Study of the Composition of Matthew 11-12* (Frankfurt am Main: Peter Lang, 1986), 112–15; Carter, *Matthew and the Margins*, 254.

5. "Not everyone who says *to me*, 'Lord, Lord,' will enter the kingdom of heaven, but the one who does the will of my Father who is in Heaven" (7:21).

The third of the triads shows a "double healing" in each instance:

1. 9:18–26 woman healed and dead girl raised;
2. 9:27–31 healing of two blind men;
3. 9:32–34 healing/exorcism of a mute man.

The conclusion to the triads is a summation of Israel's condition as sheep without a shepherd (9:35–37). The answer to this need follows with the missionary discourse (ch. 10).[6]

This Matthean profile of Jesus's authoritative words and actions is more than mere literary decorum; it is Matthew's substantiation of the messianic judge and redeemer themes that were introduced in chs. 1–3. As judge, Jesus commands the allegiance of Israel. His teaching, contrasted with that of the scribes, is with authority (7:29) and requires a positive response from those who hear him. As Israel's final eschatological judge who presides over the kingdom of heaven, Jesus has authority not only over the nation of Israel, but also over the world of spirits. His ability to cast out demons and remove physical ailments is proof of his power and authority over Israel and ultimately the world. In the case of Israel, the interworking of Jesus's words and actions illustrates God's redemptive purposes and is most evident in the first summary statement/analysis of the miracle triads (an Isaianic formula quotation). This is sharply contrasted with the response of Israel's leaders who offer their own negative assessment of Jesus's power to heal (9:1–8). Matthew combines scriptural fulfillment with healing and forgiveness of sins to present Jesus as the redeemer and liberator of his people while also providing the cause for condemnation and judgment for those who reject him.

The first summary contains a formula quotation from Isa 53:4. "That evening they brought to him many who were oppressed by demons, and he cast out the spirits with a word and healed all who were sick. This was to fulfill what was spoken by the prophet Isaiah: 'He took our illnesses and bore our diseases'" (8:16–17). Matthew's Isaianic reference explains the salvation-historical significance of the healings and sends readers back to Isa 53 to reflect upon the broader work of the servant, a salvific work that was to involve atonement and forgiveness of sins. This was explained as the goal of Jesus's work as early as Matt 1:21. It is reaffirmed in 9:1–8 where Jesus's power to heal is offered as proof of his authority to forgive sins.

---

6. As John and Jesus both preached ἤγγικεν ἡ βασιλεία τῶν οὐρανῶν (3:2; 4:17), so also did the disciples (10:7). The instructions to ἀσθενοῦντας θεραπεύετε, νεκροὺς ἐγείρετε, λεπροὺς καθαρίζετε, δαιμόνια ἐκβάλλετε (10:8) and the rejection and persecution of the disciples (10:16–33) reflect Jesus's activities in Galilee and anticipate his future sufferings. "Readers of Matthew could scarcely read the passage vv. 17–21 without being constantly reminded of the one who was the first to be handed over, who stood before the Sanhedrin and the governor, who was scourged and finally killed." Ulrich Luz, *Studies in Matthew* (Grand Rapids: Eerdmans, 2005), 157.

Healing was an important work of the Messiah.[7] The healings force the religious leaders to render a judgment. For Matthew, healing of disease and forgiveness of sins are instances of the same reality, namely Jesus as messianic redeemer and rightful judge. In the first, it is the scribes who do not believe that Jesus has such authority and therefore privately accuse him of "blasphemy" (9:3). Jesus, in turn, insists that his power to heal is proof of his authority to forgive sins.[8] Matthew offers no reassessment of the religious authorities but returns to the position of the Jewish, religious leaders in the exorcism of the mute man. A second appraisal is made and an aspersion is leveled against him: "He casts out demons by the power of the prince of demons" (9:34).

The Woes of Matthew 11

The teaching and miracles of Jesus provide the necessary background material and basis for the future damnation of the Galilean towns (11:20–24).[9] In traditional prophetic style, Jesus prefaces his condemnation with the eschatological woe of the prophets (Hos 7:13; 9:12; Amos 5:16, 18; 6:1; Mic 7:4; Nah 3:17; Hab 2:6, 12, 19; Isa 1:4; 1:24; 3:9; 5:11; and against the nations: Zeph 2:5; Isa 18:1; Jer 26:19 LXX; cf. Sib. Or. 3.303; 319; 323). The ministry of John the Baptist in both word and sign, and that of Jesus in word and miraculous sign, did not produce the required repentance and trust in God's messiah necessary to escape the judgment. It is hardly incidental that John the Baptist reemerges (for the first time) in ch. 11 as a witness with Jesus against the faithlessness of Israel, for that is how he began his ministry. The unbelieving responses of Israel to the news of the newborn king in ch. 2 are followed by John's arrival and prophetic announcement of judgment.

---

7. "For he will honour the pious upon the throne of an eternal kingdom, 8 freeing prisoners, giving sight to the blind, straightening out the twis[ted.] 9 And for[e]ver shall I cling [to those who h]ope, and in his mercy [. . .] 10 and the fru[it of . . .] . . . not be delayed. 11 And the Lord will perform marvelous acts such as have not existed, just as he sa[id,] 12 [for] he will heal the badly wounded and will make the dead live, he will proclaim good news to the poor 13 and [. . .] . . . [. . .] he will lead the [. . .] . . . and enrich the hungry. 14 [. . .] and all . . . [. . .]" (4Q521). Collins observes that Q and 4Q521 "go beyond Isaiah 61 in referring to the raising of the dead. This can hardly be coincidental." John J. Collins, "The Works of the Messiah," *DSD* 1.1 (1994): 107.

8. The purpose usage of the subjunctive: ἵνα δὲ εἰδῆτε ὅτι ἐξουσίαν ἔχει ὁ υἱὸς τοῦ ἀνθρώπου ἐπὶ τῆς γῆς ἀφιέναι ἁμαρτίας (9:6).

9. Given Matthew's penchant for parallelism, it is interesting that two previous judgments against Jesus: scribes = "he blasphemes," and Pharisees = "he casts out demons by the prince of demons," would be followed by two pronouncements of judgment by Jesus: the double woes of Chorazin and Bethsaida (compared to Tyre and Sidon and as a single unit), and then Capernaum (compared to Sodom). Tyre and Sidon are always named together in the OT which explains Matthew's coupling of Chorazin and Bethsaida cf. Isa 23; Jer 47:4; Ezek 26–28; Joel 4:4–8; Zech 9:2–4. Cf. Reiser, *Jesus and Judgment*, 226.

Matthew situates Jesus's first words of judgment against Israel within the context of John's question that further underscores this dire situation.[10]

The place that was to be the home base for Jesus (Capernaum) becomes one of the first places to receive the verdict of condemnation.[11] Though not mentioned elsewhere in Matthew, Chorazin and Bethsaida had Jesus's mighty works/δυνάμεις performed in them. Such instances of divine power, according to Jesus, should have been the occasions that caused Tyre and Sidon to repent.[12] That Jesus would compare Tyre and Sidon to these Galilean towns is a move calculated to provoke Israel. In the OT, these pagan cities were not infrequently objects of prophetic condemnation (Isa 23; Jer 25:22; 27:3; 47:4; Ezek 27:8; Joel 3:4; Zech 9:2). But it will be more tolerable for these pagan cities than for those where Jesus ministered. Matthew expands the theme of judgment by comparing Capernaum with Sodom (11:23), thereby creating a two-tier parallelism.[13] What holds true for Chorazin and Bethsaida equally applies to Capernaum. Capernaum will receive a stricter judgment than Sodom because it had the light but rejected it (4:13–16).

The most provocative statement in this pericope is that it will be *more* bearable/ ἀνεκτότερον for the gentile cities than for the Galilean towns inhabited by Israel. Rabbinic Judaism believed that both Israel and the gentiles would be judged by the same rule, namely the Torah. Citing *Sifra* 193:1.1–11, Neusner writes, "When Israel acts like gentiles, it enters the classification of gentiles; if Israel conducts itself like the gentiles, Israel will be rejected and punished as were the gentiles."[14] Here Jesus says something unprecedented, at least as far as the canonical OT is concerned: the Galilean towns will fare *worse* than the cities of the gentiles. This verdict of Jesus goes beyond the Rabbinical view that Israel acting like gentiles will receive a judgment like the gentiles. Jesus said it would be worse for Israel and his trenchant rebuke is eschatologically colored by the "concept" that John the Baptist had borrowed from his OT predecessors when addressing Israel.

The execution of the woes/οὐαί will take place ἐν ἡμέρᾳ κρίσεως (11:22, 24). This is best understood not as a temporal judgment carried out against Israel, but as the eschatological end of the age to which previous judgments likewise pointed,

---

10. In Luke the denunciation of the Galilean towns immediately follows the commissioning of the seventy-two (Luke 10:1–15), whereas John's question comes much earlier (Luke 7:17–33). Matthew's deliberate paralleling of John and Jesus might lend further support to the position of much German scholarship (in contrast to the great majority of British and American scholars) that Luke has preserved the material and sequence of Q, on which see the discussion in Reiser, *Jesus and Judgment*, 221–23.

11. Again, we observe that Jesus's move to Capernaum is prompted by John's arrest (4:12–13).

12. The ministries of John and Jesus are further unified by μετανοέω, found only on the lips of John and Jesus (3:2; 4:17; 11:20–21).

13. Paul Hoffmann, *Studien zur Theologie der Logienquelle*, NTAbh 8 (Münster: Aschendorff, 1972), 284.

14. Jacob Neusner, *Rabbinic Judaism: The Theological System* (Leiden: Brill, 2002), 67.

with Sodom being the most prominent.[15] This is the day of the Lord, like that of Mal 3–4. The contrast in v. 23 of heaven and hell suggests that the final eschatological event is in view: καὶ σύ, Καφαρναούμ, μὴ ἕως οὐρανοῦ ὑψωθήσῃ; ἕως ᾅδου καταβήσῃ. "Hell" (Hades) can refer to the grave, as it sometimes does in the OT (Gen 37:35), but this saying of Jesus denotes not a temporal reality, such as an earthly exalted or dejected status, but an eternal matter which is entirely contingent upon the acceptance or rejection of God's son. These towns, having rejected Jesus, face the ἡμέρα κρίσεως (11:24) and will not survive but will be cast into ᾅδου because they refused to repent and believe that Jesus is the Christ.

Before we take up the blasphemy of the Holy Spirit and the resulting condemnation, we point out that the judgment Jesus speaks of includes more than the three towns, owing to his description of the nation as τὴν γενεὰν ταύτην (v. 16), a designation which becomes rather significant. The term is not referring to the time of Israel so much as to the character of Israel.[16] "Generation" was first used in 1:17 to "sum up the largely unfaithful history of the people with God."[17] Having refused to repent, Jesus will go on to add the adjective πονηρά to γενεά in his descriptions of Israel. Having already performed many signs, the scribes and Pharisees ask Jesus to provide a miraculous sign. Jesus replies: γενεὰ πονηρὰ καὶ μοιχαλὶς σημεῖον ἐπιζητεῖ (12:39; cf. v. 45). No further sign will be provided than the sign of Jonah which typified the Son of Man's three-day sojourn into death (12:40). Once again the judgment is announced. Not only Nineveh, but also the Queen of the South will condemn Jesus's unbelieving listeners for their failure to repent (12:41). The Pharisees and Sadducees return to πειράζοντες Jesus by requesting a sign from heaven and again, no further sign is given to the evil and adulterous generation than the sign of Jonah (16:4).

It is important to remember that the Pharisees and Sadducees are representative of Israel. The "religious leaders" ask for a sign, but Jesus does *not* reply that only an evil and adulterous "leadership" would request such a thing, but an evil and adulterous "generation." Matthew's second modifying insertion of πονηρά to γενεά shows that national Israel bears the same epithet as the religious leaders. The woes pronounced over the Galilean towns are ultimately for the generation of Jesus's day, national Israel. Matthew builds to this conclusion in the denunciation of the Pharisees. Jesus could say that such will be sentenced to hell for their unrighteous acts that are likened to those who murdered the prophets before them (23:31–32).[18] Once again they are described as a brood of vipers (3:7; 21:33), thus continuing the persecution of God's people (21:34). The verdict nears its crescendo with the reason for God's dispatch of his servants to them: "So that on you may come all the righteous blood shed on earth, from the blood of righteous Abel to the blood of Zechariah the son of Barachiah, whom you murdered between the

---

15. Nolland, *Matthew*, 468.
16. Carter, *Margins*, 254.
17. Ibid.
18. Patte, *The Gospel According to Matthew*, 328.

sanctuary and the altar" (23:35). The words, "On you . . . all the righteous blood" (ἐφ᾽ ὑμᾶς πᾶν αἷμα δίκαιον), shows the culmination of salvation history and we should probably think here of Jesus's blood as included in the indictment.[19] That later scribes discerned an echo to αἷμα δίκαιον in Judas's lament, αἷμα ἀθῷον (27:4), and Pilate's declaration that he is innocent τοῦ αἵματος τούτου (27:24) is suggested by the textual variants.[20] In a gospel so interested in the theme of fulfillment, it is striking that Jesus would summon the religious leaders to "fill up" (πληρώσατε) the measure of their fathers (23:32). Such an action is nothing less than the culmination of a rebellious history.

The religious leaders will be held guilty for their incredulity and violence. As we have already put forward, it was not an individualistic assessment of a particular group within Israel, but a verdict reached concerning the nation: "Truly, I say to you, all these things will come upon this generation" (τὴν γενεὰν ταύτην, 23:36).[21]

Summary As with the conclusion of the Sermon on the Mount (7:15–27), so also in ch. 11, the judgment comes because of a wrong relationship to Jesus. This is a theme, which the NT writers in general and Matthew in particular do not hesitate to promote. Matthew's interest in the subject of representation is exhibited throughout. Matthew's evaluative point of view is that the religious leaders ultimately represented their generation.[22] Because of their unbelieving solidarity with their leaders, the judgment that falls upon the religious leaders is guaranteed to fall upon those they represent. It is, then, not surprising that Matthew has chosen to identify the Pharisees and Sadducees coming out to the baptism of John. They come with the nation of Israelites, and as the spiritual representatives of Israel, the nation will share in their judgment. Matthew's theology of representation also gives readers the opposite side of the spectrum. The judgment that Jesus undergoes is on behalf of his people so that the eternal life that is his, by virtue of his resurrection, would benefit them. This is why Jesus, too, is baptized by John. We now turn to the relationship of Jesus to the Spirit in judgment, and what that relationship means for Israel, as represented by their religious leaders.

---

19. Cf. David E. Garland, *The Intention of Matthew 23*, NovTSup 52 (Leiden: Brill, 1979), 184–87.

20. δικαιον B¹ L Θ ℓ 844 latt (syˢ) saᵐˢˢ mae bo; Cyp27:4 (27:4); του δικαιου τουτου ℵ K L W Γ *f*¹·¹³ 33. 565. 579. 700. 892. 1241. 1424 𝔐 lat syᵖ·ʰ saᵐˢˢ mae bo ¦ τουτου του δικαιου A Δ aur f h (27:24).

21. Jesus's lament indicates that he envisioned the approaching judgment as temporal, which we will try to show (below) as containing a final, eschatological element embedded in it. λέγω γὰρ ὑμῖν, οὐ μή με ἴδητε ἀπ᾽ ἄρτι ἕως ἂν εἴπητε· εὐλογημένος ὁ ἐρχόμενος ἐν ὀνόματι κυρίου (23:39).

22. "They are the embodiment of apostate Israel": Garland, *Intention*, 186.

Matthew 12: Blasphemy against the Spirit

The healing of the possessed blind-mute and Matt 3 share a good deal of vocabulary and themes. Motifs common to both include kingship, "Can this be the Son of David?" (12:23; 3:11,17), the kingdom of God/heaven (12:25, 28; 3:2), the Holy Spirit (12:32, πνεύματι θεοῦ = v. 28; 3:11), strong one/ἰσχυρός (12:29; 3:11), gathering/συνάγω and scattering (12:30; 3:12), good/bad trees and fruit (12:22; 3:10) and brood of vipers (12:34; 3:7). As in Matt 3, the ongoing conflict and the resulting judgment theme which permeate ch. 12 gives readers of Matthew's Gospel a further reason for the approaching eschatological crisis.

For a fourth time, Jesus's ability to heal becomes the controverted point at issue. Matthew begins with the reaction of the crowd to the exorcism and healing: μήτι οὗτός ἐστιν ὁ υἱὸς Δαυίδ; (12:23). The crowds' reaction is one of amazement, but not necessarily commitment. People have been astonished at his teaching (7:28), they have feared and have glorified God (9:8), they have laughed at Jesus (9:24), and they have declared, "Never was anything like this seen in Israel" (9:33).[23] Now they ask a question: Could Jesus be the Son of David?[24] On the surface, such a question is indicative of a crowd "groping in the dark" as they try to understand the significance of Jesus's person.[25] It could also be that Matthew intends to contrast a positive reaction of the crowd to the overtly negative reaction of the Pharisees.[26] Against this, it is often the case that μήτι anticipates a negative answer (7:16; 26:22, 25).[27]

The crowd's estimation of Jesus is quickly passed over in order to take up the negative perspective of the Pharisees. Once again, the source of Jesus's ability to cast out demons is declared to be evil: "It is only by Beelzebul, the prince of demons, that this man casts out demons" (12:24; cf. 9:34). After the reductio ad absurdum of Satan casting out his own, Jesus reveals the power behind his ability

---

23. For a survey of the uses of "crowds" in the first gospel, Warren Carter, "The Crowds in Matthew's Gospel," *CBQ* 55.1 (1993): 54–67.

24. Burger thinks that Matthew's development of Mark's "Son of David" serves a positive purpose, "Der Sohn Davids ist in dieser Darstellung immer der barmherzige Wundertäter": Christoph Burger, *Jesus als Davidssohn: Eine traditionsgeschichtliche Untersuchung* (Göttingen: Vandenhoeck & Ruprecht, 1970), 90. On the other hand, Stanton looks at the negative contexts in which the title is found and discerns an apologetic element on the part of Matthew: Graham N. Stanton, *A Gospel for a New People: Studies in Matthew* (Louisville: Westminster John Knox Press, 1993), 180–85. For the texts which anticipate that a messianic son of David would have success over the demons, as David himself did, cf. 1 Sam 16:24–23; Pss. Sol. 17.21; Josephus, *Ant.* 8.2.5 §45–49; *Pseudo Philo, Biblical Antiquities* 60.3.

25. Garland, *Reading Matthew*, 141.

26. Burger, *Jesus als Davidssohn*, 79. France suggests, "The positive reaction of the crowd is set in stark contrast to the determined opposition of the Pharisees." France, *The Gospel According to Matthew*, 478.

27. Hagner, *Matthew*, 1.342; Garland, *Reading Matthew*, 141. "The crowd raises the possibility only to dismiss it." Carter, *Matthew and the Margins*, 272.

to perform such a miracle, that heretofore could only be inferred (3:16; 12:18): πνεύματι θεοῦ ἐγὼ ἐκβάλλω τὰ δαιμόνια (12:28). Jesus's power to cast out demons is by the Holy Spirit (3:16; 12:32) and this work of the Spirit was an act of judgment (against the demonic realm). John declared that the one who would come after him would baptize in the Holy Spirit and fire (3:11). This symbol of judgment is enveloped by the imagery of the removal of trees (3:10) and chaff (3:12). The liberation of the blind-mute is at the same time an act of judgment by removal of the evil captor. Somewhat provocatively, Jesus pronounces that the kingdom that has come in judgment against the demonic realm has come "upon you" (12:28; ἔφθασεν ἐφ᾽ ὑμᾶς). The kingdom comes both to liberate and, in the case of the Pharisees, to judge. Matthew does not provide his readers with any other perspective on the Pharisees and their relationship to this kingdom (23:13). What is implied is a great reversal, such as in the sons of the kingdom statement in 9:12. What removed the demon will remove Israel. The kingdom comes upon them not in the grace of deliverance but in the removal of judgment. The reasons are given in a succession of statements and familiar images which vividly describe the fate of the listeners. Attributing Jesus's deeds to the devil, the Pharisees have unwittingly sealed their own doom: οὐκ ἀφεθήσεται αὐτῷ οὔτε ἐν τούτῳ τῷ αἰῶνι οὔτε ἐν τῷ μέλλοντι (12:32). They are a brood of vipers: γεννήματα ἐχιδνῶν (v. 34), evil: πονηροί (vv. 34, 35) and will be condemned on the day of judgment (v. 36; ἐν ἡμέρᾳ κρίσεως). What happened to the evil spirit will happen to Israel temporally, by being removed from the land (21:43–46), and eschatologically, at the final judgment when all evil is purged (13:40–43; 25:41).

Jesus is in conflict with the religious leaders ultimately because he is in conflict with Satan's kingdom. Kingsbury has noted the collusion of the religious leaders and Satan, which is repeated and developed: "Especially do the leaders of the Jews have affinity with Satan. Satan is the 'Tempter' who puts Jesus to the test (4:3), and they, too, put Jesus to the test. Satan is the 'Evil One' par excellence, and they, too, are evil. Satan is the personal 'Enemy' of Jesus (13:25, 39), and they, too, are the enemies of Jesus, bent on destroying him (12:14; 26:3–4)."[28]

This solidarity with the aims of Satan does not imply that Satan is ultimately favorable to them. In his final remark to the Pharisees and in parabolic fashion, Jesus explains the end to which the sad events of ch. 12 are headed. The unclean spirit that has gone out of a person will return with seven spirits more evil (πονηρότερα) than itself and will re-enter the house, with the result that the last state of the person will be worse than the first (12:45). There is little doubt that national Israel is the focus of the parable due to the thread that runs through this account connecting Satan and his spirits to the Pharisees and the nation by the repetition of πονηρός (the spirits = 12:45, Pharisees = 12:34; the nation/generation = 12:41, 42, 45).

It is difficult to know whether or not Jesus is referring exclusively to the judgment at the end of the age or if a temporal punishment is envisioned. Possible

---

28. Kingsbury, *Matthew as Story*, 56.

still is that temporal judgments can contain eschatological indicators of the final judgment even as the final judgment can be described with past historical events (Matt 24:37–40; cf. 2 Pet 2:4–10; Jude 5–7). While the pericopes address the eschatological judgment at the end of the age (12:38, 41,42), the house imagery of the parable (12:44) could be a reference to Jerusalem (23:38). A clear distinction between the two is not likely to be the purpose of the author. "Precision is not intended; warning is."[29] The blasphemy against the Holy Spirit includes both a historical, punitive judgment and an eschatological extirpation at the end of the age. 12:32 is suggestive that one requires the other. The sin that will not be forgiven in this age (and therefore must be punished) will be punished in the age to come, which will mete out judgment against the unforgiven. The warning and precursor is that the one who wields the Holy Spirit in judgment is the same executioner, empowered by the Holy Spirit, who will take action against a nation that refuses to repent.

The Parable of the Weeds

Matthew provides two parables that give important information concerning the coming judgment. Echoes of John's eschatological preaching can be heard in the parable of the wheat and the weeds (13:24–30, 36–43). This parable describes the wheat at the time of the harvest: the future punishment in fire and the gathering of the wheat into the barn (13:30). It also addresses a concern over the delay of the final judgment.[30] In ch. 11 John sends his disciples to ask if Jesus is the one to come. Jesus answers by referencing his mighty works, but leaves it to his audience, as well as John, to piece together their Isaianic significance.[31] Jesus is the one to come; yet his mighty deeds were seemingly devoid of the judgment that John proclaimed.

The parable of the weeds gives readers a fuller explanation of the answer given to John. Jesus explains that the characteristic of this age is one of continued conflict between the kingdom of heaven and the kingdom of Satan.[32] A similar question to John's can be found in the servants' question to the master when weeds are discovered among the wheat: "So the servants said to him, 'Then do you want us to go and gather them?'" (13:29). The master explains that they must wait until the

---

29. Nolland, *Matthew*, 515.

30. Hagner, *Matthew 14–28*, 382.

31. The blind see = Isa 29:18; 35:5; the lame walk = Isa 35:6; lepers cleansed = Isa 53:4; the deaf hear = Isa 29:18–19; 35:5; the dead are raised = Isa 26:18–19; the good news is preached to the poor = Isa 61:1.

32. Sim sees the parable of the weeds as a clear example of dualism: Sim, *Apocalyptic Eschatology*, 36–43. "There is no middle ground in the cosmic conflict between Jesus and Satan and their respective human supporters; one is either a son of the kingdom or a son of the evil one and there is no third category": Sim, *Apocalyptic Eschatology*, 79.

harvest, and then the weeds can be gathered and burned and the wheat brought into the barn.

When Jesus's disciples come to him privately and ask about the parable's meaning, Jesus explains that the good seed is sown by the Son of Man, the field is the world, and the weeds are the sons of the evil one (13:37–38). The harvest is the close of the age and harvesters are the angels sent with the task of gathering up the weeds/the sons of the evil one and throwing them into the fiery furnace (13:39–42). As it relates to the preaching of John, the ultimate removal of weeds/chaff/ fruitless trees and the eschatological ordeal by fire will not take place until συντέλεια αἰῶνός (13:39). While John was concerned to address Israel with the somber warning, the shared imagery of the parable has been broadened and extended to encompass the world: δὲ ἀγρός ἐστιν ὁ κόσμος (13:38).[33]

The fierceness of the fiery judgment producing weeping and gnashing of teeth is contrasted with the future of the righteous. Interestingly, the description of the righteous shining ὡς ὁ ἥλιος (13:43) parallels the description of Jesus's appearance in the transfiguration ὡς ὁ ἥλιος (17:2). Once readers reach ch. 17, the connection can be made: Jesus will suffer, die, and be raised (16:21), the transfiguration being a preview of his future glory (17:9). That resurrection glory will be shared with those who, borrowing the language of the parable, are sown by the Son of Man. The future glory of Jesus's followers is obtained by his suffering and resurrection. At the end of the age, when the judgment has passed and the wicked are removed, the righteous will be revealed as having the glory of the Christ. For the rest, the furnace and flames continue the symbolic ordeal described by John (13:40, 42, 50).[34] The sending out of the angels at the end of the age to gather and punish the wicked is the last and most dreadful judgment, of unending duration.

The Parable of the Tenants

The parable of the tenants is preceded by two statements concerning John the Baptist. In the temple, Jesus's authority is contested and he responds by putting a question to his interlocutors. Was the source of John's baptism ἐξ οὐρανοῦ ἢ ἐξ ἀνθρώπων (21:25)? Matthew narrates the private discussion and negative estimation of John that follows. Refusing to make their opinion of John public, Jesus responds in parables, the first of which concerns a father and his two sons. The first agrees to do the work of his father but doesn't; the second refuses, but later changed his mind and went into the vineyard to work (21:28–29). Jesus puts the question to the chief priests and the elders of the people (21:23): Which of the two did the will of his father?" They said, "The first." Jesus said to them, "Truly, I say to you, the tax collectors and the prostitutes go into the kingdom of God before you. For John came to you in the way of righteousness, and you did not believe him, but the tax collectors and the prostitutes believed him. And even when you saw it, you did not

---

33. France, *Matthew*, 533.
34. Cf. 1 En. 108:3,5,15.

afterward change your minds and believe him" (21:31–32). Jesus then turns to the parable of the tenants. The parable continues the vineyard theme and ends with Jesus's verdict about the religious leaders, who, like the second son, failed to do the will of God (cf. 21:32; 7:21–23). They refused to believe the Isaianic forerunner who came ἐν ὁδῷ δικαιοσύνης (21:25, 32). The parable of the tenants shows the intensification of their unbelief as it gives rise to hostility to the master's servants: beating, stoning, and killing them (21:35). The repeated process unfolds over a protracted period of time.[35] This salvation-historical point is confirmed when Jesus pronounces his woes over Israel's leaders for persecuting the prophets sent to them (23:34).[36] The original question (e.g., 21:25) is still the main issue, the issue of divine authority and the required response of Israel. While the vineyard is a well-known OT designation for Israel (cf. Ps 80:8–9; Isa 3:14; 5:1–17; 27:2; Hos 10:1; Mic 1:6), the emphasis here is on the disobedience of the religious leaders (cf. Jer 12:10).

After sending servants to collect his due, the owner dispatches his son who is summarily killed and tossed out of the vineyard. Readers of Matthew can interpret the son's identity since he has already been called ὁ υἱός μου (3:17; 17:5) and in both accounts John and his prophetic status is referenced (3:2, 4; 17:10–13). The sending of the son is the final and Christological moment for the vineyard workers and the reaction to the son seals their fate. To the imagery of a violent death (17:41) is added the loss of land and temple.[37] Jesus is not describing the end of the age, but the end of the nation's special status before God. This meaning is confirmed by the religious authorities' statement that after putting the tenants to death, the owner will τὸν ἀμπελῶνα ἐκδώσεται ἄλλοις γεωργοῖς, οἵτινες ἀποδώσουσιν αὐτῷ τοὺς καρποὺς ἐν τοῖς καιροῖς αὐτῶν (21:41). Their assessment and application is confirmed by the narrator (21:43, 45).

Summary Thus far we have seen how there are two aspects to the judgment of the kingdom: the end of the age and the end of the privileged status (before God) of the nation of Israel (21:41). The fulfillment of these words does not mean that every Israelite belonged to the evil one, as those first tasked with proclaiming the message of Jesus Christ were Jews.[38] But as the nations are "brought in," the nation of Israel must be judged and only after both things occur, can the end of the age and the final judgment come. This is the substance of ch. 24 where both elements (historical judgment of national Israel and the eschatological judgment of the end of the age upon the world) are brought together.

---

35. The punctiliar use of the aorist: πάλιν ἀπέστειλεν ἄλλους δούλους πλείονας τῶν πρώτων. . . (21:36).

36. The shared terminology: ἀπέστειλεν/ ἀπεσταλμένους (21:34; 23:37), ἀπέκτειναν / ἀποκτείνουσα (21:35; 23:37), ἐλιθοβόλησαν / λιθοβολοῦσα (21:35; 23:37).

37. Nolland, *Matthew*, 878–79.

38. The fulfillment means the inclusion of the gentiles and the realization of the promise made to Abraham that he would be the father of many nations (Gen 17:4; Matt 8:11–12).

The Olivet Discourse

The Olivet Discourse brings the confrontations in the temple to a close. Matthew describes Jesus's cursing of the fig tree as he made his way to Jerusalem (21:19). The cursing of the fig tree becomes a sign for the temple which will also be judged for its "fruitlessness."[39] Something greater than the temple (12:6) will ultimately abandon it, leaving it deserted and ripe for judgment (23:38).[40]

The Olivet Discourse answers two questions. Leaving the temple with his disciples, Jesus declares that not one of the temple's stones will remain upon another (24:2). His disciples respond with two questions: (1) when will these things be (πότε ταῦτα ἔσται) and (2) what will be the sign of his coming and of the end of the age (καὶ τί τὸ σημεῖον τῆς σῆς παρουσίας καὶ συντελείας τοῦ αἰῶνος; 24:3).[41] The answers Jesus gives are recapitulatory descriptions of the judgment upon Israel and the judgment upon the whole world at the end of the age.

In vv. 4–14 Jesus first describes the interadventual period, characterized by persecution, death, false prophets, and the worldwide proclamation of the gospel of the kingdom (vv. 9–12) "and then the end will come" (καὶ τότε ἥξει τὸ τέλος; v. 14). Verse 15 brings readers back to the siege and destruction of Jerusalem and descriptively carries that theme through to v. 28. Verses 29–31 recapitulate the eschatological events that bring "those days" (ἡμερῶν ἐκείνων) to a close.[42] The illustration of the fig tree and the description of "the day" (of the Lord) overtaking the world complete the characteristics of those days that lead up to the end of the age (24:36–51). The remaining two parables before the final judgment scene(s) (25:31–46) stress the anticipated but unknown time of the arrival of the Son (25:1–30). With the proposed outline of the recapitulated events in place, we now turn to some of the salient judgment features that further illustrate the judgment proclaimed by John.[43]

Jesus uses several expressions to describe the coming judgment upon Israel: the abomination of desolation (v. 15), the great tribulation (v. 21), no flesh remaining without cutting the days of judgment short (v. 22). Matthew provides no content for this desolating event. Readers would presumably be expected to infer that the trauma spoken of by Daniel was going to be repeated. Exactly what historical event

---

39. William R. Telford, *The Barren Temple and the Withered Tree*, JSNTSup 1 (Sheffield: JSOT, 1980); Alistair I. Wilson, *When Will These Things Happen? A Study of Jesus as Judge in Matthew 21-25* (Carlisle: Paternoster, 2004), 97–99.

40. France, *Matthew*, 886.

41. Sim, *Apocalyptic Eschatology*, 94.

42. "The Interadventual Period and the Advent: Matthew 24–25," in *The Collected Writings of John Murray: Select Lectures in Systematic Theology*, vol. 2 (Carlisle: Banner of Truth Trust, 1996), 389.

43. We pass over vv. 4–13, which identify the difficulties that face Jesus's followers before the end comes (24:14), understood to be the end of the age.

that is behind the cryptic "abomination of desolation" remains a subject of debate. Keener offers the following overview of Daniel's theme in Israel's history:

> The desecration of God's temple (Ps 74:3–4, 7; Is 63:18) undoubtedly constitutes a recurrent judgment motif in Israel's history; it provided the ultimate symbol of national and religious humiliation (cf. 1 Macc 3:45; 3 Macc 1:29; 2:14; 2 Bar 5:1; Test. Asher 7:2; t. Sukk. 4:28; CD 4.1718), something Jewish people resisted to death (Philo *Leg. Gai.* 209-10), except in times of national apostasy when they might cause it (Jos. *Ant.* 10,37–38; Ps. Sol. 1:8; Apoc. Abr. 27:7). The Syrian ruler had defiled the altar in the second century A.D., [*sic*] causing an "abomination" and ruining the sanctuary with "desolation" (1 Macc 4:38; cf. 1:54). Even before the first exile, the prophets recognized scattering and tribulation as a judgment designed to bring God's people to repentance (e.g., Deut 4:26–31; Jer 29;12–14; 31:9). One could also profane the temple by persecuting the righteous there. In Jerusalem, "the Wicked Priest did abominable works and defiled the sanctuary of God" (1QpHab 12.7-9); because this Qumran passage interprets Habakkuk 2:17, which refers to bloodshed, it probably refers to the persecution of the followers of the Teacher of Righteousness. (cf. 1Qphab 12.6 and context)[44]

If we consider the Danielic reference in its own literary context, we find a meaning which not only explains how such an event could provide the material for the previous referents, but also fits Matthew's eschatological purposes. Daniel's seventy weeks has been interpreted in a variety of ways.[45] During this period there is one event that is clearly set forth: "And after the sixty-two weeks, an anointed one shall be cut off and shall have nothing. And the people of the prince who is to come shall destroy the city and the sanctuary. Its end shall come with a flood, and to the end there shall be war. Desolations are decreed" (Dan 9:26). While we do not know for certain what the event is that makes desolate, the reference is to a time of extreme suffering and loss. The city and the sanctuary will be destroyed.

In the Olivet Discourse, the tribulation/θλῖψις is a time of trouble, affliction, and distress. It is the catalyst for the evacuation of Judea and Jerusalem (vv. 17–20) since it is worse than anything previously experienced: θλῖψις μεγάλη οἵα οὐ γέγονεν ἀπ᾽ ἀρχῆς κόσμου ἕως τοῦ νῦν οὐδ᾽ οὐ μὴ γένηται (v. 21). The promised judgment would be so terrible that unless the decree to shorten its duration be given, the grim result would be total annihilation (v. 22).

The interpretation of Matthew's "immediately after the tribulation of those days" (Εὐθέως δὲ μετὰ τὴν θλῖψιν τῶν ἡμερῶν ἐκείνων) is difficult, as is well known. Though the links to vv. 21–22 are easily recognizable, it is not so clear as to how the end of the age "εὐθέως" follows 70 CE. It may be, as Murray thinks, that the tribulation of those days includes the entire interadventual period as was also

---

44. Keener, *A Commentary*, 575.

45. See the summary in J. Barton Payne, *The Theology of the Older Testament* (Grand Rapids: Zondervan, 1982), 520–22.

descriptive of the experiences of the followers of Jesus.[46] "Those days" (cf. 3:1) indicate an event posterior to the downfall of Jerusalem.

Drawing from the prophetic day of the Lord materials, the end of the age is characterized by the darkening of the sun and moon, falling stars, and the shaking of the heavens (Rev 6:12; Isa 13:10; 34:4; Joel 2:10; 3:4; 4:15). In Isa 13:5 the judgment destroys the whole earth. This day of the Lord brings destruction (13:6, 9), it is cruel and full of wrath, and God's fierce anger makes the earth a desolation and destroys sinners from it (Isa 13:9). This coming of God with his army (Isa 13:4–5) is the eschatological end:

> For the stars of the heavens and their constellations will not give their light; the sun will be dark at its rising, and the moon will not shed its light. I will punish the world for its evil, and the wicked for their iniquity; I will put an end to the pomp of the arrogant, and lay low the pompous pride of the ruthless. I will make people more rare than fine gold, and mankind than the gold of Ophir. Therefore I will make the heavens tremble, and the earth will be shaken out of its place, at the wrath of the Lord of hosts in the day of his fierce anger. (Isa 13:10–13)[47]

Unlike Daniel, Matthew places the Son of Man's coming on the cloud before the judgment scene (cf. Dan 7:9–13; Matt 24:37–39). The gathering of the saints juxtaposes the terror of the nations and is accomplished by the sending of the angels to gather (ἐπισυνάξουσιν) the elect (24:31). This is the eschatological end, complete with the harvesting imagery ("the end of the age" 13:39). The angelic dispatch is sent to gather (συλλέξουσιν) the wicked to be burned in the fiery furnace while the wheat/elect are gathered into the barn/kingdom (13:41). The gathering of his people follows without mention of the fate of the wicked, which is reserved for vv. 36–40, 50–51.

The promise of the destruction of Jerusalem is then resumed with the fig tree simile and the assurance that, before the generation's end, the prophecy against the temple (not one stone left upon another) would be fulfilled (24:34).[48]

---

46. Murray, "The Interadventual Period," 389. For attempts to assign 70 CE to 24:19–31 see N. T. Wright, *Jesus and the Victory of God* (London: SPCK, 1996), 339–68; France, *Matthew*, 898–931; Michael P. Theophalis, *The Abomination of Desolation in Matthew 24.15*, LNTS 437 (London: T&T Clark, 2012), 133–45. For a critique and positive argumentation for a twofold referent (70 CE and the end of the age) in Jesus's eschatological discourse see Wilson, *When Will These Things Happen?* 109–74.

47. For parallels, see Sib. Or. 3.787–807; 4 Ezra 5.1–5.

48. *Pace* Davies and Allison who think that Matthew is speaking of the end of the age. William D. Davies and Dale C. Allison Jr., *Matthew XIX–XXVIII*, ICC (Edinburgh: T&T Clark, 1997), 366–68. Matthew is more likely returning to the days of judgment upon Jerusalem (vv. 15–28) for the following reasons: the insertion of περὶ δέ in v. 36 and the contrast of the unexpected suddenness of the parousia (vv. 37–51) to the previously mentioned "when you see all these things" of v. 33 which in recapitulatory fashion could be

It is significant to observe that Matthew finishes what he began in 1:17 with a final, negative pronouncement upon ἡ γενεὰ αὕτη (24:34). With the possible exception of the genealogy (though even there the point is to contrast the faithfulness of God to that of his people), the evaluation of Jesus's γενεά is evil, adulterous, faithless, and perverted (1:17; 11;16; 12:39, 41, 42, 45; 16:4; 17;17; 23:36).

The final examples of the parousia are the unexpected judgment of the flood (24:38–39), the thief (24:43), and the master of the servant who comes unexpectedly: καὶ διχοτομήσει αὐτὸν καὶ τὸ μέρος αὐτοῦ μετὰ τῶν ὑποκριτῶν θήσει· ἐκεῖ ἔσται ὁ κλαυθμὸς καὶ ὁ βρυγμὸς τῶν ὀδόντων (24:51). The startling διχοτομήσει before he is placed with the hypocrites in weeping and gnashing of teeth looks out of order. But the coming of God to execute his enemies need not preclude a judgment of eternal duration and proportion to follow (Matt 25:41–46, note the "eternal punishment" in v. 46). A similar eschatological scenario is provided in Rev 19–20 (esp. 19:17–21; 20:9–10).

With the promise of a division by the one to come, separating the chaff from the wheat and disposing of the former in eternal fire (3:12, πυρὶ ἀσβέστῳ), Matthew concludes his eschatological discourse with the Shepherd separating goats from the sheep and sending them into the eternal fire (25:41, εἰς τὸ πῦρ τὸ αἰώνιον) for the purpose of eternal punishment (25:46, κόλασιν αἰώνιον). The righteous inherit the kingdom (25:35–40); these go, in contradistinction to the goats, into eternal life (25:46, ζωὴν αἰώνιον).

Summary The profile of the Olivet Discourse shares common features with the parables and the preaching of John. The judgment that falls upon Israel in 70 CE serves as a warning to Jesus's followers that the eschatological end of the age will come with even greater devastation. The Son of Man (25:31) comes as king (25:34). David's son is not only a healer of Israel (9:27; 12:23), he is also the eschatological judge. Both judgment and salvation bring the eschatological discourse to a close. As in the parable of the weeds, where the righteous shine like the sun in the kingdom of the Father, so also the righteous on earth can be recognized by their deeds of mercy (25:35–40; cf. 7:12). This too is the work of judgment, as we will now seek to show.

Jesus and the Judgment

A survey of the judgment theme in Matthew would be incomplete without consideration of the experiences of Jesus, particularly upon the cross. Jesus's enigmatic statement that a prophet is not without honor except among his own

---

linked to the signs in the heavens: καὶ ὄψονται τὸν υἱὸν τοῦ ἀνθρώπου ἐρχόμενον (v. 30), or the events of the desecration of Israel (vv. 15–28): Ὅταν οὖν ἴδητε τὸ βδέλυγμα τῆς ἐρημώσεως (v. 15). The latter, in our judgment, seems more likely.

(13:57) raises an expectation that rejection and suffering will follow. Jesus's first mention of the prophets is their persecution (5:12).[49]

In another veiled reference to his death, he describes his (prophetic) sign in terms of the sign of Jonah. As Jonah was in the belly of the great fish, so would the Son of Man be three days and nights in the heart of the earth (12:40). And the "judgment" against Jonah was unmistakably by divine design (Jonah 1:4, 17).

After John the Baptist met his fate as a prophet (14:1–12), Jesus describes his own experience of rejection and ultimately his execution in a way similar to that of John. What they did to Elijah redivivus, "so also" (οὕτως καί) will the Son of Man suffer at their hands (17:12). Jerusalem is the city that kills the prophets (23:37), therefore the death of Jesus comes as no surprise.

Several times in the narrative Jesus describes his approaching death (16:21; 17:12, 22–23; 20:17–19) and each time with descriptive increase. As Matthew presents Jesus's words as trustworthy, readers can expect that his predictions of his death will come true.

Being handed over to be crucified, Jesus is identified as king (27:11, 27–29, 37). The king, in his representative role for sinners, gives his life willingly. This act on Jesus's part was more than a submission to the execution carried out by humans. It was a submission to the judgment, paradoxically of God (26:39, 42). Matthew tells us that as Jesus hung upon the cross, from the sixth hour to the ninth, darkness covered all the land (27:45). This darkness, and several of the signs that attended it, indicated that he endured the wrath of God.

Darkness in the OT As Jesus hangs upon the cross, the passersby, religious leaders, and crucified thieves all taunt the man from Galilee to unveil his messianic identity by coming down from the cross (24:39–44). Instead of unveiling his messianic identity, the land is enveloped in darkness. It was "a sign as part of a judgment on the world, namely, a warning of punishment that was now beginning."[50] The (unexplained) sign has the potential of conveying several OT meanings. Davies has put forward a return to the primordial darkness before the start of creation.[51] As he begins his gospel with an allusion to Gen 1:1, Matthew may be alluding to Genesis in order to describe a return to the darkness of Gen 1 (Gen 1:2–5).

To press further, during the plagues of Egypt darkness covers the land for three days (Exod 10:21–23):

---

49. Jesus declares that he comes to fulfill the law and the prophets (5:17) and one wonders if their experiences of persecution are not also to be included in his task of fulfillment?

50. Raymond E. Brown, *The Death of the Messiah: From Gethsemane to the Grave*, vol. 2 (New York: Doubleday, 1994), 1035.

51. W. D. Davies, *The Setting of the Sermon on the Mount* (Cambridge: Cambridge University Press, 1976), 84.

καὶ γενηθήτω σκότος ἐπὶ γῆν Αἰγύπτου (Exod 10:21)
ἐγένετο σκότος . . . ἐπὶ πᾶσαν γῆν Αἰγύπτου τρεῖς ἡμέρας) (Exod 10:22)
σκότος ἐγένετο ἐπὶ πᾶσαν τὴν γῆν (Matt 27:45)

The three hours of darkness during the time that Jesus hung upon the cross might also correspond to the three days of darkness in the events leading up to the exodus from Egypt. In similar fashion, Matthew molded Jesus's forty-day wilderness journey as the typological analogue to Israel's forty years in the wilderness (Matt 4:1).[52] It appears that he is doing the same for Jesus's suffering and death. One suspects that the darkness covering the land could portray Israel, once again, as typological Egypt (cf. Matt 2:1–15). Jesus has performed many miracles in the land of Israel, and in unbelief not unlike that of Pharaoh and his people, the signs have not been heeded. Not surprisingly, the light is removed from them before the death of the "firstborn."

Amos 8:9–10 is cited in the margins by NA[28] and might be the strongest allusion to Matthew's darkness at the sixth hour: "And on that day," declares the LORD GOD, "I will make the sun go down at noon and darken the earth in broad daylight. I will turn your feasts into mourning and all your songs into lamentation; I will bring sackcloth on every waist and baldness on every head; I will make it like the mourning for an only son and the end of it like a bitter day." Allison believes the parallels to be substantial. He writes, "Darkness falls in both; in both that darkness is at noon; and whereas there is mourning as for 'an only son' or 'a beloved one' in Amos, Jesus is, in Matthew, God's beloved Son (cf. 3:17; 12:18; 17:5), and he is confessed to be God's Son precisely at the crucifixion itself (27:54)."[53] "The day" is none other than the eschatological day of the Lord, a day of darkness and not light (Amos 5:18, 20). The Lord is the one who darkens the day into night (Amos 5:8) and comes in judgment upon his people. But the judgment announced is not a complete end of Israel, "Behold, the eyes of the LORD GOD are upon the sinful kingdom, and I will destroy it from the surface of the ground, except that I will not utterly destroy the house of Jacob" (Amos 9:8). What follows is a promise that in "that day" (of future restoration), the Lord will raise up the fallen booth of David and repair its ruins (Amos 9:11–15).

Darkness in Matthew The darkness of the crucifixion is an emblem of the day of the Lord in eschatological judgment upon the embodiment of Israel, now hanging upon the cross. The sign points backward to the prophets who spoke of

---

52. Citing Gerhardsson, Allison remarks, "It is the number, not the unit of measurement, that matters for typology." Birger Gerhardsson, *The Testing of God's Son (Matt. 4:1-11 and Par): An Analysis of an Early Christian Midrash*, ConBNT 2 (Lund: G. W. K. Gleerup, 1966), 41–43. Cited in Dale C. Allison Jr., *Studies in Matthew: Interpretation Past and Present* (Grand Rapids: Baker Academic, 2005), 80–81.

53. Allison, *Studies*, 80–81.

the darkness overtaking Israel for transgressing the covenant (Isa 13:9–16; Jer 15:9; Zeph 1:15); and in apocalyptic fashion, it points forward to the consummation of the history of this age in judgment, as the age to come prevails in victory over all opposition to the kingdom of heaven.

The return of the Son of Man is analogous to the death of the Messiah in that both events bring darkness (Matt 24:29). The darkness is a sign of God's judgment and is repeatedly spoken of as a place of weeping and gnashing of teeth and is contrasted with the kingdom of God enjoyed by the saints (8:12; 22:13; 25:30). It is a place devoid of God's favor and mercy. Matthew leads readers to conclude that Jesus experienced such an agony upon the cross. Overcome by the judgment of God, he cried out in dereliction, "Why have you forsaken me" (27:26)? The one who saves his people from their sins (1:21) undergoes the divine judgment in their place (27:45, 28), to ransom them (20:28), purchasing their freedom with his blood, poured out for many for the forgiveness of sins (26:28). *Salvation through judgment is transacted at the cross.*

The tearing of the curtain of the temple (27:51) portends the sign of the temple's demise (24:1–2).[54] But one might compare the opening up of the heavens (ἠνεῴχθησαν) and the descent of the Spirit (3:16), with the opening of the tombs and the resurrection of the saints: ἀνεῴχθησαν καὶ πολλὰ σώματα τῶν κεκοιμημένων ἁγίων ἠγέρθησαν (27:52).[55] As the darkness covered the land of Egypt before the exodus, so also in the new exodus new life issues forth from the judgment of the death. At the death of the Son of God the earth quakes (27:54) and the dead are awakened (v. 51). Preceding the resurrection of the Son of Man, an angel of the Lord, with an appearance like lightning and clothes bright like snow, descends from heaven (28:2). The earth quakes (28:2) and Jesus, risen from the dead, goes out to meet his followers (28:9–10). In Matthew's Gospel, the overlap of this age and the age to come takes place in the story of Jesus.

Conclusion

When John performed his judgment sign in the Jordan, he called upon Israel to repent and to submit to the verdict of the kingdom of heaven. While the coming of the kingdom meant that the judgment could not be forestalled, let alone stopped, it could be escaped by submitting to Jesus in faith (Matt 17:17). By stepping into the waters, Jesus committed himself to endure the reality of the sign. Those who opposed him would likewise experience the fiery Holy Spirit, but without remedy. The day of the Lord would come and remove Israel, but not before Jesus, the faithful embodiment of Israel, carried out the task of his Father. His offering was

---

54. Ibid., 86.

55. Brown thinks that Ezek 37:12–13 "may be the key passage behind Matt's description. . . . 'I will open your tombs [mnēma], and I will bring you up out of your tombs, and I will lead you into the land of Israel.'" Brown, *Death*, 1123–24.

met with the divine approbation of heaven: οὗτός ἐστιν ὁ υἱός μου ὁ ἀγαπητός, ἐν ᾧ εὐδόκησα (3:17).

With the inevitability of judgment, Matthew maps out both the temporal, eschatological judgment against Israel on the plain of history, as well as the visitation of the eschatological kingdom in the judgment at the end of the age. Matthew 11 offers a picture of the eschatological reversal for Israel as the people of God. The judgment will be more bearable for Sodom than towns of Galilee. They will rise to a greater condemnation, which indicates the judgment foretold deals with the Final Judgment. In the parable of the weeds (ch. 13), Jesus taught that the conclusion of this age will be the eternal fire for some. By contrast, the parable of the tenants (ch. 17) provides a preview of the judgment that would befall Israel and carry the Israelites away from their land. When Jesus sits upon the Mount of Olives and speaks of the future (ch. 24), the temporal and eternal judgments are described in alternation and by means of recapitulation. As terrible as 70 CE would be, something worse is expected.

Matthew only knows of one way of escape and that is only granted to the followers of Jesus. As the sin-bearing Son of Man, Jesus is authorized at the start of his ministry to be the ransom of his people (3:17). Jesus is given the Spirit to demonstrate the divine approval of his mission; a mission which includes suffering and death, the events of which purport that the judgment experienced was that of divine wrath. Upon the cross, Jesus endured what John had warned would be the fire of the Spirit, a deluge of theophanic retribution. By his death and resurrection, Jesus quenched the fire of the Spirit and opened up the way of the new exodus by his exaltation from the dead. Having undergone the baptism of the Spirit and fire, Jesus's followers would receive a baptism of favor (Matt 28:19).

Chapter 13

CONCLUSION

Our task has been to examine the meaning of the baptism in the Holy Spirit and fire. The difficulty of this expression is well known, causing Voltaire to make the laconic remark, "These words, 'He will baptize with fire,' have never been explained."[1] Those interested in John's proclamation, both past and present, would likely place the emphasis not on an absence of an explanation, but rather on the wide-ranging differences of interpretations that this enigmatic phrase has engendered. The spectrum of meaning ranges from a purely positive and gracious outpouring of the Spirit to a destructive consequence of the Spirit.

In this study we have chosen to limit our inquiry to Matthew's account.[2] Such an approach necessitated a detailed look at the grammatical structure of the logion as well as its thematic cohesiveness with the metaphors used by John (e.g., removal of trees and chaff to be burned). As OT citations and allusions are one of the hallmarks of Matthew's Gospel, attention was given to OT texts which provide plausible background material from which Matthew could draw, in order to color the Baptist narrative. We reached the conclusion that both John's preaching and baptism were eschatological in orientation.

The content of John's preaching contains standard imagery drawn from the OT. Metaphorical language, such as eschatological judgment by fire, is also found in the Second Temple literature of the first century BCE and CE. The wrathful day of the Lord and an unidentified figure who would come to judge Israel and rule over the world were also common motifs. Matthew's presentation of John's eschatological warning fits in such apocalyptic and eschatological thought of the first century CE. Ethical exhortation is the necessary application of the eschatological message, but it plays a minor role in the account (i.e., "fruits of repentance") and is not defined

---

1. Marie Francois Arouet de Voltaire, *A Philosophical Dictionary*, vol. 1 (New York: Coventry House, 1932), 195.

2. A further layer of difficulty is the question of the oral/textual development of the saying. Deciding upon an original form of the logion, lying behind the gospels and Acts, directly impacts the interpretive outcome. The difficulty of the phrase, the thorny issues of reconstructing its unmodified form, and interpretations that run in completely opposite directions could be a book-length study in and of itself.

by John. John's emphasis was on the approaching kingdom of heaven and the need to repent before "that day" arrived and the Coming One was revealed. The eschatological scenario to which the baptism in the Holy Spirit and fire pointed was the day of wrath against national Israel.

Answering the question about the meaning of the baptism in the Holy Spirit and fire is only half of the interpretive issue. Because John compares his baptism in water with the future baptism in Spirit-fire, the issue of the relationship between these two baptisms had to be probed. How does the baptism in the Holy Spirit and fire relate specifically to John's baptism with water?

Taking our cue from Matthew that John was a prophet, we analyzed the meaning of his baptism in terms of the actions performed by the OT prophets. Those scholars who have classified John's baptism as a sign-act have tended to interpret its function and meaning in terms of prophetic utterances that are detached from and not descriptive of the specific signs that the prophets performed. In other words, texts such as Jer 31; Ezek 36:25, and Joel 2 speak of a future cleansing of Israel, but such announcements are not the verbal explanations of the visual/auditory signs performed. In our judgment, these expositors are right to explain John's baptism as a performed sign, the problem has been a failure to integrate the signs of the OT prophets into their findings.

More clarification was needed to fix the parameters of what constitutes a sign-act. The work of OT scholars in this area revealed that sign-acts are actions that communicate the divine will and are also given to prompt an appropriate response in the onlookers. The OT prophets, particularly Jeremiah and Ezekiel, performed and repeated sign-acts for the nation of Israel. The great majority of the recorded sign-acts were actions that communicated the approaching judgment of Yahweh. The four sign-acts that did not communicate the wrath of God were set before Israel to show them what would take place *after* their judgment and exile. Otherwise, sign-acts communicated the disfavor of Yahweh and the impending doom of the nation.

As a prophet (Matt 11:9–13), John's fierce words and his sign-act (i.e., baptism) provide a uniform declaration of divine intent. Israel must repent because the judgment in the Spirit's fire would be like the waters that submerged those baptized. Regardless of whether or not one was baptized by John, the sign of the coming Spirit and fire deluge was for the nation as a whole. Those specifically singled out for the future eschatological baptism are, not surprisingly, the religious leaders (Pharisees and Sadducees). This Matthean context supports the interpretation of the logion offered in the present work. Were it something positive, we would not expect that these groups of leaders would be the benefactors, as Matthew's description of them is negative in outlook throughout. And as Matthew discloses, the crowds will side with their spiritual leaders against Jesus. In Matthew they are described as religious leaders τοῦ λαοῦ (Matt 2:4; 21:23; 26:3; 26:47; 27:1).

The reason for the eschatological baptism in the Spirit's fire ultimately resides in national Israel's unwillingness to believe that Jesus is the Christ. John spoke of one who would come. Like the Son of Man traditions, this "Coming One" would slay his enemies and consign them to eternal fire, while also gathering up his people for eternal life (Matt 13:38–43). But this aspect of judgment and gathering would take place in a different sequence than that conceived by John. For Matthew, Jesus would come, and he would undergo the realities of John's sign-act on behalf of his people. The cross is the eschatological event (Matt 27:45–53) that made it possible to escape the eschatological event of the end of the age. In Matthew's schema, the interim period is for the work of making disciples (Matt 28:19). The judgments Jesus spoke of would occur in the time of "this generation" (23:36) and in finality at the end of the age (12:41). The judgment upon national Israel also served as a warning to all who refuse to submit to Jesus's Davidic authority as king and savior.[3]

Following Jesus was the only way of escaping the Holy Spirit and fire. Matthew's placement of the logion in the narrative, combined with the future teachings of Jesus concerning the day of the Lord/day of judgment, indicates that the unquenchable fire was neither gracious nor refining. It was not a messianic outpouring of the Spirit that purified the righteous, nor was it a fiery stream through which all must pass. It was a judgment to be escaped or experienced, and for Matthew the determining factor is one's relationship to Jesus.

---

3. The paraenetic function has been explored in detail by Sim; cf. Sim, *Apocalyptic Eschatology*, 222–41.

BIBLIOGRAPHY

Abegg Jr., Martin G. "Messianic Hope and 4Q285: A Reassessment." *JBL* 113.1 (1994): 81–91.

Aland, Barbara et al., eds. *Novum Testamentum Graece*. Nestle-Aland 27th ed. Stuttgart: Deutsche Bibelgesellschaft, 2001.

Albright W. F., and C. S. Mann. *Matthew*. AB. New York: Doubleday, 1971.

Alford, Henry. *Matthew–John*. 4 vols. London: Rivingtons, 1844. Repr., Grand Rapids: Baker, 1980.

Allen, W. C. *Matthew*. ICC. 3rd ed. Edinburgh: T&T Clark, 1947.

Allison Jr., Dale C. "Elijah Must Come First." *JBL* 103 (1984): 256–58.

Allison Jr., Dale C. *The New Moses: A Matthean Typology*. Minneapolis: Fortress, 1993.

Allison Jr., Dale C. *Studies in Matthew*. Grand Rapids: Baker Academic, 2005.

Andersen Francis I., and David Noel Freedman. *Micah: A New Translation with Introduction and Commentary*. AB 24e. New York: Doubleday, 2000.

Anderson, Janice C. *Matthew's Narrative Web*. JSNTSup 91. Sheffield: Sheffield Academic Press, 1994.

Anderson, Robert A. *Signs and Wonders: A Commentary on the Book of Daniel*. Grand Rapids: Eerdmans, 1984.

The Ante-Nicene Fathers. Edited by Alexander Roberts and James Donaldson. 1885–1887. 10 vols. Repr., Peabody: Hendrickson, 1994.

Argyle, A. W. "An Alleged Semitism." *ET* 66 (1954–1955): 177.

Argyle, A. W. "An Alleged Semitism." *ET* 80 (1969): 285–86.

Aune, David E. *Prophecy in Early Christianity and the Ancient Mediterranean World*. Grand Rapids: Eerdmans, 1991.

Axtell, J. Stockton. *The Mystery of Baptism*. London: Bible Churchmen's Missionary Society, n.d.

Baker, David W. *Joel, Obadiah, Malachi*. NIVAC. Grand Rapids: Zondervan, 2006.

Baltzer, Klaus. "Zur formgeschichtlichen Bestimmung der Texte vom Gottesknecht im Deuterojesaja Buch." Pages 27–43 in *Probleme biblischer Theologie*. Edited by Gerhard Von Rad and Hans W. Wolff. München: Chr. Kaiser, 1971.

Barclay, William. *The Gospel of Matthew*. 2 vols. Philadelphia: Westminster Press, 1958.

Barnard, L. W. "Matt. 3.11/Luke 3.16." *JTS* 8.1 (1957): 107.

Barnes, Albert. *Notes on the New Testament: Matthew and Mark*. Grand Rapids: Baker, 1949. Repr., Grand Rapids: Baker, 1981.

Barrett, C. K. *The Holy Spirit in the Gospel Tradition*. London: SPCK, 1970.

Barnett, Paul. "The Jewish Sign Prophets – AD 40-70: Their Intentions and Origin." *NTS* 27.5 (1981): 679–97.

Barth, Gerhard. "Matthew's Understanding of the Law." Pages 58–164 in *Tradition and Interpretation in Matthew*. Edited by Günther Bornkamm, Gerhard Barth and Heinz Joachim Held. Translated by P. Scott. London: SCM, 1963.

Bauer, Walter. *A Greek-English Lexicon of the New Testament and Other Early Christian Literature*. 3rd ed. Edited by Frederick William Danker. Chicago: University of Chicago Press, 2000.

Baxter, Wayne. *Israel's Only Shepherd: Matthew's Shepherd Motif and His Social Setting.* London: T&T Clark, 2012.

Baxter, Wayne S. "Mosaic Imagery in the Gospel of Matthew." *TJ* 20.1 (1999): 69–83.

Beale, Gregory K. *Handbook on the New Testament Use of the Old Testament: Exegesis and Interpretation.* Grand Rapids: Baker Academic, 2012.

Beale, Gregory K. "The Problem of the Man from the Sea in 4 Ezra 13 and Its Relation to the Messianic Concept in John's Apocalypse." *NovT* 25.2 (1983): 182–88.

Beale, Gregory K. "The Use of Hosea 11:1 in Matthew 2:15: One More Time." *JETS* 55.4 (2012): 697–715.

Beare, Francis W. *The Gospel according to Matthew.* Oxford: Basil Blackwell, 1981.

Beasley-Murray, George R. *Baptism in the New Testament.* Grand Rapids: Eerdmans, 1962.

Beasley-Murray, George R. "The Interpretation of Daniel 7." *CBQ* 45 (1983): 44–58.

Beaton, Richard. *Isaiah's Christ in Matthew's Gospel.* SNTS 123. Cambridge: Cambridge University Press, 2002.

Becker, Joachim. *Messianic Expectation in the Old Testament.* Translated by D. Green. Minneapolis: Fortress, 1977.

Becker, Jürgen *Jesus von Nazaret.* Berlin: Walter de Gruyter, 1996.

Becker, Jürgen. *Johannes der Täufer und Jesus von Nazareth.* BS 63. Neukirchen-Vluyn: Neukirchener, 1972.

Belleville, Linda L. "'Born of Water and Spirit': John 3:5." *TJ* 1 (1980): 125–41.

Ben Zvi, Ehud. "'Twelve Prophetic Books' or 'The Twelve'? A Few Preliminary Considerations." Pages 125–56 in *Forming Prophetic Literature.* Edited by John D. Watts and Paul R. House. Sheffield: Sheffield Academic Press, 1996.

Bergin, Liam O. *Propheticum Lavacrum: Baptism as Symbolic Act of Eschatological Salvation.* Analecta Gregoriana 277. Rome: Gregorian University, 1999.

Best, Ernest. "Spirit-Baptism." *NovT* 4 (1960): 236–43.

Betz, Hans D. *The Sermon on the Mount: A Commentary on the Sermon on the Mount, Including the Sermon on the Plain.* Hermenia. Minneapolis: Fortress, 1995.

Betz, Otto. "Was John an Essene?" Pages 205–14 in *Understanding the Dead Sea Scrolls: A Reader from the Biblical Archeology Review.* Edited by H. Shanks. New York: Random House, 1992.

Beuken, Willem A. M. "The Emergence of the Shoot of Jesse: An Eschatological or a Now Event?" *CTJ* 39 (2004): 88–108.

Black, David A. "New Testament Semitisms." *TBT* 39 (1988): 215–23.

Black, Matthew. *An Aramaic Approach to the Gospels and Acts.* Oxford: Oxford, 1979.

Black, Stephanie L. "How Matthew Tells the Story: A Linguistic Approach to Matthew's Narrative Syntax." Pages 24–52 in *Built Upon the Rock: Studies in the Gospel of Matthew.* Edited by Daniel M. Gutner and John Nolland. Grand Rapids: Eerdmans, 2008.

Black, Stephanie L. *Sentence Conjunctions in Matthew's Gospel.* JSNTSup 216. Sheffield: Sheffield Academic Press, 2002.

Blenkinsopp, Joseph. *Creation, Un-creation, Re-creation: A Discursive Commentary on Genesis 1-11.* London: T&T Clark, 2011.

Blenkinsopp, Joseph. *Prophecy and Canon: A Contribution to the Study of Christian Origins.* Indiana: University of Notre Dame Press, 1977.

Blenkinsopp, Joseph. "Prophesy and Priesthood in Josephus." *JJS* 25.2 (1974): 239–62.

Blomberg, Craig L. "Matthew." Pages 1–110 in *Commentary on the New Testament Use of the Old Testament.* Edited by Gregory K. Beale and D. A. Carson. Grand Rapids: Baker, 2007.

Blomberg, Craig L. *Matthew: An Exegetical and Theological Exposition of Holy Scripture.* NAC 22. Nashville: Broadman Press, 1992.

Böcher, O. "Wilderness." In *Dictionary of New Testament Theology and Exegesis.* Edited by Moisés Silva. Grand Rapids: Zondervan, 2014. Accordance Bible Software 11.1.6.

Bock, Darrell L. "Dating the *Parables of Enoch: A Forschungsbericht.*" Pages 58–113 in *Parables of Enoch: A Paradigm Shift.* Edited by James H. Charlesworthand Darrell L. Block. London: Bloomsbury, 2013.

Bock, Darrel L. *Luke 1:1-9:50.* ECNT 1. Grand Rapids: Baker, 1994.

Bockmuehl, Markus. "A 'Slain Messiah' in 4Q Serekh Milhamah (4Q285)?" *TynBul* 43 (1992): 155–69.

Bornkamm, Günther. "End-Expectation and Church in Matthew." Pages 15–51 in *Tradition and Interpretation in Matthew.* Edited by Günther Bornkamm, Gerhard Barth and Heinz Joachim Held. London: SCM, 1963.

Bretscher, Paul G. "Exodus 4:22-23 and the Voice from Heaven." *JBL* 87 (1968): 301–11.

Briggs, Charles. *Messianic Prophecy: The Prediction of the Fulfillment of Redemption through the Messiah.* New York: Scribner's, 1886. Repr., Peabody: Hendrickson, 1988.

Brooks, Oscar S. *The Drama of Decision: Baptism in the New Testament.* Peabody: Hendrickson, 1987.

Brown, Colin, ed. *New International Dictionary of New Testament Theology.* 4 vols. Grand Rapids: Zondervan, 1974–1985.

Brown, Raymond E. *Birth of the Messiah: A Commentary on the Infancy Narratives of Matthew and Luke.* Rev. ed. New York: Doubleday, 1993.

Brown, Raymond E. *The Death of the Messiah: From Gethsemane to the Grave.* New York: Doubleday, 1994.

Brown, Raymond E. *New Testament Essays.* London and Dublin: Geoffrey Chapman, 1965.

Brownlee, W. H. "John the Baptist in the Light of Ancient Scrolls." Pages 33–53 in *The Scrolls and the New Testament.* Edited by Krister Stendahl and James H. Charlesworth. New York: Crossroad, 1992.

Brueggemann, Walter. *Isaiah 1-39.* Louisville: Westminster John Knox Press, 1998.

Brueggemann, Walter. *The Land: Place as Gift, Promise, and Challenge in Biblical Faith.* Minneapolis: Fortress, 2002.

Brueggemann, Walter. *Theology of the Old Testament: Testimony, Dispute, Advocacy.* Minneapolis: Fortress, 1997.

Bruner, Frederick D. *The Christ Book: A Historical/Theological Commentary, Matthew 1-12.* Waco: Word, 1987.

Bultmann, Rudolph. *The History of the Synoptic Tradition.* Oxford: Basil Blackwell, 1963.

Burger, Christoph. *Jesus als Davidssohn: Eine traditionsgeschichtliche Untersuchung.* Göttingen: Vandenhoeck & Ruprecht, 1970.

Butterworth, M. "Daniel." *New Bible Commentary.* Edited by D. A. Carson et al. Downers Grove: IVP, 1994. Accordance Bible Software 11.1.6.

Cage, Gary T. *The Holy Spirit: A Sourcebook with Commentary.* Reno: Charlotte House, 1995.

Calvin, John. *Commentary on the Prophet Isaiah.* Translated by William Pringle. Grand Rapids: Baker, 2003.

Calvin, John. *Harmony of the Gospels Matthew, Mark and Luke.* Vol. 1. Translated by William Pringle. Grand Rapids: Eerdmans, 1972.

Cameron, Peter S. *Violence and the Kingdom: The Interpretation of Matthew 11:12.* Frankfurt: Peter Lang, 1984.

Capes, David B. "Intertextual Echoes in the Matthean Baptismal Narrative." *BBR* 9 (1999): 37–49.

Caragounis, Chrys C. *The Son of Man*. WUNT 38. Tubingen: J. C. B. Mohr, 1986.

Carson, Donald A. *Matthew*. EBC 1. Grand Rapids: Zondervan, 1995.

Carter, Warren. "The Crowds in Matthew's Gospel." *CBQ*, 55.1 (1993): 54–67.

Carter, Warren. "Evoking Isaiah: Matthean Soteriology and an Intertextual Reading of Isaiah 7-9 and Matthew 1:23 and 4:15-16." *JBL* 119.3 (2000): 503–20.

Carter, Warren. *Matthew and the Margins: A Sociopolitical and Religious Reading*. Maryknoll: Orbis, 2005.

Casey, Maurice. "General, Generic and Indefinite: The Use of the Term 'Son of Man' in Aramaic Sources and in the Teaching of Jesus." *JSNT* 29 (1987): 21–56.

Casey, Maurice. "The Jackals and the Son of Man." *JSNT* 23 (1985): 3–22.

Casey, Maurice. "Method in Our Madness, and Madness in Their Methods: Some Approaches to the Son of Man Problem in Recent Scholarship." *JSNT* 42 (1991): 17–43.

Casey, Maurice. *The Solution to the 'Son of Man' Problem*. Edinburgh: T&T Clark, 2009.

Casey, Maurice. *Son of Man: The Interpretation and Influence of Daniel 7*. London: SPCK, 1979.

Catchpole, David. *The Quest for Q*. Edinburgh: T&T Clark, 1993.

Charette, Blaine. *The Theme of Recompense in Matthew's Gospel*. JSNTSup 79. Sheffield: JSOT, 1992.

Charles, R. H. *A Critical and Exegetical Commentary on the Book of Daniel*. Oxford: Clarendon, 1929.

Charlesworth, James H. "John the Baptizer and the Dead Sea Scrolls." Pages 1–35 in *The Bible and the Dead Sea Scrolls*. Vol. 3 of *The Scrolls and Christian Origins*. Edited by James H. Charlesworth. Waco: Baylor University Press, 2006.

Charlesworth, James H. *The Old Testament Pseudepigrapha and the New Testament: Prolegomena for the Study of Christian Origins*. Cambridge: Cambridge University Press, 1985.

Chester, Andrew. *Messiah and Exaltation*. WUNT 207. Tübingen: Mohr Siebeck, 2007.

Childs, Brevard S. *Biblical Theology of the Old and New Testaments*. Minneapolis: Fortress, 1993.

Childs, Brevard S. *Introduction to the Old Testament as Scripture*. Minneapolis: Fortress, 1979.

Childs, Brevard S. *Isaiah*. Louisville: Westminster John Knox, 2001.

Chilton, Bruce D. *The Isaiah Targum: Introduction, Translation, Apparatus and Notes*. TAV 11. Wilmington: Michael Glazier, 1987.

Chrysostom. *Homilies on the Gospel of Saint Matthew*. Vol. 10 of *The Nicene and Post-Nicene Church Fathers*. Series 1. Edited by Philip Schaff. 1886–1889. 14 vols. Repr., Peabody: Hendrickson, 1994.

Clarke, Howard. *The Gospel of Matthew and Its Readers*. Bloomington: Indiana University Press, 2003.

Clements, Ronald. *Isaiah 1-39*. Grand Rapids: Eerdmans, 1980.

Collins, Adela Y. "Son of Man." Pages 341–48 in *The New Interpreters Dictionary of the Bible*. Edited by Katherine D. Sakenfeld et al. Nashville: Abingdon, 2009.

Collins, Adela Y., and John J. Collins. *King and Messiah as Son of God*. Grand Rapids: Eerdmans, 2008.

Collins, John J. *The Apocalyptic Vision of the Book of Daniel*. HSM. Missoula: Scholars Press, 1977.

Collins, John J. *Daniel: A Commentary on the Book of Daniel*. Hermeneia. Minneapolis: Fortress, 1993.

Collins, John J. *The Scepter and the Star: Messianism in Light of the Dead Sea Scrolls*. Grand Rapids: Eerdmans, 2010.

Collins, John J. *Seers, Sibyls and Sages in Hellenistic-Roman Judaism*. Leiden: Brill, 1997.

Collins, John J. "The Works of the Messiah." *DSD* 1.1 (1994): 98–112.

Cook, Stephen L. *Prophecy and Apocalypticism: The Postexilic Setting*. Minneapolis: Fortress, 1995.

Cooper, Ben. *Incorporated Servanthood: Commitment and Discipleship in the Gospel of Matthew*. London: T&T Clark, 2013.

Craigie, Peter C. *The Book of Deuteronomy*. NICOT. Grand Rapids: Eerdmans, 1976.

Crowe, Brandon D. *The Obedient Son: Deuteronomy and Christology in the Gospel of Matthew*. BZNW 188. Berlin: De Gruyter, 2012.

Cullmann, Oscar *Christology of the New Testament*. London: SCM, 1963.

Cullmann, Oscar. *Die Tauflehre des Neuen Testaments*. Zurich: Zwingli-Verlag, 1948.

Dapaah, Daniel S. *The Relationship between John the Baptist and Jesus of Nazareth: A Critical Study*. Lanham: University Press of America, 2005.

Daube, David. *The Exodus Pattern in the Bible*. London: Faber and Faber, 1963.

Davies, D. P. "An Alleged Semitism." *ET* 81 (1970): 150–51.

Davies, William D. *The Setting of the Sermon on the Mount*. Cambridge: Cambridge University Press, 1963.

Davies, William D., and Dale C. Allison Jr. *Matthew I-VII*. ICC. Edinburgh: T&T Clark, 1988.

Davies, William D., and Dale C. Allison Jr. *Matthew VIII-XVIII*. ICC. Edinburgh: T&T Clark, 1991.

Davies, William D., and Dale C. Allison Jr. *Matthew XIX-XXVIII*. ICC. Edinburgh: T&T Clark, 1997.

Day, John. *God's Conflict with the Dragon and the Sea: Echoes of a Canaanite Myth in the Old Testament*. Cambridge: Cambridge University Press, 1985.

Delling, Gerhard. "ΒΑΡΤΙΣΜΑ ΒΑΠΓΙΣΘΗΝΑΙ." *NovT* 2 (1958): 92–115.

Dempster, Stephen G. *Dominion and Dynasty*. NSBT 15. Downers Grove: IVP, 2003.

Dennert, Brian C. *John the Baptist and the Jewish Setting of Matthew*. WUNT 403. Tübingen: Mohr Siebeck, 2015.

Devries, Simon J. *Yesterday, Today and Tomorrow: Time and History in the Old Testament*. Grand Rapids: Eerdmans, 1975.

Dillard Raymond B., and Tremper Longman III. *An Introduction to the Old Testament*. Grand Rapids: Zondervan, 1994.

Driver, S. R. *Daniel*. Cambridge: Cambridge University Press, 1936.

Drummond, James. *The Jewish Messiah*. London: Longmans Green, 1877.

Drury, John. "Mark 1.1-15: An Interpretation." Pages 25–36 in *Alternative Approaches to the New Testament Study*. Edited by Anthony E. Harvey. London: SPCK, 1985.

Duguid, Ian. "Ezekiel." Pages 229–32 in *New Dictionary of Biblical Theology*. Edited by T. Desmond Alexander et al. Downers Grove: IVP, 2000.

Dumbrell, William J. *The Faith of Israel: A Theological Survey of the Old Testament*. Grand Rapids: Baker, 2002.

Dumbrell, William J. *The New Covenant: The Synoptics in Context*. Singapore: The Bible Society of Singapore, 1999.

Dumbrell, William J. *The Search for Order: Biblical Eschatology in Focus*. Grand Rapids: Baker, 1994.

Dunn, James D. G. *Baptism in the Holy Spirit: A Re-examination of the New Testament Teaching on the Gift of the Spirit in Relation to Pentecostalism Today.* Philadelphia: Westminster Press, 1970.

Dunn, James D. G. "Spirit-and-Fire Baptism." *NovT* 14 (1972): 81–92.

Dunn, James D. G. *Jesus Remembered: Christianity in the Making.* Vol. 1. Grand Rapids: Eerdmans, 2003.

Edsman, Carl-Martin. *Le baptême de feu.* Uppsala: Lundsquistska Bokhandeln, 1940.

Eggler, Jürg. *Influences and Traditions Underlying the Vision of Daniel 7:2-14.* OBO 177. Göttingen: Vandenhoeck & Ruprecht, 2000.

Eggleston, Chad L. "Wilderness, Desert." Pages 843–47 in *Dictionary of Old Testament Prophets.* Edited by Mark J. Boda and J. Gordon McConville. Downers Grove: IVP, 2012.

Eissfeldt, Otto. *The Old Testament: An Introduction.* Translated by Peter R. Ackroyd. New York: Harper & Row, 1965.

Ellis, E. Earle. *The Gospel of Luke.* NCBC. Grand Rapids: Eerdmans, 1987.

Ernst, Josef. *Johannes der Täufer: Interpretation, Geschichte, Wirkungsgeschichte.* Berlin: Walter de Gruyter, 1989.

Evans, Christopher F. *Saint Luke.* TPINTC. London: SCM, 1990.

Evans, Craig A. "Messianism." Pages 698–707 in *Dictionary of New Testament Background.* Edited by Craig A. Evans and Stanley E. Porter Jr. Downers Grove: IVP, 2000.

Evans, Craig A. "The Baptism of John in a Typological Context." Pages 45–17 in *Baptism, The New Testament and the Church.* JSNTSup 171. Edited by S. E. Porter and A. R. Cross. Sheffield: Sheffield Academic Press, 1999.

Everson, A. Joseph. "The Days of Yahweh." *JBL* 93 (1974): 329–37.

Faierstein, Morris M. "Why Do the Scribes Say That Elijah Must Come First?" *JBL* 100 (1981): 75–86.

Farmer, William R. *The Synoptic Problem.* New York: Macmillan, 1964.

Feldman, Louis H. "Prophets and Prophecy in Josephus." Pages 210–39 in *Prophets, Prophecy, and Prophetic Texts in Second Temple Judaism.* Edited by M. H. Floyd and R. D. Haak. New York: T&T Clark, 2006.

Ferguson, Everett. *Baptism in the Early Church: History, Theology, and Liturgy in the First Five Centuries.* Grand Rapids: Eerdmans, 2009.

Fesko, John V. *Word, Water, and Spirit: A Reformed Perspective on Baptism.* Grand Rapids: Reformation Heritage Books, 2010.

Filson, Floyd V. *The Gospel according to St. Matthew.* London: A&C Black, 1975.

Fishbane, Michael. *Biblical Text and Texture: A Literary Reading of Selected Texts.* Oxford: Oneworld Publications, 1998.

Fishbane, Michael. *Text and Texture: Close Readings of Selected Biblical Texts.* New York: Schocken Books, 1979.

Fitzmyer, Joseph A. *The Gospel according to Luke 1-9.* AYBC. New York: Doubleday,1995, p. 467.

Fitzmyer, Joseph A. "More about Elijah Coming First." *JBL* 104 (1985): 295–96.

Flemington, William F. *The New Testament Doctrine of Baptism.* London: SPCK, 1948.

Flusser, David. "The Baptism of John and the Dead Sea Sect." Pages 209–38 in *Essays on the Dead Sea Scrolls: In Memory of E. L. Sukenik.* Edited by C. Rabin and Y. Yadin. Jerusalem: Hehal Ha-Sefer, 1961.

Fohrer, Georg. "Die Gattung der Berichte über symbolische Handlungen der Propheten." *ZAW* 64. 2 (1952): 101–20.

France, R. T. *The Gospel according to Matthew.* NICNT. Grand Rapids: Eerdmans, 2007.

Friebel, Kelvin G. *Jeremiah's and Ezekiel's Sign-Act*. JSOTSup 283. Sheffield: Sheffield Academic Press, 1999.

Fuller, Reginald H. *The Foundations of New Testament Christology*. London: Collins, 1969.

Funk, Robert W. "The Wilderness." *JBL* 78 (1959): 205–14.

Gaffin, Richard B. "Justification in Luke-Acts." Pages 106–25 in *Right with God: Justification in the Bible and the World*. Edited by D. A. Carson. Grand Rapids: Baker, 1992.

Gage, Warren A. *The Gospel of Genesis: Studies in Protology and Eschatology*. Winona Lake: Carpenter Books, 1984.

Gallagher, Edmon L. "The Blood from Abel to Zechariah in the History of Interpretation." *NTS* 60.1 (2014): 121–38.

Garland, David E. *Reading Matthew: A Literary and Theological Commentary*. Macon: Smyth & Helwys, 2001.

Geldenhuys, Norval. *The Gospel of Luke*. NICNT. Grand Rapids: Eerdmans, 1979.

Gerhardsson, Birger. *The Testing of God's Son (Matt. 4:1-11 and Par): An Analysis of an Early Christian Midrash*. ConBNT 2. Lund: G. W. K. Gleerup, 1966.

Gibbs, Jeffrey A. "Israel Standing with Israel: The Baptism of Jesus in Matthew's Gospel (Matt 3:13-17)." *CBQ* 64 (2002): 511–26.

Gibbs, Jeffery A. *Matthew 1:1-11:1*. Saint Louis: Concordia, 2006.

Gilmore, Alec. *Christian Baptism: A Fresh Attempt to Understand the Rite in Terms of Scripture, History, and Theology*. Chicago: The Judson Press, 1959.

Glazier-McDonald, Beth. *Malachi: The Divine Messenger*. SBL 98. Atlanta: Scholars Press, 1987.

Gnilka, Joachim. *Das Matthäusevangelium*. Vol. 1. HTKNT. Freiburg: Herder, 1986.

Goguel, Maurice. *Au seuil de l'évangile Jean-Baptiste*. Paris: Payot, 1928.

Goldingay, John. *Isaiah*. NIBC. Peabody: Hendrickson, 2001.

Goldingay, John, and David Payne. *A Critical and Exegetical Commentary on Isaiah 40-55*. 2 vols. ICC. London: T&T Clark, 2006.

Goldingay, John, and Pamela J. Scalise. *Minor Prophets II*. NIBCOT. Peabody: Hendrickson, 2009.

Goldingay, John E. *Daniel*. WBC 30. Nashville: Thomas Nelson, 1989.

Goodacre, Mark. M. *The Case against Q*. Harrisburg: Trinity Press International, 2002.

Goppelt, Leonhard. *Theologie des Neuen Testaments*. Göttingen: Vandenhoeck & Ruprecht, 1980.

Goulder, Michael D. "Is Q a Juggernaut?" *JBL* 115 (1996): 667–81.

Goulder, Michael D. *Luke: A New Paradigm*. JSNTSup 20. Sheffield: Sheffield Academic Press, 1989.

Goulder, Michael D. *Midrash and Lection in Matthew*. London, SPCK, 1974.

Grabbe, Lester L. "Thus Spake the Prophet Josephus…: The Jewish Historian on Prophets and Prophecy." Pages 240–47 in *Prophets, Prophecy, and Prophetic Texts in Second Temple Judaism*. Edited by M. H. Floyd and R. D. Haak. New York: T&T Clark, 2006.

Gray, George Buchannan. *A Critical and Exegetical Commentary on the Book of Isaiah 1-27*. ICC. Edinburgh: T&T Clark, 1911.

Gressmann, Hugo. *Der Messias*. FRLANT 26. Göttingen: Vandenhoeck und Ruprecht, 1929.

Gundry, Robert H. *Matthew*. Grand Rapids: Eerdmans, 1982.

Gurtner, Daniel M. "Interpreting Apocalyptic Symbolism in the Gospel of Matthew." *BBR* 22.4 (2012): 525–45.

Hagner, Donald. "Apocalyptic Motifs in the Gospel of Matthew: Continuity and Discontinuity." *HBT* 7.2 (1985): 53–82.

Hagner, Donald A. *Matthew 1-13*. WBC 33A. Nashville: Thomas Nelson, 2000.

Hagner, Donald A. *Matthew 14-28*. WBC 33b. Nashville: Thomas Nelson, 1995.

Hamilton, James M. *God's Glory in Salvation through Judgment: A Biblical Theology*. Wheaton: Crossway, 2010.

Hannan, Margaret. *The Nature and Demands of the Sovereign Rule of God in the Gospel of Matthew*. LNTS 308. London: T&T Clark, 2006.

Hare, Douglas R. *Matthew*. IBC. Louisville: Westminster John Knox, 1993.

Hare, Douglas R. A. *The Son of Man Tradition*. Minneapolis: Fortress, 1990.

Harrington, Daniel J. *The Gospel of Matthew*. SPS 1. Collegeville: Liturgical Press, 1991.

Harris, R. Laird, Gleason L. Archer Jr., Bruce K. Waltke. *Theological Workbook of the Old Testament*. Chicago: Moody, 1982. Accordance Bible Software 4.

Harrison, Ronald K. *Introduction to the Old Testament*. Peabody: Prince Press, 1999.

Hartman, L. F., and A. A. Di Lella, *The Book of Daniel*. AB 23. New York: Doubleday, 1978.

Hastings, James. *The Great Texts of the Bible: St. Matthew*. Edinburgh: T&T Clark, 1951.

Hengel, Martin. *The Charismatic Leader and His Followers*. Translated by James Greig. Spring Valley: Crossroad, 1981.

Hengstenberg, Ernst W. *Christology of the Old Testament*. 2nd ed. Translated by J. Martin. Edinburgh: T&T Clark, 1864.

Hill, Andrew E. *Daniel – Malachi*. EBC. Rev. ed. Grand Rapids: Zondervan, 2008.

Hill, Andrew E. *Malachi: A New Translation with Introduction and Commentary*. New York: Doubleday, 1998.

Hill, David. "False Prophets and Charismatics: Structure and Interpretation in Matthew 7:15-23." *Biblica* 57.3 (1976): 327–48.

Hill, David. *The Gospel of Matthew*. NCBC. Grand Rapids: Eerdmans, 1984.

Hillers, Delbert R. *Micah*. Hermeneia. Minneapolis: Fortress, 1984.

Hoffmann, Paul. *Studien zur Theologie der Logienquelle*. NTAbh 8. Münster: Aschendorff, 1972.

Hoffmann, Yair. "The Day of the Lord as a Concept and a Term in the Prophetic Literature." *ZAW* 93.1 (1981): 37–50.

Hooker, Morna D. "John's Baptism: A Prophetic Sign." Pages 22–40 in *The Holy Spirit and Christian Origins: Essays in Honor of James D. G. Dunn*. Edited by Graham Stanton, Bruce W. Longenecker and Stephen C. Barton. Grand Rapids: Eerdmans, 2004.

Hooker, Morna D. *Jesus and the Servant: The Influence of the Servant Concept of Deutero-Isaiah in the New Testament*. London: SPCK, 1959.

Hooker, Morna D. *The Signs of a Prophet: The Prophetic Actions of Jesus*. Harrisburg: Trinity Press, 1997.

Horsley, Richard A. *The Liberation of Christmas: The Infancy Narratives in Social Context*. New York: Continuum, 1989.

Horsley, Richard A. "'Like One of the Prophets of Old' Two Types of Popular Prophets at the Time of Jesus." *CBQ* 47 (1985): 435–63.

Hossfeld, Frank-Lothar, and Erich Zenger. *Psalms 2: A Commentary on Psalms 51-100*. Minneapolis: Fortress, 2005.

House, Paul R. *The Unity of the Twelve*. Sheffield: Almond Press, 1990.

Huizenga, Leroy A. *The New Isaac: Tradition and Intertextuality in the Gospel of* Matthew. SNT. Leiden: Brill, 2009.

Hutchinson, John C. "Was John the Baptist an Essene from Qumran?" *BSac* 159 (2002): 187–200.

Hutton, Rodney R. "Magic or Street-Theater? The Power of the Prophetic Word." *ZAW* 107 (1995): 247–60.

Jamieson, Robert, and A. R. Fausset. *A Commentary: Critical, Experimental and Practical on the Old and New Testament*. Vol. 5. Grand Rapids: Eerdmans, 1948.

Jeremias, Joachim. *Infant Baptism in the First Four Centuries*. Philadelphia: Westminster Press, 1960.

Jeremias, Joachim, and Walther Zimmerli, *The Servant of God*. London: SCM, 1957.

Johnson, Luke T. *The Acts of the Apostles*. SPS 5. Collegeville: The Liturgical Press, 1992.

Jones, Alexander. *The Gospel according to St Matthew*. London: Geoffrey Chapman, 1965.

Jones, Barry A. *The Formation of the Book of the Twelve: A Study in Text and Canon*. Atlanta: Scholars Press, 1995.

Jones, Brian C. "Wilderness." Pages 848–52 in *The New Interpreters Dictionary of the Bible*. Edited by Katherine D. Sakenfeld et al. Nashville: Abingdon, 2009.

Kasier, Otto. *Isaiah 1-12*. 2nd ed. Translated by John Bowden. Philadelphia: Westminster, 1974.

Keener, Craig S. *A Commentary on the Gospel of Matthew*. Grand Rapids: Eerdmans, 1999.

Keener, Craig S. *Matthew*. NTCS. Downers Grove: Inter Varsity Press, 1997.

Keener, Craig S. *The Spirit in the Gospels and Acts*. Peabody: Hendrickson, 1997.

Keil, Carl F. *Daniel*. Translated by M. G. Easton. Edinburgh: T&T Clark, 1866–91. Repr., Peabody: Hendrickson, 2001.

Keil, Carl Friedrich, and Franz Delitzsch. *Commentary on the Old Testament*. Peabody: Hendrickson, 1996.

Kennedy, Joel. *The Recapitulation of Israel: Use of Israel's History in Matthew 1:1-4:11*. WUNT 257. Tübingen: Mohr Siebeck, 2008.

Kienzier, Johnathan. *The Fiery Holy Spirit: The Spirit's Relationship with Judgment in Luke-Acts*. JPTSup 44. Dorchester: Deo Publishing, 2015.

Kim, Seyoon. *The Son of Man as Son of God*. Grand Rapids: Eerdmans, 1985.

Kingsbury, Jack D. "The Developing Conflict between Jesus and the Jewish Leaders in Matthew's Gospel." *CBQ* 49 (1987): 57–73.

Kingsbury, Jack D. *Matthew as Story*. 2nd ed. Philadelphia: Fortress, 1988.

Kingsbury, Jack D. *Matthew: Structure, Christology, Kingdom*. Philadelphia: Fortress, 1975.

Kittel, Gerhard, and Gerhard Friedrich, eds. *Theological Dictionary of the New Testament*. 10 vols. Translated by Geoffrey W. Bromiley. Grand Rapids: Eerdmans, 1964–1976.

Kline, Meredith G. "Oath and Ordeal Signs." *WTJ* 27.2 (1965): 115–39.

Kline, Meredith G. *By Oath Consigned*. Grand Rapids: Eerdmans, 1968.

Kline, Meredith G. *Treaty of the Great King: The Covenant Structure of Deuteronomy*. Eugene: Wipf & Stock, n.d.

Kloppenborg, John S. *The Formation of Q: Trajectories in Ancient Wisdom Collections*. Harrisburg: Trinity Press International, 1987.

Kobelski, Paul J. *The Royal Son of God: The Christology of Matthew 1-2 in the Setting of the Gospel*. Göttingen: Vandenhoeck & Ruprecht, 1979.

Kraeling, Carl H. *John the Baptist*. New York: Charles Scribner's Sons, 1951.

Kümmel, Werner G. *The Theology of the New Testament*. London: SPCK, 1974.

Lacocque, André. "Allusions to Creation in Daniel 7." Pages 114–31 in *The Book of Daniel: Composition and Reception*. Vol. 1. Edited by John J. Collins and Peter W. Flint. Leiden: Brill, 2001.

Ladd, George Eldon. *A Theology of the New Testament*. Rev. ed. Grand Rapids: Eerdmans, 1993.

Lampe, Geoffrey W. H. *The Seal of the Spirit: A Study in the Doctrine of Baptism and Confirmation in the New Testament and the Fathers.* London: SPCK, 1967.

Leal, Robert B. *Wilderness in the Bible: Toward a Theology of Wilderness.* SBL 72. New York: Peter Lang, 2004.

LeCureux, Jason T. *The Thematic Unity of the Book of the Twelve.* Sheffield: Sheffield Phoenix Press, 2012.

Lenski, Richard C. H. *The Interpretation of Saint Matthew's Gospel.* Minneapolis: Augsburg, 1943.

Lentzen-Deis, Fritzleo. *Die Taufe nach den Synoptikern: Literarkritische und gattungsgeschichtliche Untersuchungen.* Frankfurt am Main: Joseph Knecht, 1970.

Leuchter, Mark. "Another Look at the Hosea/Malachi Framework in the Twelve." *VT* 64 (2014): 249–65.

Levenson, John D. *Creation and the Persistence of Evil: The Jewish Drama of Divine Omnipotence.* Princeton: Princeton University Press, 1996.

Lewis, Scott M. *What Are They Saying about New Testament Apocalyptic?* Mahwah: Paulist Press, 2004.

Lindblom, Johannes. *Jesu Missions- och Dopbefallning, Mt. 28, 18-20 Tillika en Studie over det kristna Dopeti Ursprung.* Uppsala, 1919.

Lohmeyer, Ernst. *The Lord's Prayer.* Translated by John Bowden. London: William Collins Sons & Co., 1965.

Longman III, Tremper, and Daniel G. Reid. *God Is a Warrior.* Grand Rapids: Zondervan, 1995.

Lowery, David K. "A Theology of Matthew." Pages 19–63 in *A Biblical Theology of the New Testament.* Edited by Roy B. Zuck. Chicago: Moody, 1994.

Lucas, Ernsest C. *Daniel.* AOTC. Downers Grove: IVP, 2002.

Luz, Ulrich. *Matthew 1-7.* Hermeneia. Edited by Helmut Koester. Translated by James E. Crouch. Minneapolis: Fortress, 1985.

Luz, Ulrich. *Matthew 8-20.* Hermeneia. Edited by Helmut Koester. Translated by James E. Crouch. Minneapolis: Fortress, 2001.

Luz, Ulrich. *Studies in Matthew.* Grand Rapids: Eerdmans, 2005.

Maier, Gerhard. *Matthäus-Evangelium,* BKZNT 1. Stuttgart: Hänssler, 1983.

Manson, T. W. *The Sayings of Jesus: As Recorded in the Gospels according to St. Matthew and St. Luke.* Grand Rapids: Eerdmans, 1979.

Marguerat, Daniel. *Le jugement dans l'Evangile de Matthieu.* Geneva: Labor et Fides, 1981.

Marshall, I. Howard. *The Gospel of Luke,* NIGTC. Exeter: Paternoster, 1978.

Marshall, I. Howard. "The Meaning of the Verb 'Baptize.'" Pages 8–24 in in *Baptism, The New Testament and the Church.* JSNTSup 171. Edited by S. E. Porter and A. R. Cross. Sheffield: Sheffield Academic Press, 1999.

Martinez, Florentino Garcia, and Eibert J. C. Tigchelaar. *The Dead Sea Scrolls Study Edition.* Leiden: Brill, 1999.

Mathewson, David. "The Apocalyptic Vision of Jesus according to the Gospel of Matthew: Reading Matthew 3:16-4:11 Intertextually." *TynBul* 62.1 (2011): 89–108.

Mauser, Ulrich. *Christ in the Wilderness: The Wilderness Theme in the Second Gospel and Its Basis in the Biblical Tradition.* London: SCM, 1963.

McDonald, J. Ian H. "What Did You Go Out to See? John the Baptist, the Scrolls and Late Second Temple Judaism." Pages 53–64 in *The Dead Sea Scrolls in Their Historical Context.* Edited by T. Lim. London: T&T Clark, 2004.

McKenzie, Steven L., and Howard N. Wallace. "Covenant Themes in Malachi." *CBQ* 45 (1983): 549–63.

Meier, John P. "John the Baptist in Josephus: Philology and Exegesis." *JBL* 111.2 (1992): 225–37.

Meier, John P. "John the Baptist in Matthew's Gospel." *JBL* 99.3 (1980): 383–405.

Meier, John P. *Matthew.* NTM. Wilmington: Michael Glazier, 1980.

Meier, John P. *Mentor, Message, and Miracles.* Vol. 2 of *A Marginal Jew: Rethinking the Historical Jesus.* New York: Doubleday, 1994.

Meier, John P. *The Vision of Matthew: Christ, Church, and Morality in the First Gospel.* Eugene: Wipf and Stock, 1991.

Metzger, Bruce. *A Textual Commentary on the Greek New Testament.* Stuttgart: United Bible Society, 1975.

Meyer, Heinrich A. W. *Critical and Exegetical Hand-Book to the Gospel of Matthew.* Vol. 1. Edinburgh: T&T Clark, 1844. Repr., Peabody: Hendrickson, 1983.

Montgomery, James A. *A Critical and Exegetical Commentary on the Book of Daniel.* ICC. Edinburgh: T&T Clark, 1927.

Morris, Leon. *The Gospel according to Matthew.* Grand Rapids: Eerdmans, 1992.

Motyer, Alec. *The Prophecy of Isaiah.* Downers Grove: IVP, 1993.

Moule, C. F. D. *An Idiom Book of the New Testament.* Cambridge: Cambridge University Press, 1982.

Moule, C. F. D. "The Judgment Theme in the Sacraments." Pages 464–81 in *The Background of the New Testament and Its Eschatology.* Edited by W. D. Davies and D. Daube. Cambridge: Cambridge University Press, 1964.

Moulton James H., and Wilbert F. Howard, *A Grammar of the Greek New Testament.* Edinburgh: T&T Clark, 1929.

Mounce, Robert H. *Matthew.* NIBC. Peabody: Hendrickson, 1991.

Mowinckel, Sigmund. *He That Cometh: The Messiah Concept in the Old Testament and Later Judaism.* Translated by G. W. Anderson. Grand Rapids: Eerdmans, 2005. Repr., Nashville: Abingdon Press, 1956.

Muller, Mogens. *The Expression 'Son of Man' and the Development of Christology: A History of Interpretation.* London: Equinox, 2008.

Murray, John. "The Interadventual Period and the Advent: Matthew 24-25." Pages 387–400 in *The Collected Writings of John Murray: Select Lectures in Systematic Theology.* Vol. 2. Carlisle: Banner of Truth Trust, 1996.

Neusner, Jacob. *Rabbinic Judaism: The Theological System.* Leiden: Brill, 2002.

Newman, Barclay M., and Philip C. Stine, eds. *A Handbook on the Gospel of Matthew.* UBSHS. New York: United Bible Societies, 1988.

Nickelsburg, George W. E., and James C. Vanderkam. *1 Enoch 2: A Commentary on the Book of 1 Enoch, Chapters 37-82.* 2 vols. Hermeneia. Edited by Klaus Baltzer. Minneapolis: Fortress, 2012.

Nixon, Robin E. *The Exodus in the New Testament.* London: Tyndale Press, 1963.

Nogalski, James D. "The Day(s) of YHWH in the Book of the Twelve." Pages 192–213 in *Thematic Threads in the Book of the Twelve,* BZAW 325. Edited by P. L. Redditt and A. Schart. New York: W. de Gruyter, 2003.

Nogalski, James D. "Recurring Themes in the Book of the Twelve: Creating Points of Contact for a Theological Reading." *Int* 127 (2007): 125–36.

Nolland, John. *The Gospel of Matthew.* NIGTC. Grand Rapids: Eerdmans, 2005.

Nolland, John. "'In Such a Manner It Is Fitting for Us to Fulfill All Righteousness': Reflections on the Place of Baptism in the Gospel of Matthew." Pages 63–80 in *Baptism, The New Testament and the Church.* JSNTSup 171. Edited by S. E. Porter and A. R. Cross. Sheffield: Sheffield Academic Press, 1999.

Noth, Martin. "The Holy Ones of the Most High." Pages 215–28 in *The Laws in the Pentateuch and Other Essays.* Translated by D. R. Ap-Thomas. London: Oliver and Boyd, 1966. Repr., London: SCM, 1984.

Osborne, Grant R. *Matthew.* ZECNT. Grand Rapids: Zondervan, 2010.

Oswalt, John N. *The Book of Isaiah, Chapters 1-39.* NICOT. Grand Rapids: Eerdmans, 1986.

Patte, Daniel. *The Gospel according to Matthew: A Structural Commentary on Matthew's Faith.* Minneapolis: Fortress, 1987.

Patzia, Arthur G. "Did John the Baptist Preach a Baptism of Fire and the Holy Spirit?" *EQ* 40.1 (1968): 23–27.

Payne, J. Barton. *The Theology of the Older Testament.* Grand Rapids: Zondervan, 1982.

Pennington, Jonathan. *Heaven and Earth in the Gospel of Matthew.* Grand Rapids: Baker, 2007.

Petersen, David L. "A Book of the Twelve?" Pages 3–10 in *Reading and Hearing the Book of the Twelve.* Edited by James D. Nogalski and Marvin A. Sweeney. Atlanta: SBL, 2000.

Petersen, David L. *The Prophetic Literature: An Introduction.* Louisville: Westminster John Knox, 2002.

Petersen, David L. *Zechariah 9-14 and Malachi.* Louisville: Westminster John Knox, 1995.

Plummer, Alfred. *The Gospel according to St. Luke.* ICC. 5th ed. Edinburgh: T&T Clark, 1981.

Polhill, John B. *Acts.* NAC 26. Nashville: Broadman, 1992.

Polley, Max E. "The Place of Henry Wheeler Robinson among Old Testament Scholars." *Baptist Quarterly* 24.6 (1972): 271–83.

Porter, Stanley E. *Idioms of the Greek New Testament.* Sheffield: Sheffield Academic Press, 1996.

Przybylski, Benno. *Righteousness in Matthew and His World of Thought.* SNTSM 41. Cambridge: Cambridge University Press, 1980.

Rad, Gerhard von. *Theology of the Old Testament.* Vol. 2. Translated by D. M. G. Stalker. London: Oliver and Boyd, 1965.

Redditt P. L., and A. Schart, eds. *Thematic Threads in the Book of the Twelve.* BZAW 325. New York: W. de Gruyter, 2003.

Reiser, Marius. *Jesus and Judgment: The Eschatological Proclamation in Its Jewish Context.* Translated by Linda M. Maloney. Minneapolis: Fortress, 1997.

Rendtorff, Rolf. "How to Read the Book of the Twelve as a Theological Unity." Pages 75–90 in *Reading and Hearing the Book of the Twelve.* Edited by James D. Nogalski and Marvin A. Sweeney. Atlanta: SBL, 2000.

Ridder, Richard R. de. *Discipling the Nations.* Grand Rapids: Baker, 1971.

Ridderbos, Herman. *Matthew.* Translated by R. Togtman. Grand Rapids: Zondervan, 1987.

Ridderbos, Jan. *Isaiah.* Translated by John Vriend. Grand Rapids: Zondervan, 1985.

Riesner, Rainer. *Jesus als Lehrer: Eine Untersuchung zum Ursprung der Evangelien-Überlieferung.* WUNT 2. Tübingen: Mohr Siebeck, 1981.

Robertson, A. T. *A Grammar of the Greek New Testament.* Nashville: Broadman, 1934.

Robertson, A. T., and William H. Davis. *A New Short Grammar of the Greek New Testament.* Grand Rapids: Baker, 1985.

Robinson, H. Wheeler. "Hebrew Sacrifice and Prophetic Symbolism." *JTS,* 43 (1942): 129–39.

Robinson, H. Wheeler. "Prophetic Symbolism." Pages 1–17 in *Old Testament Essays.* Edited by D. C. Simpson. London: Charles Griffin and Company, 1927.

Robinson, J. A. T. "The Baptism of John and the Qumran Community: Testing a Hypothesis." *HTR*, 50.3 (1957): 175–92.

Robinson, J. A. T. *12 New Testament Studies*. London: SCM, 1962.

Robinson, James M. *The Critical Edition of Q*. Edited by Paul Hoffmann, John S. Kloppenborg and Milton C. Moreland. Hermeneia. Minneapolis: Fortress, 2000.

Rothchild, Clare K. *Baptist Traditions and Q*. WUNT 190. Tübingen: Mohr Siebeck, 2005.

Rowland, Christopher. *The Open Heaven: A Study of Apocalyptic in Judaism and Early Christianity*. London: SPCK, 1982.

Rowley, Harold H. *From Moses to Qumran: Studies in the Old Testament*. New York: Association Press, 1963.

Sabourin, Leopold. "Apocalyptic Traits in Matthew's Gospel." *RSB* 3.1 (1983): 19–36.

Sailhamer, John H. *The Pentateuch as Narrative* (Grand Rapids: Zondervan, 1992).

Sanders, E. P. *The Historical Figure of Jesus*. London: The Penguin Press, 1993.

Sanders, E. P. *Jesus and Judaism*. Minneapolis: Fortress, 1985.

Schmidt, Nathaniel. "The 'Son of Man' in the Book of Daniel." *JBL* 19 (1900): 22–28.

Schweizer, Eduard. *Das Evangelium nach Matthäus*. Göttingen: Vandenhoeck & Ruprecht, 1973.

Schwemer, Anna Maria. "Prophet, Zeuge und Märtyrer: Zur Entstehung des Märtyrerbegriffs im frühesten Christentum." *ZTK* 96.3 (1999): 320–50.

Scobie, Charles H. H. *John the Baptist*. London: SCM Press, 1964.

Seitz, Christopher R. *Isaiah 1-39*. Louisville: John Knox Press, 1993.

Shepherd, Michael B. "Daniel 7:13 and the New Testament Son of Man." *WTJ* 68 (2006): 99–111.

Sim, David C. *Apocalyptic Eschatology in the Gospel of Matthew*. SNTSMS 88. Cambridge: Cambridge University Press, 1996.

Simonetti, Manlio, ed. *Matthew 1-13*. ACCS 1a. Downers Grove: Inter Varsity Press, 2001.

Smith-Christopher, Daniel L. "The Book of Daniel." *The New Interpreter's Bible*. Vol. 7. Edited by Leander K. Keck et al. Nashville: Abingdon Press, 1996.

Smith, Gary V. *Isaiah 1-39*. NAC 15a. Nashville: B&H, 2007.

Smith, Ralph L. *Micah-Malachi*. WBC 32. Grand Rapids: Zondervan, 1984.

Smith, Robert H. *Matthew*. ACNT. Minneapolis: Augsburg, 1989.

Soggin, J. Alberto. *Introduction to the Old Testament*. 2nd ed. Translated by John Bowden. Philadelphia: Westminster Press, 1980.

Sollamo, Raija. "Messianism and the 'Branch of David.'" Pages 357–70 in *The Septuagint and Messianism*. BETL 195. Edited by M. A. Knibb. Leuven: Leuven University Press, 2004.

Stacey, W. David. *Prophetic Drama in the Old Testament*. London: Epworth Press, 1990.

Stanton, Graham. "The Gospel of Matthew and Judaism." *BJRL* 66 (1984): 264–84.

Stanton, Graham N. *A Gospel for a New People: Studies in Matthew*. Louisville: Westminster John Knox Press, 1993.

Steck, Odil. *Israel und das gewaltsame Geschick der Propheten*. WMANT 23. Neukirchen-Vluyn: Neukirchener Verlag, 1967.

Stein, Robert H. *Jesus the Messiah*. Downers Grove: IVP, 1996.

Stein, Robert H. *The Synoptic Problem*. Grand Rapids: Baker, 1987.

Steinmann, J. *Saint John the Baptist and the Desert Tradition*. New York: Harper and Brothers/Longmans, n.d.

Stendahl, Krister. "Quis et unde? An Analysis of Matthew 1-2." Pages 56–66 in *The Interpretation of Matthew*. Edited by Graham Stanton. Minneapolis: Fortress, 1983.

Stenning, J. F., ed. and trans. *The Targum of Isaiah*. Oxford: Clarendon Press, 1949.

Strecker, George. *Der Weg der Gerechtigkeit: Untersuchung zur Theologie des Mattäus.* Göttingen: Vandenhoeck & Ruprecht, 1962.

Stromberg, Jacob. "The 'Root of Jesse' in Isaiah 11:10: Postexilic Judah, or Postexilic Davidic King?" *JBL* 127.4 (2008): 655–69.

Stuart, Douglas. *Malachi,* in *The Minor Prophets.* 3 vols. Edited by Thomas E. McComiskey. Grand Rapids: Baker, 2003.

Stuart, Moses. *A Commentary on the Book of Daniel.* Boston: Crocker & Brewster, 1850.

Sweeney, Marvin A., Jerome T. Walsh and Chris Franke. *The Twelve Prophets: Hosea, Joel, Amos, Obadiah, Jonah.* Vol. 1. Collegeville: The Liturgical Press, 2000.

Tate, Marvin. *Psalms 51-100.* WBC 20. Grand Rapids: Zondervan, 1990.

Tatum, W. Barnes. *John the Baptist and Jesus: A Report of the Jesus Seminar.* Sonoma: Polebridge Press, 1994.

Taylor, Joan E. *The Immerser: John the Baptist within Second Temple Judaism.* Grand Rapids: Eerdmans, 1997.

Taylor, Richard A., and E. Ray Clendenen. *Haggai, Malachi.* NAC 21a. Nashville: Broadman & Holman, 2004.

Taylor, Vincent. *The Gospel according to St. Mark.* New York: Macmillan, 1955.

Terrien, Damuel. *The Psalms: Strophic Structure and Theological Commentary.* Grand Rapids: Eerdmans, 2003.

Theophalis, Michael P. *The Abomination of Desolation in Matthew 24.15.* LNTS 437. London: T&T Clark, 2012.

Thompson, G. H. P. "Called-Proved-Obedient: A Study in the Baptism and Temptation Narratives of Matthew and Luke." *JTS* 11.1 (1960): 1–12.

Tilborg, Sjef van. *The Jewish Leaders in Matthew's Gospel.* Leiden: Brill, 1979.

Tinsley, E. J. *The Gospel according to Luke.* CBC. Cambridge: Cambridge University Press, 1965.

Torrance, T. F. "Proselyte Baptism." *NTS* 1 (1954): 50–54.

Trilling, Wolfgang "Die Täufertradition bei Matthäus." *BZ* 3 (1959): 271–89.

Trumbower, Jeffry A. "The Role of Malachi in the Career of John the Baptist." Pages 28–41 in *The Gospels and the Scriptures of Israel.* Edited by Craig A. Evans and W. Richard Stegner. JSNTSup 104. London: Sheffield Academic Press, 1994.

Tull, Patricia K. *Isaiah 1-39.* Macon: Smyth & Helwys Publishing, 2010.

Turner, David L. *Israel's Last Prophet: Jesus and the Jewish Leaders in Matthew 23.* Minneapolis: Fortress, 2015.

Turner, David L. "Matt 21:43 and the Future of Israel." *Bsac* 159 (2002): 46–61.

Turner, David L. *Matthew.* BECNT. Grand Rapids: Baker Academic, 2008.

Turner, Nigel. "An Alleged Semitism." *ET* 66 (1955): 252–54.

Turner, Nigel. *A Grammar of New Testament Greek.* Edinburgh: T&T Clark, 1976.

Verhoef, Peter A. *The Books of Haggai and Malachi.* Grand Rapids: Eerdmans, 1987.

Vermes, Geza. "The Oxford Forum for Qumran Research Seminar on the Rule of War from Cave 4 (4Q285)." *JJS* 43 (1992): 85–90.

Vermes, Geza. *Scripture and Tradition in Judaism: Haggadic Studies.* Leiden: Brill, 1973.

Vermes, Geza. "The Use of בר נש / בר נשא in Jewish Aramaic." Pages 147–65 in *Post-Biblical Jewish Studies.* Edited by Geza Vermes. Leiden: Brill, 1975.

Verseput, Donald J. *The Rejection of the Humble Messianic King: A Study of the Composition of Matthew 11-12.* Frankfurt am Main: Peter Lang, 1986.

Voltaire, Marie Francois Arouet de. *A Philosophical Dictionary.* Vol. 1. New York: Coventry House, 1932.

Vos, Geerhardus. *Biblical Theology: Old and New Testament*. Edinburgh: The Banner of Truth Trust, 1975.

Vos, Geerhardus. *Redemptive History and Biblical Interpretation*. Edited by Richard B. Gaffin. Phillipsburg: Presbyterian & Reformed, 1980.

Wallace, Daniel. *Greek Grammar beyond the Basics*. Grand Rapids: Zondervan, 1996.

Waltke, Bruce K., "Micah." Pages 591–764 in *An Exegetical and Expository Commentary: The Minor Prophets*. Vol. 2. Edited by Thomas E. McComiskey. Grand Rapids: Baker, 2000.

Waltke, Bruce K., and Charles Yu. *An Old Testament Theology: An Exegetical, Canonical, and Thematic Approach*. Grand Rapids: Zondervan, 2007.

Walton, John H. "The ANZU Myth as Relevant Background for Daniel 7?" Pages 69–90 in *The Book of Daniel: Composition and Reception*. Vol. 1. Edited by John J. Collins and Peter W. Flint. Leiden: Brill, 2001.

Watts, John D. W. *Isaiah 1-33*. WBC 24. Nashville: Thomas Nelson, 1985.

Watts, Rikk E. "Immanuel: Virgin Birth Proof Text or Programmatic Warning of Things to Come (Isa 7:14 in Matt 1:23)?" Pages 92–113 in *From Prophecy to Testament: The Function of the Old Testament in the New*. Edited by Craig A. Evans. Peabody: Hendrickson, 2004.

Webb, Robert L. "Jesus' Baptism: Its Historicity and Implications." *BBR* 10.2 (2000), 261–309.

Webb, Robert L. *John the Baptizer and Prophet: A Socio-Historical Study*. JSNTSup 62. Sheffield: Sheffield Academic Press, 1991.

Wegner, Paul D. *An Examination of Kingship and Messianic Expectation in Isaiah 1-35*. Lewiston: The Edwin Mellen Press, 1992.

Wellhausen, Julius. *Das Evangelium Matthaei*. Berlin: Georg Reimer, 1904.

Wenham, Gordon J. *Genesis 1-15*. WBC 1. Nashville: Thomas Nelson, 1987.

Wildberger, Hans. *Isaiah 1-12*. CC. Translated by T. H. Trapp. Minneapolis: Fortress, 1991.

Wilkins, Michael. *Matthew*, NIVAC. Grand Rapids: Zondervan, 2003.

William R. Telford. *The Barren Temple and the Withered Tree*. JSNTS 1. Sheffield: JSOT, 1980.

Wills, Lawerence M. "Scribal Methods in Matthew and Mishnah Abot." Pages 183–97 in *Biblical Interpretations in Early Christian Gospels*. Vol. 2. LNTS 310. Edited by Thomas R. Hatina. Edinburgh: T&T Clark, 2008.

Wilson, Alistair I. *When Will These Things Happen? A Study of Jesus as Judge in Matthew 21-25*. Carlisle: Paternoster, 2004.

Wink, Walter. *John the Baptist in the Gospel Tradition*. Cambridge: Cambridge University Press, 1968.

Witherington III, Ben. "Jesus and the Baptist—Two of a Kind." *Society of Biblical Literature 1988 Seminar Papers*. SBLSP 27. Atlanta: Scholars Press, 1988.

Witherington III, Ben. "John the Baptist." Pages 383–91 in *Dictionary of Jesus and the Gospels*. Edited by Joel B. Green, Scot McKnight and I. Howard Marshall. Downers Grove: IVP, 1992.

Witherington III, Ben. *Matthew*. Macon: Smyth & Helwys, 2006.

Witherington III, Ben. *New Testament History: A Narrative Account*. Grand Rapids: Baker Academic, 2001.

Wright III, Benjamin G. "A Note on Statistical Analysis of Septuagintal Syntax." *JBL* 104.1 (1985): 111–14.

Wright, N. T. *Jesus and the Victory of God*. London: SPCK, 1996.

Wright, N. T. *The New Testament and the People of God*. Minneapolis: Fortress, 1992.

Yamasaki, Gary. "Broken Parallelism in Matthew's Parable of the Two Builders." *Direction* 13.2 (2004): 143–49.

Yamasaki, Gary. *John the Baptist in Life and Death: Audience-Oriented Criticism of Matthew's Narrative*. JSNTSup 167. Sheffield: Sheffield Academic Press, 1998.

Zevit, Ziony. "The Structure and Individual Elements of Daniel 7." *ZAW* 80 (1968): 385–96.

Zimmerli, Walther. *Ezekiel 1: A Commentary on the Book of the Prophet Ezekiel, Chapters 1-24*. Translated by R. E. Clements. Philadelphia: Fortress, 1969.

Zimmerli, Walther. *The Fiery Throne: The Prophets and Old Testament Theology*. Minneapolis: Fortress, 2003.

INDEX